MW00669062

San Antonio

City on a Mission

by Henry G. Cisneros and
Catherine Nixon Cooke
Introduction by Red McCombs
and including a photo journal
featuring the work of Al Rendon

J Robert Towery – Publisher/Designer
James Tomlinson – Executive Publisher
Ardith Bradshaw – Editor
Nikki Sepsas – Profile Writer
Noah Towery – Associate Publisher
Jacques Verhaak – President & CFO

an Urban Renaissance Book
Published by Cityink Company
www.cityink.com

San Antonio

photo by Noah Towery

photo by Noah Towery

City on a Mission

photo by Noah Towery

photo by Noah Towery

photo by Al Rendon

photo by Al Rendon

Library of Congress Control Number: 2022941696

ISBN-13: 978-0-9741374-6-9

Henry G. Cisneros (1947-). and
Catherine Nixon Cooke, (1950-)
The eleventh volume in CityInk's Urban Renaissance Books series, ***San Antonio–City on a Mission*** recounts the city's explosive growth in recent decades. Known for its cultural diversity, San Antonio is a place where inclusiveness is a powerful catalyst for innovation, and a booming bioscience ecosystem is fueling its future.

Fireworks cover photo by Al Rendon

published by cityink company
www.cityink.com
Memphis, TN 901-483-2001

URBANRenaissanceBOOKS a series created by cityink
Printed in Korea

Contents

photo by Al Rendon

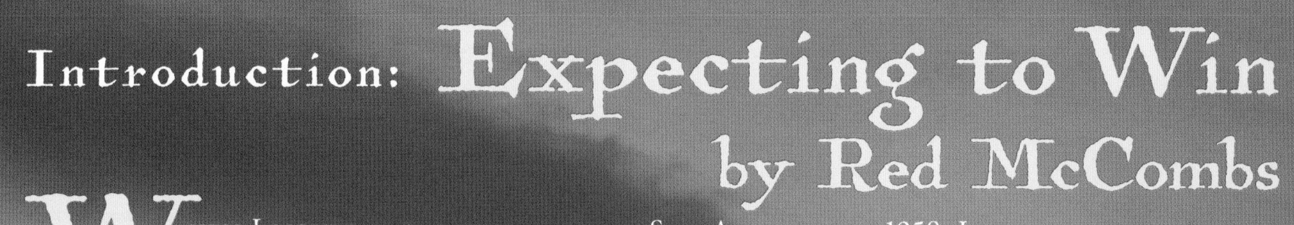

Introduction: Expecting to Win by Red McCombs

When I moved with my family to San Antonio in 1958, I was advised by well-placed people that this was a 'closed town'—that politically, economically, and socially it was controlled by 'old families.' I found that to be erroneous; I found San Antonio to be a very open city that welcomed people willing to work hard.

I did that. As a young auto dealer, I worked hard to build a successful business—selling Ford Edsels of all things! People bought my cars, and eventually, the McCombs Automotive Group became the largest automobile conglomerate in the United States. I became involved in the Chamber of Commerce early in my new life here—convinced that San Antonio was a great place. I also recognized that it was not a city that had a presence on the national 'radar screen.' A decade later, HemisFair would become a watershed moment for San Antonio that would change that.

I was chairman of the Chamber of Commerce in 1963 when the idea of a world's fair began to hatch. I credit people like U.S. Representative Henry B. González and businessman Bill Sinkin for dreaming up the idea, and Marshall Steves and Tom Frost for believing that finding underwriting for the fair should encompass the entire community. They came up with a plan that could involve every single business, regardless of size. I worked closely with the Executive Committee for the fair, and we tackled some big challenges.

We had to secure both federal and state approval and funding; and we had to convince at least twenty- three corporations to participate by sponsoring exhibits that were thematic to the fair, which was entitled "Confluence of Civilizations."

The political intrigue was substantial. US Representative

Henry B. González was a huge proponent on the national level, but US Senator Ralph Yarborough was not forthcoming with his support. And our Governor, John Connally—who was the honorary commissioner for the fair—did not want to be in the same room with Senator Yarborough. But John Connally worked it out with the help of another US senator from Texas—John Tower—and the fair got the needed federal approval and funding. The Governor did the same thing at the state level, and we passed that hurdle of support and funding. The next challenge was securing major exhibitors, which I thought would be easy.

We got three immediately—General Electric (GE), thanks to committee member Jim Gaines, who was president of our local radio/television station WOAI; IBM, thanks to another local connection; and Southwestern Bell, which was a real coup. Then we hit a real dry spell; we did not get any more for months. Because my company had achieved record sales for the Ford Motor Company, I had worked directly with its president, Lee Iacocca. I told him Ford should be part of HemisFair. We had acquired ninety-seven acres for the fair's location in downtown San Antonio. I explained that each national exhibitor would lease a small tract to build a pavilion for their company and staff it over the six months that the fair would operate. Lee balked at the commitment; instead, he offered that Ford would make a quarter-million-dollar contribution for some art object for the fair. I continued to press for an exhibition pavilion, and he finally told me, "Red, that dusty ass town of yours has no political or economic significance to Ford Motor Company."

I called John Connally to report that disheartening conversation. John told me to call Lee back and tell him he would be getting a telephone call from Lyndon (President Johnson) within forty-eight hours to explain the significance of the fair and Texas. I did that with great pleasure.

Lee said, "You're pulling my chain."

I told him, "Just sit back, relax, and watch it happen." It happened. Ford agreed to build a pavilion, and others followed like falling dominoes.

Virtually none of those exhibitors had any interest in coming to San Antonio in 1968. But when we inaugurated the major exhibits, Henry Ford and other Fortune 500 CEOs showed up in their corporate jets. They gave impassioned speeches about how important Texas and San Antonio were to them.

photos by Al Rendon

▲ Businessman Bill Sinkin (l) and Mayor Walter W. McAllister (r) were early proponents of a World's Fair in San Antonio.

▼ Red McCombs, former Spurs coach Larry Brown, and then Mayor Henry Cisneros believed an NBA championship team would help transform the city and they were right.

Before HemisFair, the Fortune 500 companies did not even know San Antonio existed. It's not that we had a bad reputation. We had no reputation at all. As that old saying goes, perception is reality, so when I saw this reaction from big corporations, I began to think about ways to change their perception of San Antonio.

In the mid-to-late 1960s, several cities that had not been particularly visible suddenly became household names—Atlanta, Minneapolis, and San Diego, for example. They had catapulted to national recognition because they had major league sports teams. Sports are great unifiers—fans from every corner of a community become united. I knew that residents of San Antonio were ready for a team. And the arena that we'd built for HemisFair had been sitting empty since the fair closed.

In 1973 I negotiated a lease-buy deal with Dallas Mayor Robert Folsom to take over a basketball team called the Dallas Chaparrals. Fifty local investors joined me, and when we got the team to San Antonio, we held a contest to change its name. Local sportscasters, athletes, and the media made suggestions—we were looking for something short that captured the flavor of our region. The winning name was the 'Spurs' (I was born in Spur, Texas, but that's not why the name was chosen). The rest is history; we became an NBA team.

We bought a star player, George Gervin, "The Iceman," from the Virginia Squires and then won the lottery by getting David Robinson. It took until 1999 to win our first NBA championship, but we've won four more since then. The Spurs were the catalyst for two more sports arenas in San Antonio—the Alamodome and the AT&T Center.

HemisFair was also a catalyst for San Antonio's now-booming hospitality industry. We discovered that people really liked coming here and we were good at welcoming them. Introducing them to our unique cultural charm was enhanced by a refurbished River Walk and new hotels. Developments like the La Quinta chain created by the Barshop family and the Hilton Palacio del Rio constructed by Zachry Company in record time for HemisFair using an innovative new modular system led the way.

About the same time, we saw years of work for a public university and a state-supported medical school come to fruition. Early in our campaign for a branch of the University of Texas, I spoke with Frank Erwin, a friend who was also chairman of the UT Board of Regents. Frank told me there was no need for a UT component in San Antonio because Austin was only seventy miles away and could meet San Antonio's needs. I called Governor Connally again to argue our city's case, and again, he helped. And when it came to the medical school idea, he believed that San Antonio could become the medical hub for all of south Texas.

If it sounds like I'm singing John Connally's praises, I am. He was very modest, not looking for credit; he believed that Texas could grow in tourism, that HemisFair was a big move to awaken the rest of the country, and that our city could develop a world-class medical center.

HemisFair, the Spurs, the medical school, a one thousand room hotel downtown, and our new highway interchanges positioned San Antonio for exciting progress as the 1970s got underway. The communications industry helped tell San Antonio's story. I jumped into that business with Lowry Mays when we co-founded Clear Channel Communications in 1972, eventually building it to ownership of twelve hundred radio stations around the country. We also had two major newspapers: *The San Antonio Express-News* and *The Light*.

San Antonio's population had grown to over 700,000. The city was on the rise. We saw inclusion become a part of city government when citizens approved single-member

photo courtesy of Red McCombs

districts in 1975. In 1981, we elected a visionary mayor, Henry Cisneros, who pushed an agenda of economic development and high expectations for San Antonio.

About that time, the renowned evangelist Oral Roberts invited me to visit his university campus in Tulsa, Oklahoma. I noticed that there were signs all over the place—they all read "Expect a Miracle." When I asked him about the placards, he told me, "You'll never get a miracle unless you expect it." When I returned to San Antonio, I had a new motto of my own; and I've lived by it ever since: "Expect to Win"!

Sports teams offered an excellent opportunity for me to put my motto to work. When I owned the Denver Nuggets and later the Minnesota Vikings in the 1990s, my wife Charline and I did a lot of cheering and saw some wonderful wins and some not-so-wonderful losses. But there is no doubt that those teams helped build visibility for their hometowns of Denver and Minneapolis like the Spurs have done for San Antonio. An even faster-paced sport caught my attention just a few years ago, and I invested in the Circuit of Americas outside of Austin. It opened in 2012 and is the first racetrack in the country purpose-built for Formula One cars. Watching those cars zoom around the track during the U.S. Grand Prix, hearing the deafening roar of those engines—I love the excitement. But I am always happy to return to my home in San Antonio, with its tall oak trees and native limestone, filled with all the memories of watching both my family and my city grow up. It is an extraordinary place to live.

San Antonio has had some big "wins" over the years, beyond its Spurs-related endeavors. Because San Antonio is an 'open town,' new industries moved here, bringing the obvious benefits like new buildings and more jobs. But we also got the gift of talent that came with those companies—people from other places with innovative ideas. In the 1980s and 1990s, SeaWorld, DLSI, and Sony came to San Antonio, and when Southwestern Bell (which later became AT&T) put its headquarters here, it was a signal event for the city, "a shot heard around the world" by Fortune 500 types.

The new millennium brought more action to San Antonio: a Toyota manufacturing plant came to San Antonio's south side, creating 3000 new jobs; Rackspace moved its international cloud computing company to a huge, abandoned mall near Windcrest; and organizations like the Texas Research and Technology Foundation worked to attract data centers, research laboratories and technology firms to the city.

It's happening.

Microsoft came to San Antonio in 2014 as an anchor tenant; it will expand on a hundred and fifty-eight additional acres over the next few years, creating a billion-dollar facility on what was once Texas prairie. Today there are so many new real estate projects—high-tech renovations in older parts of town, all kinds of new construction as San Antonio's outer boundaries expand—it's hard to keep up. It's exhilarating to see all that action in the city I love.

When reflecting on the most significant "wins" for San Antonio as well as for myself, I have this list:

- The biggest boost for our city in recent history—getting the San Antonio Spurs. Despite finishing tenth in the 2021 basketball season, I am sure that they'll be back on top once the new rookies mature. After all, their coach, Gregg Popovich, led the US basketball team to Olympic gold in Tokyo in 2021;
- The best mayor for this city's forward momentum during my time here—Henry Cisneros;
- With the Covid-19 pandemic still on our minds, I've admired how mayor Ron Nirenberg and County Judge Nelson Wolff have communicated with our citizens and pushed for vaccinations;
- The best decision of my life—marrying my wonderful wife, Charline, who passed away in 2019.
- My most significant honor—having the Business School at UT-Austin named for me.

As for San Antonio's future, it depends on leadership and its continuance as an inclusive community. The city has every right to expect to win. Its rich history and unique persona, captured in the ensuing pages, will prove it.

▼ Red McCombs and his wife, Charline, made ranching and Texas Longhorns part of their legacy.

photo courtesy of Red McCombs

Chapter One:
A New Start

In the 1960s it was clear that the nation was changing. San Antonio recognized that the old order and the old ways had to change here too. City leaders hit upon the idea of a large endeavor that would involve the entire city—a world's fair. They selected a theme that brilliantly captured the city's essence: Confluence of Civilizations. And San Antonio was onto a new path.

— Henry G. Cisneros

Until 1930, San Antonio was the largest city in Texas. A growing military presence had blessed it—an army post that became Fort Sam Houston was built in 1876 to guard and protect the country's southern border with Mexico during the ongoing Indian Wars. After the United States entered World War I, the U.S. Army recognized the need for trained flying instructors. Because of its consistently clear weather, abundance of water, and good transportation, San Antonio was chosen as an ideal aviation training site; and Kelly Field, which later became Kelly Air Field, was built in December 1917.

Construction of Brooks Field (later Brooks Air Force Base) was completed in 1918, and in 1931 Randolph Air Field was constructed to expand pilot training facilities. During World War II, the San Antonio Aviation Cadet Center (SAAC) became a basic training center for the Army Air Corps. Renamed Lackland Air Force Base in 1947, it transitioned into the only basic training for the U.S. Air Force.

By the late 1950s, the five bases elevated employment opportunities that helped create a new Latino middle class. But the civil service wage-based economy of San Antonio made competing with the explosive growth of Texas's other population centers challenging. Over the next few decades, the city slipped behind Dallas and Houston, focusing their economies on banking, energy, and new businesses that rewarded education and entrepreneurial thinking.

When San Antonio native Henry B. González was elected to the U.S. Congress in 1961 and presented his "20th Century Plan" for his 20th Congressional District, they listened. The plan called for broadening the economic base and outlined a bold first step—hosting

The Menger Hotel pioneered the hotel industry in San Antonio in 1859.

Courtesy of Institute of Texan Cultures/UTSA Special Collections

a world's fair in 1968, celebrating its founding 250 years before, and generating national and international visibility. City leaders welcomed the plan and quickly formed an executive committee to make the world's fair a reality, envisioning it as a catalyst for recognition and growth. They named it HemisFair—believing that most of its exhibitors would come from the Americas—and chose the theme of "Confluence of Civilizations" to celebrate the diversity that has always been an essential characteristic of San Antonio.

Author and poet Sidney Lanier had astutely and humorously described the diversity of San Antonio during an 1873 trip to the city where he hoped the warm climate might cure his tuberculosis. Staying at the famous Menger Hotel—the first hotel in town to offer its guests electricity and running water—Lanier wrote, "If peculiarities were quills, San Antonio would be an entire porcupine." The porcupine he described was many centuries in the making.

Author and poet Sidney Lanier had astutely and humorously described the diversity of San Antonio during an 1873 trip to the city, where he hoped the warm climate might cure his tuberculosis. Staying at the famous Menger Hotel—the first hotel in town to offer its guests electricity and running water—Lanier wrote, "If peculiarities were quills, San Antonio would be an entire porcupine." The porcupine he described was many centuries in the making.

A thousand years before Spanish army expeditions came north in the late 1600s, indigenous peoples lived along the river, an oasis of clear water surrounded by beautiful cottonwood trees. When missionaries and colonizers discovered this idyllic setting in the 1700s, with the help of the native Payayas, they built a waterway system using stone acequias; they constructed forts and missions including San Antonio de Valero (the Alamo); and they established the first municipality of San Antonio de Bexar in 1721.

Spain looked to other places in its empire for additional colonizers. When the Canary Islands experienced economic difficulties in the early part of the 18th century, the Spanish crown offered land grants and promises of a better life in San Antonio de Bexar. Those early pioneers arrived in 1731. Encountering snakes, coyotes, and Indian raids, they persevered to add still another quill to the porcupine.

After Mexico's independence from Spain in 1810, the new nation continued to colonize its northern territory, granting land in 1821 to three hundred Anglo-American families, led by Stephen F. Austin. They came south from the Trans-Appalachia states, including Virginia, Tennessee, and North Carolina. Among those "Old Three Hundred" colonists was Asa Mitchell, who acquired slaves and cattle and purchased additional acres near Mission Espada. Today that 700-acre site is the campus of Texas A&M University–San Antonio, a four-year public university. Constructed in 2009, its architecture reflects the past of the historic Spanish missions nearby.

Former slaves constituted a significant African-American presence in San Antonio. They joined Latinos, Anglo-Americans, Germans, Poles, Alsatians, Czechoslovakians, Irish, Italian, Chinese, and others to create the confluences that Lanier described in his famous quote—words memorialized on a plaque that has hung in the Menger Hotel for more than a century.

HemisFair was envisioned as a dramatic way to recognize those

Photos Courtesy of Institute of Texan Cultures/UTSA Special Collections

Randolph AFB (upper photo) was built in 1931 during the Great Depression; Kelly Field (lower photo) was built more than a decade earlier to train World War I pilots. Eventually San Antonio became home to five military bases.

▲ San Antonio de Bexar was established in 1721.

▼ Mission San Francisco de Espada was constructed in 1731.

unique confluences that were San Antonio's fiber. It would emphasize the cultural and economic advantages of people working together. Leading the planning process were department store owner Jerome Harris and businessman Bill Sinkin, both friends of Congressman González. They enlisted powerhouses in the San Antonio business community, an impressive list including:

H.B. "Pat" Zachry, Zachry Company built freeways, bridges, power plants, an expansion of Randolph Air Force Base, and diverse construction projects around the world; Marshall Steves, a descendant of Canary Island settlers, whose family established its lumber company in 1866 to provide building materials to south Texas and Mexico; Tom Frost, whose family founded the city's first bank in 1868; Jim Gaines, President of WOAI Radio; Frank Manupelli, general manager of Howard Aero; and Mayor Walter W. McAllister.

All were part of the committee of visionaries who made HemisFair a reality and started San Antonio's march toward a modern future.

By 1963, forty-eight more community leaders had joined the committee—working to secure official approvals, raise money, attract exhibitors, and commission public artwork for the fair, which would be built on ninety-seven acres of downtown neighborhoods. Scheduled to open in April 1968, HemisFair promised to be a turning point for San Antonio, but the fast-approaching deadline was daunting. Miraculously, the money was raised. The U.S. government

photo courtesy of Mission Espada

sanctioned the fair, hotels and a convention center were built, exhibit pavilions were erected, and more than 30 countries from both hemispheres participated, along with major corporations including Eastman Kodak, General Electric, Ford, General-Motors, Coca-Cola, and IBM.

Mayor McAllister recruited a young entrepreneurial caterer named Rosemary Kowalski to handle the celebrations planned for more than 100 exhibit pavilions at HemisFair. In the decades that followed, her company expanded to become the now-legendary RK Group, providing food, equipment rentals, floral designs, event planning and management, and hospitality services worldwide.

With pavilions, fountains, and artwork completed, hotels built in record time, guest services in place, and VIPs ready to travel to San Antonio in April 1968, tragedy struck. Two days before the scheduled opening, the Reverend Martin Luther King, Jr. was assassinated in Memphis, Tennessee. Riots, burning, and looting erupted in cities around the country. Anger, sadness, and frustration permeated the national psyche. Desegregation was less than a decade old in San Antonio and minority populations were not yet proportionally represented in city government. Both the Latino and African-American populations struggled to have their voices heard as their city evolved during these troubled times. Atlanta was the center of the African-American civil rights movement; San Antonio was about to become the cradle of the Latino civil rights movement. The scales were tipping; diverse voices would soon level the playing field, changing the way decisions would be made in San Antonio forever.

Against this backdrop, HemisFair embraced inclusion, welcoming the world. Visitors ranged from President and Mrs. Lyndon Johnson to world-famous musician Louis Armstrong, from actors Roy Rogers, Dale Evans, and Raquel Welch to foreign leaders from Mexico, Canada, China, Italy, Argentina, and Spain. Many more countries in the Americas and Europe were represented and citizens from every neighborhood in San Antonio supported it with their attendance. Passengers who rode the all-glass elevator to the top of the 750-foot Tower of the Americas (the tallest observation tower in the country at the time) were told by a tour guide that HemisFair was "a symbol of cultural diversity that carries with it the hope of unity for humanity."

During the summer of 1968, as the number of total visitors to HemisFair climbed to nearly 7,000,000, a

▲ Govenor John Connally, H.B. "Pat" Zachry, Frank Manupelli, Mayor Walter McAllister planning HemisFair.

▼ Congressman Henry B. González, Lady Bird Johnson, and Mayor Walter W. McAllister on opening day of HemisFair. City Councilwoman and future mayor Lila Cockrell is in background in pink suit and white gloves.

photos this page courtesy of Institute of Texan Cultures/UTSA Special Collections

Brigadier General Robert F. McDermott (USAF Retired) brought with him ideas that would be transformational.

newcomer arrived in San Antonio. Brigadier General Robert F. McDermott (USAF Retired) brought with him ideas that would build upon this turning point that would be transformational. The General had been recruited as the new CEO of the United Services Automobile Association (USAA). Established in San Antonio in 1922, the company was created by twenty-five Army officers who recognized the challenges military families encountered when seeking automobile insurance due to their recurring assignments to new locations.

By 1963 when then-CEO Col. Charles E. Cheever, Sr., decided to retire, it had branched into home insurance. Cheever had served as a judge advocate at Fort Sam Houston in 1937 and taught military law at West Point before returning to San Antonio, where he joined USAA and was promoted to president in 1953. After a decade at the helm, he'd seen significant growth in memberships and assets and was ready to retire to join the family-run Broadway Bank, where his son, Charles Cheever, Jr. was president. Established in 1941 as the city's first suburban bank, it focused on military customers, many of whom were members of USAA.

Cheever knew exactly who his successor at USAA should be. Cheever had been McDermott's law professor at West Point. He went on to become a fighter pilot in World War II, served on President Eisenhower's staff post-war, attended Harvard Law School, and taught briefly at West Point before being tapped as the Dean of the new Air Force Academy in Colorado Springs in 1954. McDermott liked his work with the bright young students there and did not accept USAA's overtures when Cheever approached him nine years later. Cheever agreed to wait, extending his time as CEO. Like the planning and construction of HemisFair, McDermott's recruitment took five years; and just as one catalyst prepared to close its gates, the next one arrived in the Alamo City in human form.

The timing was perfect. HemisFair had illustrated the critical benefits of outside interaction and inclusion. McDermott embraced a leadership model that turned that philosophy into action and success at USAA and in San Antonio. Like the many generals who came to San Antonio over the years, including Dwight Eisenhower, he followed a "military model" of advancement based on meritocracy—not on color, race, or gender. As diverse sectors of San Antonio were awakening to the growing necessity of equitable representation, the old guard recognized that change had come.

▼ The Cheever family opened the first suburban bank in San Antonio in 1941 with an investment of $60,000.
▶ Today Broadway Bank is the largest independently-owned bank headquartered in San Antonio, with financial centers in Austin, San Marcos, Wimberley, Kyle, and Buda.

Courtesy of Broadway Bank

Courtesy of Institute of Texan Cultures/UTSA Special Collections

More than 1000 hotel rooms and 2000 motel rooms sprang up to accommodate expected visitors to HemisFair. The Hilton Palacio del Rio Hotel was built by H.B. Zachry Company in just 202 days, using modular construction. It was one of the first buildings with an entrance on the San Antonio River Walk, which became a major attraction for both tourists and residents in 1968.

toohool wikimedia commons

Larry D. Moore wikimedia commons

The 750-foot Tower of the Americas was built for HemisFair '68; today the iconic landmark offers guests a spectacular view of the city from its revolving restaurant.

Chapter Two:
The Road to Inclusion

ONCE PEOPLE ARE AT THE TABLE OF DECISION-MAKING AND THEY KNOW THEY HAVE A VOICE, THE QUESTION OF REPRESENTATION ITSELF IS RESOLVED, AND TOGETHER WE CAN START TO WORK ON THE CONTENT OF INVESTMENTS AND PROGRESS."

— HENRY G. CISNEROS

▲ The 45-ton Torch of Friendship, created by Mexican sculptor Sebastian, was a gift to the city from Los Empresarios, a local Mexican business organization, in 2002.

▶ COPS (Communities Organized for Public Service) worked to increase minority access to government and education in the 1980s.

The consensus during the decades following HemisFair was that San Antonio was enjoying its best times. Between 2007 and 2017, it became the third fastest-growing city in the United States, with a 24 percent increase in employment in just a decade. Between July 1, 2016 and July 1, 2017, San Antonio was the fastest-growing city in the nation, according to the U.S. Census Bureau. The journey to this pinnacle of success was not without road bumps.

As the divided economy that defined San Antonio in the 1950s and 1960s slowly gave way to a new dialogue in the 1970s, the city became an incubator for ambitious Latino organizations raising their voices for the first time. Their precursor was the League of United Latin American Citizens (LULAC), established as the first Hispanic civil rights organization in 1929 in Corpus Christi, Texas. It had worked for decades to combat ethnic discrimination against Latinos in the United States. By the 1960s, the organization had moved its headquarters to Washington, DC, to increase awareness and take its affirmative action agenda to a national level. It supported newer organizations like the Mexican American Legal Defense and Educational Fund (MALDEF), established in 1968, and the Southwest Voter Registration Education Project (SVREP) and Communities Organized for Public Service (COPS), both established in 1974.

In the barrios of San Antonio's West Side, it was clear that change was underway, nurtured largely by local churches. When San Antonio-born activist Ernesto (Ernie) Cortés, Jr. founded COPS in 1974, he noted that all social change begins at the local level, around institutions that people trust. Polls showed there was no more trusted institution among Latinos than the Roman Catholic Church; activists recognized a powerful constituency ready to be enlisted in the cause.

When Francis James Furey was appointed the Catholic Archbishop of San Antonio in 1969, he joined the growing movement supporting inclusion within city government and society; and he established one of the first diocesan commissions for Mexican Affairs in the country. He was a mentor to Patrick Flores, who was ordained as a priest in 1956 and eventually became the first Mexican-American Catholic bishop in the United States. When Furey met Cortés, he offered his support to COPS and encouraged neighborhood churches to become places where Latino dreams and demands could be heard.

The same year that COPS was established Robert McDermott was elected Chairman of the San Antonio Chamber of Commerce. In the five years since he had assumed the leadership at USAA, the military insurance company had doubled in size, and his introduction of an innovative four-day workweek and employee childcare revolutionized the workplace. He established the nonprofit San Antonio Economic Development Foundation in 1974 to promote new businesses coming to San Antonio and to urge minority hiring and the equalization of wages. In 2021, the foundation changed its name to greater: SATX Regional Economic Partnership. The scales appeared to be tipping; diverse voices were beginning to level the playing field.

Since the 1950s, city government had been controlled by a group of business leaders whose Good Government League (GGL) proposed its hand-picked slate of candidates for the city council. Typically, six businessmen from the city's North Side were chosen for the slate, along with three representatives from other sections of town. But by the 1975 election, the GGL was aware of changing dynamics when an opposition slate called the "Independent Team" offered stiff competition. In a strategic move, the GGL created a nine-candidate ticket that broke with its tradition.

In 1975, I ran for Place 3 on the City Council as part of the West Side Good Government League ticket. My campaign focused on economic development, instead of social welfare programs, as the means to lift San Antonio out of poverty.

— Henry G. Cisneros

Almost immediately after arriving from Mexico in 1926, my grandparents, Carolina and Jose Mungia were active in social welfare initiatives for Hispanics living on San Antonio's West Side; and both had colorful histories. My grandfather was from Jalisco; he became a revolutionary journalist who fought in the Mexican Revolution. My grandmother was from Puebla; she was a teacher and later a school principal in Orizaba until political unrest closed the school. They left Mexico in 1926 to make a new life on the West Side of San Antonio, where they created several remarkable enterprises aimed at honoring their Mexican heritage and promoting understanding for it. The family established Munguia Printers in 1936—some of its early clients were the city's Chinese grocers, who were denied service by Anglo printers, and Father Carmelo Tranchese who published the first Spanish archdiocesan Sunday newsletter, *La Voz de Parroquia*. Known as the "housing priest," Father Tranchese was a major force behind the country's first public housing project—the Alazán-Apache Courts, completed on San Antonio's West Side in 1942.

— Henry G. Cisneros

photo courtesy of Institute of Texan Cultures/UTSA Special Collections

▲ Spurs basketball star Sean Elliott (center), Henry Cisneros, and Mayor Lila Cockrell participated in the 1990 groundbreaking for the Alamodome.

Mayor Cockrell appointed the tri-chairs of United San Antonio. She chose General McDermott, the CEO of USAA, to represent private business, and Raúl Jiménez, a food magnate whose contributions to the Latino community, were well known, to represent the civic sector. She told them that there was 'a new kid on the council' who she wanted to represent the government sector, and I was catapulted into what became a powerful step towards inclusion. Our group met every Thursday at seven o'clock in the morning in General McDermott's office at USAA's new 286-acre campus in northwest San Antonio. We interacted with leaders from every part of town and with ordinary citizens willing to share ideas for building a better city and region. Slowly, diverse voices began to find common ground.

— Henry G. Cisneros

In that same election, Lila Banks Cockrell was elected as the first woman mayor of a major U.S. city. She had served on the city council, was skilled at debate, listened to all sides of an argument, and was known for her gracious demeanor and unwavering courtesy.

In her 2019 memoir, *Love Deeper Than a River*, she wrote about her first encounter with a COPS group shortly after her election. "I remember a big public meeting that COPS staged in a West Side church," Cockrell wrote. "To get their agenda items through, the group embraced what they called pressure methods, believing those tactics were necessary for their success. I did not like those methods because they did not encourage coming in, sitting down, and trying to negotiate... while this political strategy differed from mine, I realized that the COPS constituency was making its needs and aspirations known, something that had not really happened before in San Antonio."

These were turbulent times in city governance systems throughout the country. When the U.S. Justice Department objected to San Antonio's system, citing its lack of minority representation, the city conducted a referendum on the idea of single-member districts rather than taking on a federal court battle. In a very close vote, citizens approved a "Ten-One Plan" where city council representatives would be elected by constituents from ten districts. As a result, the election of 1977 produced the first minority-dominated city council, with five Latinos and one African- American representative.

The years immediately following this shift in political power were at times rocky, and Mayor Cockrell sought advice and guidance from some of San Antonio's wisest leaders. One of those was McDermott, who suggested establishing United San Antonio—an organization designed to include all sectors—private, public, and civic—to bring progress and growth to the city.

The vision of an improved public transportation system was one goal that emerged from United San Antonio, championed by City Councilman Glen Hartman, and citizens voted in favor of a one-half-cent sales tax to fund it. The VIA Metropolitan Transit Authority began operating in 1978, improving transportation services for citizens without their own vehicles. It won the Best Transit System award in North America in 1990; today, its modern fleet of more than 500 buses serves San Antonio the area with more than 100 routes and 7,193 buses. But the infrequency of buses creates long commutes for many—to work, school, the grocery store, medical appointments, and church—and the city continues to look for new solutions. VIA's new Keep SA Moving plan proposes a $38 million investment to make transportation a high priority for this fast-growing city. Its CNG-powered (compressed natural gas) fueling station is the largest in North America.

More than 500 people participated in Target 90; they generated 140 goals for the city to achieve over the next seven years. While the goals were undoubtedly important, the most valuable part of the process was that people worked together. Everyone was invited to come into a shared space and dream together. It was a turning point; some of the city's most influential businessmen began to see the potential for economic transformation through inclusion. They understood the strategy and supported it, which was instrumental in San Antonio's growth in the last decades of the twentieth

H.B. "Pat" Zachry (right) not only helped plan HemisFair; his construction company also built much of it. Since the 1920s the Zachry Company has built civil engineering projects and today its roads, airports, power plants, and other construction projects stretch across the globe.

Courtesy of Institute of Texan Cultures/UTSA Special Collections century. Other community leaders like Raúl Jiménez from the West Side and Reverend Claude Black, and LouNelle Sutton from the East Side added diversity. They were the right people on the scene at the right time, united in that critical moment for our city.

• H.B. "Pat" Zachry (1901 – 1984) was born in Laredo, Texas, and earned a degree in civil engineering from Texas A&M University in 1922. He founded the H.B. Zachry Company in 1924 and oversaw worldwide construction projects that included roads, dams, bridges, airplane runways, and power plants. He is remembered for building the Hilton Palacio del Rio Hotel in just 202 days, in time for the 1968 opening of San Antonio's HemisFair, and for his many civic contributions that helped produce a modern city.

• Brigadier General Robert F. McDermott (1920 – 2006) was born in Boston, Massachusetts, and graduated from the United States Military Academy. After distinguished service as a fighter pilot during World War II, he was appointed Dean of the Air Force Academy by President Eisenhower in 1959. He retired from the Air Force in 1968 to become the CEO of USAA in San Antonio. His civic contributions to the city include chairmanship of the Greater San Antonio Chamber of Commerce and the establishment of United San Antonio and the San Antonio Economic Development Foundation.

• General William V. McBride (1922—), born in Wampum, Pennsylvania, was the former Vice Chief of Staff of the United States Air Force. A four-star general, he is a decorated veteran of both World War II, where he served as a bomber squadron navigator in the European Theater, and the Korean War, where he commanded both the 2nd Air Rescue Group and the 8th Rescue Group. After retirement in 1978, he moved to San Antonio, where he has served as President of the San Antonio Chamber of Commerce and as a board member of a long list of civic organizations.

• Red McCombs (1927-) was born in Spur, Texas, and is the founder of the Red McCombs Automotive Group, co-founder of Clear Channel Communications, and a former owner of the San Antonio Spurs, Denver Nuggets, and Minnesota Vikings. The McCombs School of Business at the University of Texas at Austin is named in his honor. His contributions to San Antonio since moving here in 1958 are recognized in every corner of the city. When he arrived a little more than fifty years ago, he wanted to see San Antonio become a nationally recognized city and worked hard to make that happen.

• Tom C. Frost (1927 – 2018) was born in San Antonio and graduated from Washington and Lee University in Virginia. He was the fourth generation to lead Frost Bank, established in 1868 by his great grandfather. Legendary for his crucial role in the success of both HemisFair and the South Texas Medical Center, he also spearheaded the development of Project Quest and the Free Trade Alliance; served on many civic boards; and received the Aguila Azteca medal, the highest honor bestowed on a foreign citizen by Mexico. Shortly before he died in 2018, he helped plan the Frost Tower, a new 24-story headquarters for the 150-year-old bank, developed by Weston Urban and completed in 2019.

The new dreams formulated in the 1980s for the decades ahead reshaped both the skyline and the soul of San Antonio. The Economic Development Foundation actively recruited new businesses. It funded exploratory trips to California's Silicon Valley and Japan's innumerable manufacturing plants, looking for companies that might recognize

> When I ran for mayor in 1981, on a platform of economic growth and job creation, I thought of myself as a 'two-fisted boxer.' Fist number one had to grow the economy, and the second fist had to harness it to work for everybody. After I won the election, building on the momentum of United San Antonio, I created Target 90 to set goals for our city for the remainder of the decade. I used the same tri-chair model to be sure all sectors of San Antonio could participate. I selected Bob Marbut, CEO of the Harte-Hanks media conglomerate, a traditional Texan; Roy Kaiser, a Latino who had been a leader in COPS, and Lou Nelle Sutton, a State Representative trailblazer in the African-American community—along with her much-respected husband, G.J. Sutton.
>
> — Henry G. Cisneros

Robert Gordon Marbut (1935-2022) helped build modern San Antonio through diverse roles in business and civic leadership.

photo by Susan Riley; courtesy of Janette McDonald Marbut

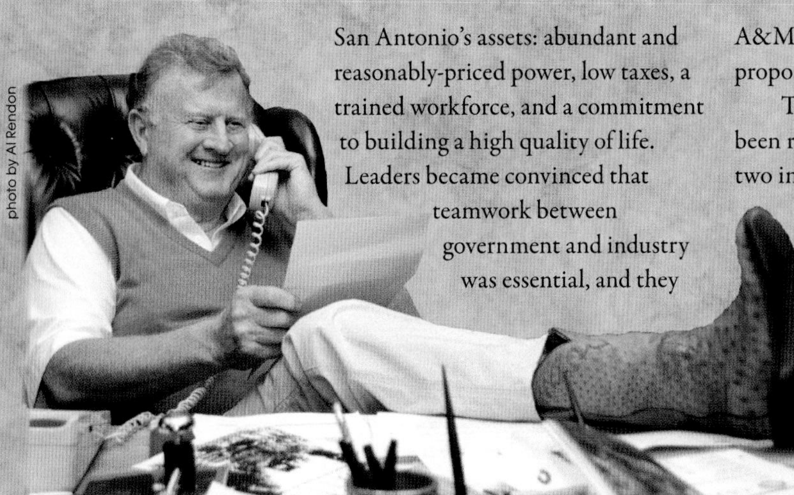

photo by Al Rendon

San Antonio's assets: abundant and reasonably-priced power, low taxes, a trained workforce, and a commitment to building a high quality of life. Leaders became convinced that teamwork between government and industry was essential, and they recognized that San Antonio could benefit from looking beyond its city limits for opportunities.

SeaWorld San Antonio was an opportunity that came from afar; it built its action-packed 250-acre complex on the far west side of San Antonio in 1988, and the Hyatt Regency Hill Country Resort opened nearby a few years later. An unexpected visit to the mayor's office started the process.

In the fast-growing northwest quadrant of the city, Fiesta Texas—now Six Flags Fiesta Texas—opened its gates to world-class rollercoasters and other exciting rides in 1992, not far from USAA. Nearby, the University of Texas at San Antonio (UTSA) and the South Texas Medical Center (both established in 1969) were expanding dramatically, accompanied by booming residential and commercial development in the area.

Downtown, the Alamodome welcomed sports fans to its new arena in 1993; and the city's NBA basketball team, the San Antonio Spurs, won its first league championship six years later. Early negotiations were underway to bring a Toyota manufacturing plant to the far South Side, thanks to the city's developing international relationship with Japan. The decades-long dream of state senator Frank L. Madla, Jr., to see a four-year public university in the same area was becoming a reality, with plans to construct a standalone campus for Texas A&M–San Antonio not far from the proposed Toyota site.

To the west, on what had been ranchland until the 1940s, two institutes founded by oilman/philanthropist Tom Slick were early pioneers in charting San Antonio's future ventures into biosciences and technology. Southwest Foundation for Biomedical Research (now the Texas Biomedical Research Institute) established a large primate research colony to search for new vaccines to combat infectious diseases. Southwest Research Institute quickly became one of the most extensive applied research facilities in the world, engineering products ranging from artificial heart valves to deep-sea submersibles to rocket parts. The fields of bioscience, technology, and cybersecurity were about to explode with possibilities for new companies. San Antonio was ready to meet the future.

▲ Red McCombs

▶ Tom Frost

▶ Southwest Research Institute and the Foundation for Applied Research (today Texas Biomedical Research Institute) were founded by Tom Slick (right) in the 1940s; he hired Harold Vagtborg (left) to oversee some of the first science and technology endeavors in San Antonio.

Courtesy of Southwest Research Institute

photo courtesy of Sea World

I was sitting in my office on a Monday afternoon, waiting for a scheduled appointment with someone named William Jovanovich. I did not know who he was, but of course, I welcomed him when he arrived. He brought a piece of paper with him—it was a draft of a press release. The headline announced that SeaWorld was coming to San Antonio, followed by a sentence about when the park would open. There was a blank space for the date. He told me that he wanted to build his theme park in San Antonio, and it was up to me to fill in the blanks. I had never heard of SeaWorld. He told me he had a plane at the airport and was flying to Orlando, Florida that night; he asked me to come with him to see a SeaWorld in action. I agreed to do it; we flew to Florida in record time; I saw the park, and he flew me back to San Antonio the next day. And the rest is history.

— Henry G. Cisneros

SeaWorld San Antonio was the city's first theme park; it attracted more than 16 million visitors in 2019, pre-pandemic. The park's new Tidal Surge ride is pictured above.

photo courtesy of Sea World

Chapter Three: A Vibrant Core

The River Walk accented with neon captures the excitement experienced by millions of tourists each year.

A RIBBON OF WATER FLOWS THROUGH THE HEART OF SAN ANTONIO, UNITING MODERN DREAMS WITH THE CITY'S HISTORICAL PAST. THE FAMOUS RIVER WALK ATTRACTS MORE THAN ELEVEN MILLION VISITORS TO SAN ANTONIO'S BUSTLING DOWNTOWN EVERY YEAR.

— CATHERINE NIXON COOKE

In 1959, nearly a decade before HemisFair introduced the world to San Antonio, businessman David Straus listened to the San Antonio Chamber of Commerce board describe the growing dangers along the downtown stretch of the San Antonio River. When twenty-eight-year-old architect Robert Hugman designed arch bridges and walkways along the river in the 1930s, he envisioned continued development that would add beauty and charm to the downtown and attract business and tourism. Over the years, that dream had faded; crime was rampant, and by the late 1950s, it was considered so dangerous that military bases in San Antonio declared it off-limits. Straus volunteered to tackle the problem, and Chamber President Walter Corrigan asked him to organize and chair a committee. At the time, only two buildings had access to the River Walk; several others backed up to the river, but their entrances were at the street level. After extensive research and trips to other cities protecting their historic districts, Straus made an out-of-the-box suggestion that changed the face of downtown San Antonio and the city's future. He reminded community leaders that the waterway running through town had attracted early settlers, provided water and power, and united a population with its beauty and utility. He proposed that new downtown businesses be encouraged to design entrances on the river level rather than the streets above. The chamber committee realized it needed a master

photo by Al Rendon

plan to illustrate to property owners what the River Walk could become, and the local chapter of the American Institute of Architects was enlisted to design one. For four months, a committee of architects—Cy Wagner, Ed Mok, Brooks Martin, Walter Mathis, Thomas Presley, Boone Powell, and Ignacio Torres—met weekly and drew their ideas on a chalkboard.

At the time, only Casa Rio—the oldest restaurant on the river—had made the waterway part of its identity—landscaping the banks between two bridges and introducing colorful dinner barges. Established by German entrepreneur Albert Beyer in 1946, Casa Rio originally was the basement of a centuries-old Mexican hacienda ruined by the famous flood of 1921. Beyer excavated the mud and silt and began to serve cantina- like Mexican food. He operated barges that floated along the river. Those planning the refurbishment of the river in the early 1960s recognized the appeal of the barges and created a new city operating concession, which Casa Rio held until 1995. Still family-run, the restaurant is managed by the fourth generation of the Beyer/Lyons family and is an icon on the San Antonio River, serving more than 500,000 customers a year.

The most recent competition for the barge concession was fierce. In 2019 the City awarded the contract to Go Rio San Antonio River Cruises, owned by Esperanza "Hope" Andrade. Before venturing into tourism, he was well-known in San Antonio having served as Texas's Secretary of State from 2008-2012 and as a

photo Courtesy of Bill Lyons/Casa Rio

Historic Casa Rio was the first restaurant on the River Walk.

The Alamo, San Antonio's most iconic landmark, attracts 2.5 million visitors annually.

Commissioner on the Texas Workforce Commission. In anticipation of millions of visitors, the riverfront was reinvented.

The whirlwind planning to accommodate HemisFair in 1968 had a profound effect on the pace of the River Walk development. New hotels like the Hilton Palacio del Rio and La Mansion del Rio hugged the landscape, the walkways at river level were lighted, restaurants and shops sprang to life. In the decades that followed, the massive Rivercenter Mall and Marriott Rivercenter incorporated the old Joske's Department Store parking lot creating the curve where colorful barges turn around.

Today, more than 37,000,000 tourists visit San Antonio each year; only the Alamo surpasses the River Walk as the city's number one attraction. As Andrade recalls, "HemisFair brought the world to San Antonio; and now that I'm in the tourism industry, I'm convinced it really put our city on the map. I'm so proud of tourism and grateful to all the workers in hospitality—-in restaurants, hotels, and on our barges. They are our ambassadors; they are the friendly, kind faces of San Antonio. During the Covid-19 pandemic, tourism was hit hard; and I really thought this might be the end for Go Rio. But I'm an optimist; I've seen visitors returning to San Antonio, and I think there will be a bounceback for tourism; in 2021, conventions started booking again for 2022 and 2023...we are such a unique city!"

Another magnet that energized the city post-HemisFair made use of the existing arena that had been built for exposition. Red McCombs, a local automobile dealer and a member of the fair's executive committee, suggested that bringing a sports team to San Antonio could provide a way for the city to build its visibility once the fair closed. He put together a group of thirty-six local investors to purchase a basketball team called the Dallas Chaparrals in 1973.

Renamed the San Antonio Spurs, the team joined the National Basketball Association three years later, facilitated by the American Basccketball Association-NBA merger. Despite some problematic early seasons, the Spurs began a climb to success, including five league championships and worldwide recognition. McCombs saw San Antonio as a great city needing local unification and a national image; he hoped the Spurs might be the solution. The team attracted fans from all over town—everyone cheered for the Spurs.

By the late 1980s, the team needed a larger arena, and sports fans pushed hard for a new complex that could accommodate a professional football team, should that longtime dream be realized. Construction of the Alamodome, just east of downtown, began in 1990. Three years later, the Spurs played their first game in the new arena.

That same year, Julianna Hawn Holt and Peter M. Holt, chairman of HOLT CAT Machinery Company, bought the majority interest in the Spurs from a consortium of owners led by McDermott; and the push for a national championship began. When in 1999 the team won the NBA championship, Holt parlayed that success into convincing a powerful group of county and city leaders to build what became the AT&T Center.

Because tourism, the convention business, and the military have historically fueled San Antonio's economy, it has not experienced the central business growth of other cities. The downtown skyline has not changed much; modern skyscrapers of glass and mirrors have not replaced the historic architectural gems built in the late 1920s. The upside is a human scale that remains constant in downtown San Antonio, where water,

"On June 25, 1999, the Spurs won the NBA championship, and the city went crazy. Tim Duncan was named the finals MVP. More than 300,000 citizens showed up at a parade to celebrate the victory; as the floats passed by, fans chanted, 'Arena, arena, arena.' The process to approve a new arena for San Antonio was complex and controversial, but thanks to the leadership of Cyndi Krier, who served as Bexar County Judge from 1993 to 2001, and a remarkable team of elected officials, business leaders, and the citizens of Bexar County, the new SBC Center became a reality."

— Nelson Wolff, Bexar County Judge

foliage, and natural limestone are the key landscape components. There has always been a delicate dance in San Antonio, its unlikely partners being the desire for an expanding economy and the determination to protect its historical, cultural character.

That character is reflected in the limestone headquarters for H-E-B, a grocery chain that was ranked number eleven on *Forbes* magazine's list of America's largest private companies in 2019. With more than 400 stores across Texas and in Mexico, H-E-B moved to San Antonio from Corpus Christi in 1985. It converted an Army arsenal complex constructed in 1859 into a modern corporate compound on the banks of the San Antonio River. H-E-B is now the state's largest private employer, with more than 135,000 people on its payroll. It is also one of this city's most generous corporate citizens.

Tony Kent–Wikimedia Commons

Rivercenter Mall was part of downtown San Antonio's post-HemisFair boom; three decades later more than 100 stores and restaurants comprise the Shops at Rivercenter

Cultural character is evident in other renovated landmark buildings downtown. The Aztec and Majestic Theatres, both built in the late 1920s, were restored in recent decades as state-of-the-art modern venues for Broadway productions, music concerts, and various special events while retaining the magnificent atmospheric ambiance of their historic pasts.

New structures also have added to the vibrancy of San Antonio's downtown. One of the most striking is the colorful Central Library, completed in 1995 and funded by a $28 million city bond along with more than $10 million in private donations. San Antonio residents proudly call it "the red enchilada" as a fond reference to a favorite local food that celebrates the city's Latino heritage. Renowned Mexican architect Ricardo Legorreta designed the library in partnership with the local firms of Sprinkle-Robey Architects and Johnson-Dempsey Associates. Utilizing design features from Mexico, Legorreta included plazas, lush landscaping, and fountains as part of the 240,000-square-foot facility, determined to "break the concept that libraries are imposing."

The Municipal Auditorium, designed by celebrated architect Atlee Ayres in 1926 as a memorial to American soldiers killed in World War I, was transformed into the Tobin Center for the Performing Arts in 2014. Its Spanish Colonial Revival façade was preserved as a salute to its historical past. Still, the new 183,000 square-foot facility, designed by the Seattle-based LMN architectural firm in partnership with San Antonio's Marmon-Mok Architecture, is a world-class performing arts center for the twenty-first century and beyond. Located just steps from the San Antonio River, with three separate

photo Courtesy of Las Casas Foundation

Built in 1929, the Majestic Theatre is Antonio's oldest and largest atmospheric theater. It was renovated to full glory in 1989 by Las Casas Foundation, led by civic leader Joci Straus.

photo by Al Rendon

The Central Library, known for its bold style and color, was designed by Mexican post-modernist architect Ricardo Legorreta.

theaters of varying sizes, the Tobin Center for the Performing Arts presents programming as diverse as San Antonio itself.

While a booming hospitality and entertainment scene evolved downtown in the decades following HemisFair, real estate developers saw significant potential in the large tracts of land in San Antonio's suburbs. Most of the city's business and residential growth occurred in the northern quadrants. In 1969, plans to build the new South Texas Medical Center and the city's first four-year public university in northwest San Antonio were announced. Texas Governor Preston Smith—standing in front of the Alamo—signed the bill authorizing the new University of Texas at San Antonio (UTSA). Six years later, it welcomed its first students to its 700-acre campus located nearly fifteen miles from downtown. It would be several decades later until a second campus was built in the heart of San Antonio.

In 1993, UTSA acquired the abandoned Fiesta Plaza Mall on the edge of downtown San Antonio as a donation from Bill Miller Bar-B-Q Enterprises. The eleven-acre site enabled the University to move forward with its "UTSA Downtown" initiative. The initiative was in response to a landmark lawsuit filed by the Mexican-American Legal Defense Fund against the State of Texas in 1987, demanding equal access to quality higher education for Mexican-Americans. The case resulted in the South Texas Border Initiative, which allocated more than $90 million in funding for UTSA and stipulated that $20 million be used to build a second campus downtown.

The first classes were held on the new campus designed by Humberto Saldana & Associates in 1997; acquisition of additional acreage and development of a long-range expansion plan was begun. Two decades later, Graham Weston, the co-founder of the cloud computer firm Rackspace, donated $15 million to the next iteration. It includes relocating the UTSA Business School downtown and building a $33 million National Security Collaboration Center and a $57 million School of Data Science—timely additions for a society increasingly conscious of the growing need for cybersecurity expertise.

Before Weston sold Rackspace to Apollo Global Management in 2016, he established Geekdom, a co-working space in downtown San Antonio that promotes entrepreneurial start-up companies focusing on technology. His real estate development company, Weston Urban, also has several residential and commercial projects under construction, fulfilling his vision of creating a vibrant tech district in a booming downtown.

In 2009, a few years before Weston added his innovative ideas and financial clout to business development downtown, San Antonio elected a new mayor who vowed to focus on residential equity in the

◀ The Municipal Auditorium was built in 1926, designed by architect Atlee Ayres.
photo courtesy of Institute of Texan Cultures/UTSA Special Collections

city's core. Thirty-five-year-old Julián Castro announced that "The Decade of Downtown" had begun, outlining plans for increasing housing options in the heart of San Antonio and assuring his constituents that the strategy would create new vibrancy. Ed Cross, a longtime inner-city developer, supported the idea wholeheartedly. He told *The Rivard Report*, established in 2012 as an online source of public service journalism, that San Antonio must become a city where educated professionals want to live, work, and raise their families. Great cities have great downtowns. Other developers agreed. By 2019, more than 7,000 new downtown residential units had been added to San Antonio's inventory.

Some of the most innovative new growth has taken place in an abandoned brewery on the edge of downtown—simply called The Pearl, it is an exciting smorgasbord taking mixed-use development to a new level. It has transformed the face of San Antonio. When Christopher "Kit" Goldsbury sold Pace Picante Sauce to Campbell Foods in 1994, a creative idea for expanding San Antonio's economy and showcasing its multi-cultural heritage began to percolate in his imagination. With family roots in Texas and Mexico, he dreamed of a privatized mixed-use development—a blended neighborhood. It would be a community with plazas, shops, restaurants, entertainment, galleries, residences, a hotel, and a culinary institute—on the historic site of Pearl Brewery, just north of the city core. It would be perched above the San Antonio River, with a landscaped turnaround for colorful barges traveling from downtown. The Pearl's original buildings from the late 1800s blend with modern structures designed by the award-winning architectural firm Lake Flato, many primarily powered by solar energy. Goldsbury's dream has become a national model for "place-making" and is the recipient of the Urban Land Institute's highest award. More than 30,000 people visit the complex weekly. It has become the crown jewel of San Antonio's downtown revitalization.

Today San Antonio's vibrant core is buzzing with activity. The

▼ The Auditorium became the Tobin Center for the Performing Arts in 2014, with a modern expansion designed by Seattle-based LMN Architects and the local firm Marmon Mok Architecture.

photo by Al Rendon

photo by Al Rendon

photo by Al Rendon

dramatic Frost Tower opened in 2019, just blocks from the bank's 1868 location and adjacent to the historic San Fernando Cathedral, which has been at the at the city's heart since 1731.

The cathedral, located in Main Plaza, has been the city's core since its earliest days as a Spanish settlement; and many consider it the soul of San Antonio. A limestone plaque located in front of the altar in the nave documents the historic cathedral's importance with seven simple words: "This is the heart of the city." Today, its long history is reflected in a spectacular light show, projecting dramatic images accompanied by sound, viewed from Main Plaza.

CPS Energy has maintained its headquarters downtown on the banks of the San Antonio River since 1860, when—as the San Antonio Gas Company—it began manufacturing gas from tree resin for the city's first gaslights on Main Plaza. Historically it has had several names and downtown locations, but for more than 160 years, it has powered the city and the larger metropolitan area. It is the nation's largest municipally-owned utility that generates and distributes power. Its diverse and generous community involvement is based on

Courtesy of Silver Ventures

photo by Robin Jerstad

its motto, "People First." When its new 494,000 square-foot headquarters building opened in 2020, CPS focused on energy efficiency in all aspects of its modern design.

Ironically, the complex is located on land once occupied by Valero Energy, a Fortune 500 company that the City of San Antonio and CPS Energy won in a 1975 lawsuit against their gas provider, Coastal States, and LoVaca Gathering, owned by Oscar Wyatt. As part of the landmark settlement, Coastal States was forced to divest itself of LoVaca and create a new entity whose shares were allocated to San Antonio. Wyatt's young vice President, Bill Greehey,

The Pearl Brewery Development has been globally recognized for its transformational repurposing of a 19th century brewery located along the San Antonio River, just north of downtown. Envisioned by Christopher "Kit" Goldsbury, CEO of Silver Ventures, and designed by Lake/Flato Architects, this vibrant urban district is home to more than a dozen restaurants, a bustling weekend farmer's market, residences, plazas and green spaces, and the five-star Hotel Emma.

photo by Al Rendon

photo by Al Rendon

Hemisfair Park Area Redevelopment and the Hemisfair Conservancy are working together to redevelop and energize the downtown site of the 1968 World's Fair. The Yanaguana Garden, a popular and innovative children's playground, was completed in 2015. Construction of the 8-acre Civic Park, just west of the Henry B. González Convention Center, is underway. The Zachry Hospitality Group's proposed mixed-use development project would bring new retail and housing to the heart of San Antonio.

moved to San Antonio to lead the new company, Valero Energy. He oversaw the construction of its first headquarters in 1984, where CPS Energy's new compound stands today. Valero's assets have increased to more than $50 billion and in 1995 it moved to a 200-acre campus in the North West quadrant. Today, both CPS Energy and Valero Energy are among the city's most generous corporate citizens, supporting education, the arts, medical research, and countless community service projects enriching the quality of life in San Antonio.

The San Antonio River Improvements Project has provided significant enhancements in recent years. The immense public-private partnership focuses on the thirteen-mile stretch of the waterway that drew the area's earliest inhabitants and allowed them to survive. It promises today and tomorrow's populations a respite from urban life—an escape from concrete and steel. With its flowing ribbon of water, it becomes a sacred space for San Antonians. Bexar County, the City of San Antonio, the U.S. Army Corps of Engineers, the San Antonio River Authority, and the San Antonio River Foundation, began the massive $380 million public works project in 2005. By the end of the decade, the four-mile Museum Reach, north of downtown, was fully operational, with landscaped walkways and public art stretching from the heart of downtown to the river's headwaters just below Pearl. Mission Reach, the seven-mile extension southward toward the missions, completed Confluence Park in 2018. It includes a learning center and walking trails through a restored ecosystem that ends at beautiful Mission Espada.

San Pedro Creek Culture Park also celebrates the waterway that is such an essential part of San Antonio. Located on a tributary of the river just west of downtown, it was once a beautiful oasis where the Payaya people lived for thousands of years before the Spanish settlements. It became a favorite destination for city residents at the end of the nineteenth century, reached via mule-driven streetcars. But during the twentieth century, it deteriorated into little more than a drainage ditch. A $125 million transformation has brought it back to life. Today, it showcases the works of prominent local artists, murals, ceramic art, tiled benches, and historical text and poetry depicting a colorful past and vibrant present. It has earned national praise as San Antonio's own "Latino High Line."

Artists Lionel and Kathy Sosa are described as a renaissance couple and rightly so. They have blazed trails in Hispanic marketing, education, art, and philanthropy. Lionel was selected as part of The Smithsonian's American Enterprise Series and named one of the twenty-five most influential Hispanics in the U.S. by *Time Magazine*. In

photo by Al Rendon

2021, they created a five-panel mural for San Pedro Creek's Culture Park, reflecting the unique spirit that is San Antonio—a bilingual depiction with themes featuring immigration, confluence, and restoration.

Similar to the way San Pedro Creek was restored to an important place in San Antonio's modern existence, the ninety-seven-acre site of the HemisFair, where San Antonio's march toward becoming a modern international city began, had experienced a rebirth. HemisFair's Tower of the Americas still stands tall; its all-glass elevator continues to transport passengers to the observation deck, located 750 feet above the Alamo City. But on the grounds below, a second transformation is underway. The new Henry B. González Convention Center opened in 2016, and the HemisFair Park Area Redevelopment Corporation began its revitalization of the surrounding area with modern enhancements and lively fun. The Yanaguana Garden opened in 2015. Featuring a children's playground, splash pad, fountains, and climbing structures, the Civic Park was transformed in 2019 into an urban green space with a towering canopy of oak trees. This site of culinary festivals and music performances is creating new energy in the once-vibrant plazas that had gone dormant in recent decades.

Andres Andujar, CEO of the HPARC, expects the final result to be "one of the world's great places," a walkable urban district with multiple parks, residences, and local businesses. The '68 apartments, designed by Lake Flato Architects opened in late 2019 as an aesthetic homage to the original fair, couples a hefty dose of modernism with affordable living spaces.

Mayor Castro's "Decade of Downtown" exceeded expectations; San Antonio's citizens recognized its successful results—both economic and intrinsic. Robert Rivard, an award-winning journalist and founder of the city's first online public service news source San Antonio Report, explains that Castro's vision "stretched into two decades; and it saved San Antonio from becoming a forgotten city." The momentum continued; San Antonio is among the top five fastest-growing cities in America.

Despite the Covid-19 pandemic, San Antonio's growth continues, outpacing that of Texas and the nation. It is a "city on a mission"— both literally and figuratively. Its five historic missions, shaded by ancient trees, remind residents and visitors of a history steeped in community. Its mission for the future is equally powerful; important tasks are ahead for San Antonio as it pushes beyond its vibrant core into every corner of the city.

photo by Al Rendon

image courtesy of Hemisfair

Chapter Four: A City of Neighborhoods

Tree-lined streets, frozen paletas, vine-covered porches, corner baseball games, sizzling kielbasas, manicured golf courses, urban parks, and spaghetti dinners at San Francesca di Padua— all are part of San Antonio's tapestry of neighborhoods... each unique thread deserves equity in city services; and San Antonio has made that a focus.

— Catherine Nixon Cooke

A city at large is an abstraction. To a child, the idea of a city is beyond understanding—what is real are those people and things immediately around us. We feel connected to our neighborhoods; they define how we see the world and find our place in it, how we access information, how we develop our identities and how we relate to others. They are the building blocks of cities.

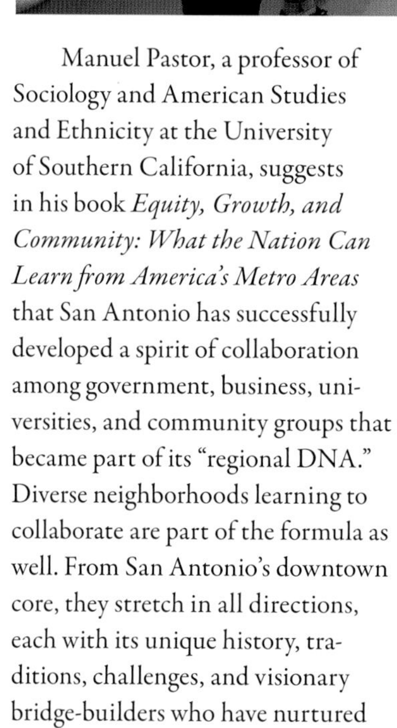

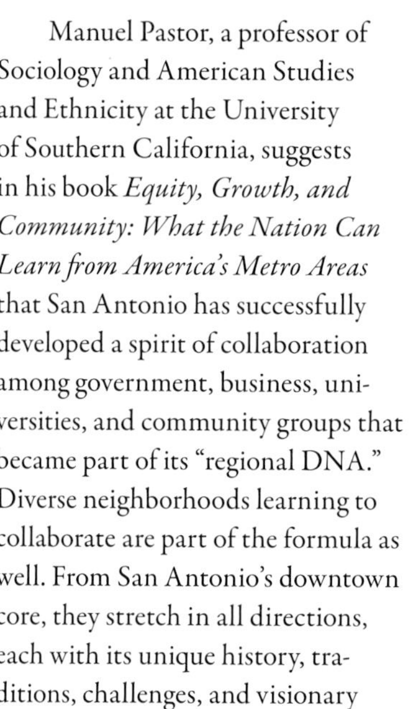

photos Courtesy of Contemporary at Blue Star

The Contemporary at Blue Star is a vibrant part of the bustling art scene of Southtown.

San Antonio's myriad neighborhoods can be understood as a cluster of small villages—each with unique assets and challenges. Often competing for services and opportunities, they eventually learned to work together to form a better city. Natural boundaries —like railroad tracks and freeways— shaped the geography of those "villages" as well as other boundaries created by economic status and ethnicity. Like most cities in the United States, San Antonio experienced its share of discrimination. Segregated neighborhoods and workplaces dominated until incomes rose, and integrated housing and school districts became realities late in the twentieth century. When it adopted a more inclusive form of city government in the mid-1970s, the city began to broaden into the "brotherhood" described by President Lyndon Johnson. However, the journey has been tumultuous and remains tenuous.

Manuel Pastor, a professor of Sociology and American Studies and Ethnicity at the University of Southern California, suggests in his book *Equity, Growth, and Community: What the Nation Can Learn from America's Metro Areas* that San Antonio has successfully developed a spirit of collaboration among government, business, universities, and community groups that became part of its "regional DNA." Diverse neighborhoods learning to collaborate are part of the formula as well. From San Antonio's downtown core, they stretch in all directions, each with its unique history, traditions, challenges, and visionary bridge-builders who have nurtured mutual respect and collaboration.

King William District/Southtown

The historic King William District is just to the south of downtown, with stately homes built by the German entrepreneurs who, more than 200 years ago, established Pioneer Flour Mills, several breweries, early streetcar lines, and newspapers. Many grand houses have been restored, including the Steves' Homestead, built in 1876 by Edward Steves, a German immigrant who established the city's first lumber company in 1866. Today it operates as the Villa Finale Museum and Gardens; its antiques and opulent furnishings transport visitors back to nineteenth century San Antonio, when the wealthiest citizens lived on the South Side of town.

The first neighborhood in Texas to be declared historical, the King William District treasures its quiet and elegant tree-lined streets. In 1984 it expanded to include a mix of more modest cottages in "Baja King William" and the Lavaca area, where

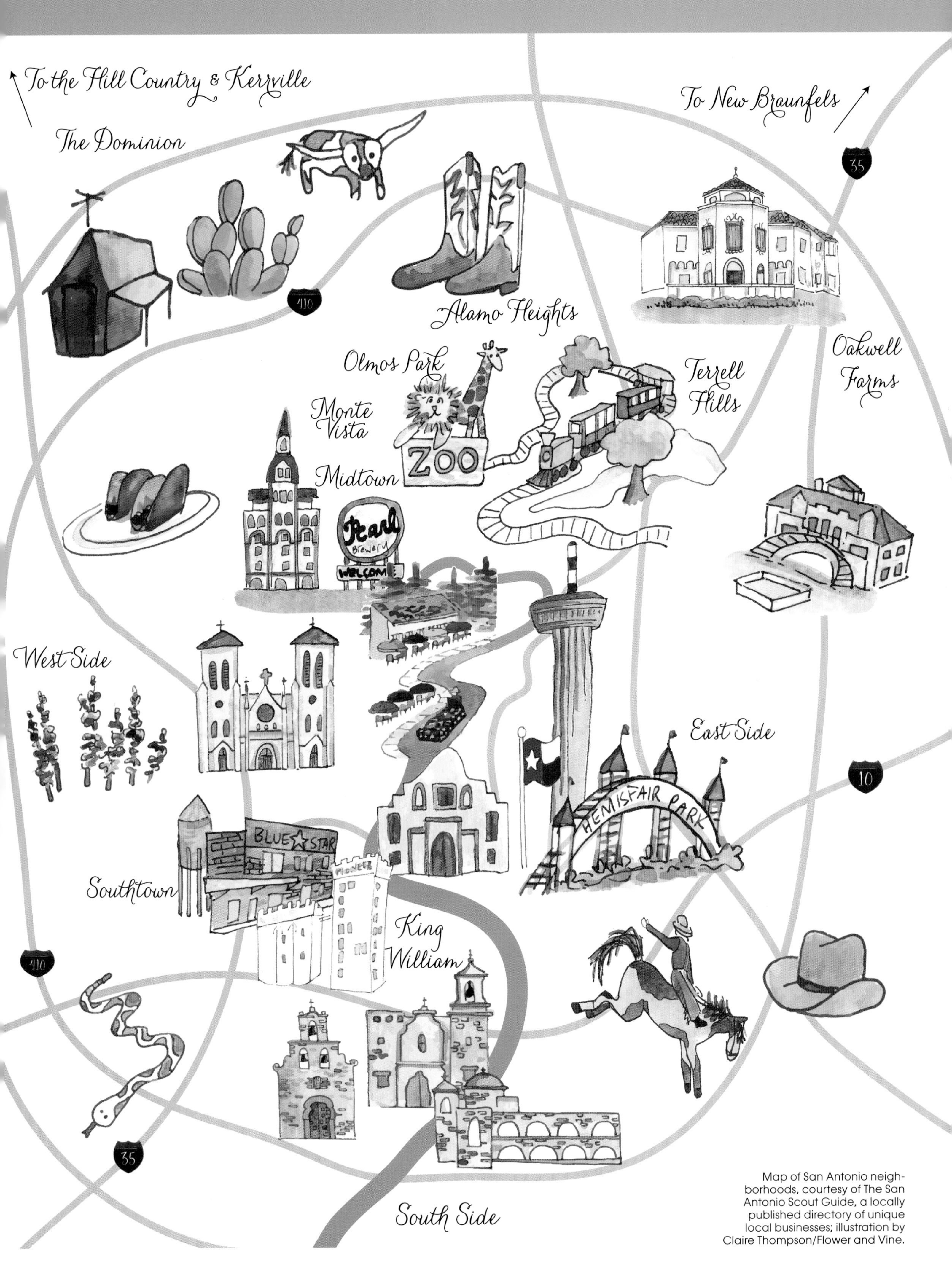

Map of San Antonio neighborhoods, courtesy of The San Antonio Scout Guide, a locally published directory of unique local businesses; illustration by Claire Thompson/Flower and Vine.

photo by Al Rendon

Villa Finale in the King William neighborhood reflects the history and architecture of San Antonio's grand houses of the mid-19th century.

some of San Antonio's best-known artists, poets, and writers live. The modernization of surrounding SouthTown, with its ultra-hip cafes, lively bars, and new residential developments such as the Flats at Big Tex and the Cevallos Lofts have enlivened the entire area. A sizzling contemporary art scene anchored by Blue Star Arts Center and Ruby City (designed by Britain's Sir David Adjaye) adds distinct energy to a once-neglected part of town on the edges of the wealthier King William District.

"The only bad childhood memory I have is of the wind blowing the wrong way. When that happened, we could smell the horrible odor of everyone's waste, which had been deposited in Mitchell Lake south of our home after being processed at the Rilling Road Wastewater Treatment Plant a short distance upstream. Much later, during my first year on the city council in 1987, we closed the Wastewater Plant and created the Mitchell Lake wetlands out of what had once been a sewage lagoon. We flooded more than 200 of the 589 acres with treated wastewater to provide a year-round refuge for more than 300 species of migratory birds."

—Bexar County Judge Nelson Wolff
The Changing Face of San Antonio

South Side

Farther south, neglect was more profound; freeways on the city's far South Side were not lighted until the 1970s. Its residents were underserved in terms of infrastructure, health care, and educational opportunities. But there has always been a magical ambiance to this part of San Antonio, first settled by the Payayas thousands of years ago. It's also where the Spanish first settled in the 1700s, and later by immigrants from Poland and Czechoslovakia who also settled in nearby Panna Maria. Its canopies of massive pecan trees and cottonwoods shading the riverbank, cottages with vine-covered porches and family gardens, and baseball games played in quiet streets are memories that delight Richard Perez, CEO and President of the San Antonio Chamber of Commerce. He grew up in the Gillette area, where his father established a small landscaping company. Decades later, he still lives in the neighborhood, surrounded by familiar shade trees and family. The Fairway Landscape and Nursery remains a thriving southside business run by his siblings and cousins.

Bexar County Judge and former San Antonio mayor Nelson Wolff, also recalls baseball games during his childhood there. He remembers it as a safe and friendly neighborhood, where homes could be left unlocked. A summer highlight was a refreshing swim at the nearby Hot Wells Spa now undergoing significant restoration. Wolff's German-American grandparents moved with their three children from Pflugerville to San Antonio's South Side in the 1930s. His grandfather found work as a janitor, and his father, like many young people growing up during the Great Depression, left school after eighth grade to help support his family. Wolff was the first in his family to attend high school and college; he chose a career of public service and was a member of the City Council, mayor of San Antonio, a member of the Texas House of Representatives, and Bexar County Judge.

In the late 1980s and 1990s, efforts were made to reverse a languishing South Side, including constructing a new subdivision and golf course, improvements to nearby coal-generating electric plants, and new drainage projects. At the same time, the neighborhood's historic past received further attention. Funding from the city and state for the Mission Trails project resulted in ten miles of hike-and-bike connections from the iconic Alamo to the four San Antonio missions situated south of town—San Jose, Concepcion, San Juan Capistrano, and San Francisco de Espada.

Crumbling limestone walls and bell towers, built by indigenous people for the Spaniards in the eighteenth century, underwent restoration; and in 2015, the missions were designated as a UNESCO World Heritage Site. Echoes of ancient artisans working in the fields along stone acequias are part of the South Side's unique culture. Those echoes inspired the design for the city's first four-year public university just a few miles from Mission Espada. The new Texas A&M University–San Antonio campus opened its doors in 2009, bringing a boost of energy and expanded opportunity to the historic landscape.

Frank Madla, Jr. was a champion for development on the South Side for decades; he lobbied for economic growth and infrastructure as both a State Representative and a State Senator. Other bridge-builders, including Nelson Wolff, pushed hard too; and in 2003, the City Council adopted its City South Master Plan. Former Mayor Ed Garza points to the plan as an example of Pastor's description of San Antonio's spirit

> "When I was mayor, Bob Marbut was CEO of Harte-Hanks Communications and a Target 90 Task Force co-chair. He was also on the board of "Up With People," where he knew Mrs. Naoko Mitsui Shirane, a cousin-in-law of Dr. Shoichiro Toyoda, whose father founded Toyota Motors. He introduced us; she fell in love with San Antonio, helped us organize a trade delegation to Japan in 1985, and was instrumental in promoting our city in her country. It was friendships and careful relationship-building that brought Toyota to San Antonio."
>
> —-Henry G. Cisneros

photo by Al Rendon

photo courtesy of TAMUSA

Texas A&M University–San Antonio

> 'I am proud to be a native of San Antonio's South Side. My parents met while attending South San Antonio Iigh School. Back then, options for higher education in that eighborhood were limited. Now, in 2020, there are a number uality education options—made possible by the audaciousness nd creativity of so many champions like the great senator 'rank L. Madla, Jr., who had a vision to bring a university o the South Side of San Antonio. He knew that access to uality educational programs was the key to building economic rosperity throughout the region. It is an honor to be part of his legacy."
>
> — Dr. Cynthia Teniente-Matson, President, Texas A&M–University

of collaboration. Garza noted it was "based on the South Side's longing for economic growth, good schools, and modern amenities and on the North Side's frustration with the rapid growth that had caused congested roadways and massive zoning problems."

A big win for the plan was the decision by Japanese automaker Toyota to build a new manufacturing plant on the South Side in 2003. The relationship with Toyota had been making for nearly two decades, initiated in 1985 when a San Antonio trade delegation went to Japan.

In 2002, after that long courtship, the final negotiations with

"In the new frontier of outer space, history is being made every day by the men and women of the Aerospace Medical Center without whom there could be no history. Americans make the mistake that space research has no value on earth. Nothing could be further than the truth....We have a long way to go; many weeks and months and years of tedious work lie ahead. There will be setbacks and frustrations and disappointments; there will be, as there always are, pressures in this country to do less and temptations to do something else that is perhaps easier. But this research here must go on; this space effort must go on; the conquest of space must and will go ahead. That much we know and can say with confidence and conviction.

Frank O'Connor, the Irish writer, in one of his books that I read as a boy, said that he and friends would make their way across the countryside, and when they came to an orchard wall that seemed too high, too hard to climb, they took off their hats and tossed them over the wall, and had no choice but to follow them. This nation has tossed its cap over the wall of space, and we have no choice but to follow it."

—-President John F. Kennedy

photo courtesy of Brooks

Brooks is a 1,300-acre mixed-use community with homes, businesses, shops and restaurants, education and research facilities, and recreation centers; it serves as a major economic engine for San Antonio.

Toyota began; they were complex and intense. In his book *Transforming San Antonio*, Wolff shares the details of the auto maker's decision to locate its new plant on a 2,600-acre site in San Antonio, leading to the eventual employment of more than three thousand people. "Those were frantic and exhilarating days," he says, adding, "Who would have believed that in less than five short months a city could alter its future and a major international corporation could adjust its course for the coming century?"

As the twentieth century concluded, the decision to close many of the country's military bases also changed San Antonio's future. The Kelly, Lackland, and Brooks bases were located on the city's South and West sides. Brooks Air Force Base had operated on the South Side for eighty five years, first as the Primary Flying School for the Army Air Corps in 1918, then as the Advanced Flying School during World War II. After the war, its School of Aerospace Medicine became a national center that provided teaching, clinical medicine, and research. It also worked closely with NASA to support orbital space flight and America's journey to the Moon.

President John F. Kennedy visited Brooks Air Force Base on November 21, 1963, just one day before being assassinated in Dallas. He praised the base's historic contributions to the country during both World Wars and the Korean War. He told his audience how important the new field of space research would be in the future—an uplifting and unforgettable moment for Brooks Air Force Base and San Antonio, followed by tragedy the next day.

As base closures became a reality in the mid-1990s, city and state officials, military leaders, and community planners realized the dramatic impact of the move on San Antonio's employment and the overall economy. They worked hard to design a transition plan for the privatization of the base; the result was the establishment of the Brooks Development Authority in 2002.

During its first decade of privatization, it successfully promoted

photo courtesy of George Cisneros

A neon spur designed by artist George Cisneros adorns the AT&T Center.

The San Antonio Stock Show and Rodeo (opposite page) brings two weeks of western thrills to San Antonio each winter.

economic development. It attracted retail businesses, research and distribution facilities for DPT Laboratories, the South Texas Center for Emerging Infectious Diseases, a STEM charter school, a hospital, and several research partnerships with local universities, including a UIW medical school on the site of the School of Aerospace Medicine. No longer associated with the Air Force, the mixed-use development provides long-overdue public amenities and is an example of successful repurposing.

"I was born here in San Antonio at Lackland Air Force Base, and I am proud to have been raised here. My humble parents brought me from Wilford Hall Hospital to the first and only home they ever owned. We lived in a very small and friendly four-street neighborhood on the east side of town. Even so, my world felt big in every way. My no-nonsense parents kept me busy—old school style. In addition to our schoolwork, we all had chores that were nonnegotiable, ranging from cleaning the house top-to-bottom to extensive yard work to some summers painting our whole house. While we were taught to prioritize hard work, from time to time, we also had fun. My mother loved cooking big meals during the holidays. She would invite our extended family and friends to drop by whenever they could. In the background, we either had sports playing on the television or Motown records spinning on the stereo. Again, my world was plenty big. Most everything I needed and knew was on the east side of town. It was where I learned the merits of hard work and the importance of "putting people first," which became our motto at CPS Energy during my tenure."

—Paula Gold-Williams, former CEO of CPS Energy

East Side

The East Side of San Antonio has experienced some repurposing as well. Once the destination for African-Americans moving to San Antonio from rural areas at the turn of the century, it's now a magnet of attraction for sports fans, concert-goers, and rodeo aficionados.

Rodeo photos by Al Rendon

San Antonio's championship NBA team, the Spurs, plays basketball in the state-of-the-art AT&T Center, opening as the SBC Center in 2002. The Rampage, the city's American Hockey League team, delivers fast-paced action on its ice rink; and the arena also stages regular concerts featuring performers ranging from Rod Stewart to Andrea Bocelli to Snoop Dog. It is also the site for one of the country's award-winning rodeos and livestock expositions, attracting more than two million people sporting cowboy boots and hats

photo by Al Rendon

The Alamodome became San Antonio's pre-eminent arena in 1993.

during its two-and-a-half-week run each February. It encompasses music performances by top country-western and rock singers, barns full of animals, bull and bronco riding, calf roping, a carnival, food stands, and a fancy VIP dining club. Still, there is more to the San Antonio Livestock Exposition. Its proceeds support education in the community; over the years, SALE has provided more than $210 million in scholarships and grants to Texas college students. Even the pandemic of 2020-2021 could not stop the rodeo—with "can do" spirit and safety protocols, it awarded all of its scholarships.

Nearby, in the older Alamodome, football dominates the vast arena, home to the University of Texas-San Antonio Roadrunners and the annual Alamo Bowl.

The Carver Community Cultural Center was built in 1918 as a community center in the heart of the East Side. Its performances and educational programs celebrate the diverse cultures of our world, with emphasis on the community's African-American heritage. Just a few blocks away, historic St. Paul's Square is anchored by Sunset Station, constructed in 1903 by the Southern Pacific Railroad to replace its original small depot that was built when steam locomotives first stopped in San Antonio in 1877. They delivered a steady flow of enterprising men and women ready to start a new life in a town on the rise; in the first decade of the twentieth century, San Antonio's population nearly doubled, to 96,614.

Not far from St. Paul's Square, the historic residential neighborhoods of Dignowity Hill, Knob Hill, and Government Hill are experiencing revitalization with an influx of young professionals. Dignowity Hill, just east of downtown, was settled in the mid-1800s by Dr. Anthony Michael Dignowity, a Czech immigrant, physician, and outspoken abolitionist whose political views nearly cost him his life in 1861 when he narrowly escaped being hanged in the Main Plaza.

After the Civil War and emancipation, freed slaves began moving to town from rural areas. The city saw a surge in its African-American population, followed by the establishment of Ellis Alley, the first neighborhood where freed slaves could own land. Over time, the impacts of poverty and neglect took the historic enclave to the brink of demolition. It was saved by a partnership between San Antonio for Growth on the East Side (SAGE), the San Antonio Conservation Society, VIA, and the Department of Planning and Community Development Tax Increment Reinvestment Zone. In 2016 the refurbished Ellis Alley was recognized by Preservation Texas.

Tuesdae Knight, President and CEO of SAGE, says her organization worked harder in 2020 than ever before. "Even though we had to close our physical doors because of the Covid-19 pandemic, we touched so many more people on a one-to-one basis. We helped hundreds apply for the PPE grants; it was intense and non-stop. The East Side still has the lowest annual income rates in the city—about twenty-nine thousand dollars—but rates are rising.

▶ Tuesdae Knight, CEO of San Antonio for Growth on the Eastside (SAGE)

photo courtesy of SAGE

According to realtor.com, in 2019 our neighborhood had become the most gentrified. That's both good news and bad news; there is a fear that trend will mean long-time residents can no longer afford to live here."

Knight is encouraged by developers like Randy Hartwig, who founded Velocity TX in 2019 as a "bioglobal accelerator" in the abandoned 55,000 square-foot Merchants Ice complex on Houston Street. "He's hiring on the East Side," she says, "and that is good for the neighborhood." Paula Gold-Williams, former President and CEO of CPS Energy—a company with more than 3,000 employees and revenues of more than $2.5 billion a year—spent her childhood in that neighborhood and still resides there.

Several stately mansions built in the 1880s in the Government Hill neighborhood have been restored in recent years; modern housing is part of the "gentrification" that Knight describes. The "Castle", designed by famed architect Alfred Giles for Edwin Holland Terrell, borders Fort Sam Houston and is a popular event site today. Terrell was educated at DePauw University, Harvard Law School, and the Sorbonne in Paris. As vice President of the San Antonio Gas Company in 1877, Terrell saw to it that the neighborhood was among the first to receive gas and water from the city. Two decades later, his sons each built homes a few miles to the north as San Antonio expanded.

North Central/Mahncke Park

A wealthy entrepreneur named George Washington Brackenridge owned rural land just beyond Fort Sam Houston, where Apache chief Geronimo was once incarcerated. His privately-owned company, San Antonio Water Works, was located there, close to the headwaters of the San Antonio River. Water was drawn from the river and pumped through an eighteenth-century acequia, up a hill to a storage reservoir which delivered water to San Antonio's East Side, where affluent friends like Edwin Terrell had built their homes. Decades later, the thirty-eight-acre San Antonio Botanical Center was built where the reservoir once stood. Today, it offers visitors a vast array of native plants, trees, and flowers of every color and size. Populated by butterflies during their annual migrations, the winding walkways and striking architecture enchant the senses.

Brackenridge loved nature; he was influenced to donate land to San Antonio for some of its earliest parks by his friend Ludwig Mahncke, the city's first paid parks commissioner. In 1899, Brackenridge deeded nearly 200 acres that included the waterworks property to the city, envisioning the creation of a "zoo without cages" at the bottom of the hill, where bison, African lions, deer, and monkeys could roam free. Emma Koehler, whose husband owned the nearby Pearl Brewery, donated land as well. Today, the 343-acre Brackenridge Park is home to a world-class zoo, the beautifully restored Sunken Gardens/

The Japanese Tea Garden in Brackenridge Park offers a quiet escape, with walkways, stone bridges, a 60-foot waterfall, and ponds filled with koi.

photo by Al Rendon

The Witte Museum has focused on the nature, science, and culture of South Texas since the 1920s; its interactive, hands-on exhibits have made it one of the top museums in the country.

Courtesy of the Witte Museum

The San Antonio Botanical Garden is recognized nationally for its botanical diversity and experiences that connect people to the natural world.

photo by Al Rendon

Japanese Tea House, and the Witte Museum, an award-winning natural history and education repository.

Constructed in 1926, with an ultra-modern addition completed in 2019, the Witte is home to dinosaurs, exhibits about the early indigenous people, and flora and fauna of the state's diverse regions. The area features a ceiling that changes from a bright blue sky to the dark hues of a Texas thunderstorm through high-tech sound and lighting.

Across the street from the Witte and its surrounding park lies the much smaller Mahncke Park. It was another gift from Brackenridge and was named in honor of his friend. In the 1920s and 1930s, cottages were built beside its narrow boundaries. The Mahncke Neighborhood Association is one of the most active in the city. Just a few blocks down Broadway, the DoSeum, a children's museum that opened in 2015, delivers hands-on excitement to the younger set. It has an outdoor pond and high technology interactive exhibits inside its colorful, futuristic building.

Alamo Heights/Terrell Hills/Olmos Park

Brackenridge built his own mansion—Fernridge—directly north of Brackenridge Park, on land now part of the University of the Incarnate Word. Because it was on slightly higher terrain than downtown San Antonio, it was less likely to be affected by the floods that plagued the city's center during heavy rains—he called his new residential area Alamo Heights.

The Terrell family also owned considerable acreage nearby. Just a few miles north of Edwin Terrell's "castle" in Government Hill, the family farm was considered a remote rural area in the early 1900s. Edwin's sons, Henry and Frederick, both built homes there in 1912, establishing another neighborhood on higher ground less prone to flooding and more likely to offer cooler breezes during the hot months. They called it Terrell Hills.

Alamo Heights, Terrell Hills, and Olmos Park (a similar enclave to the west) became magnets for affluent citizens. They offered large lots for spacious homes, and eventually, the advantages of excellent public schools and recreational amenities, including the city's first private country club. In 1939, Mayor Maury Maverick was running for re-election; he campaigned to initiate higher taxes in San Antonio's new "silk stocking" areas. Terrell Hills residents, led by Pat Swearingen, began the legal process to incorporate the neighborhood as a township and the city of San Antonio approved the petition on March 31.

Maverick was re-elected in May but could not tax the new city, which now had its own mayor—Wilbur L. Matthews. Alamo Heights and Olmos Park followed suit; all three are incorporated cities surrounded by San Antonio and remain home to many "old money" families who have helped shape the city.

Over the years, restaurants, museums, and high-end retail boutiques have added to the area's appeal. The beautiful mansion built in 1927 by arts patron Marion Koogler McNay was transformed into a museum in 1954–the first modern art museum in Texas. It showcases a vast art collection ranging from paintings and drawings by old masters and impressionists to contemporary works and sculpture. Temporary exhibits are wonderfully varied—ranging from Hollywood costumes to "Immersed: Local to Global Art Sensations," celebrating San Antonio as a "place of deep history, local values, and global thinking."

Northside/Northwest side

In the 1980s and 90s, development pushed farther northeast as newer neighborhoods sprang to life. Growth along the Austin corridor of Interstate 35 included Randolph Air Force Base. It produced the incorporated cities of Schertz, Cibolo, Universal City, Live Oak, and Selma; all included among San Antonio's "villages." Initially settled by immigrants from Alsace-Lorraine, France, the area is booming today, dominated by shopping malls, car dealerships, theater complexes, an 800,000-square-foot Amazon distribution center, and IKEA. Just a little farther north, New Braunfels and San Marcos have become the fastest-growing cities in the United States in their categories.

The continued growth of the South Texas Medical Center, USAA, UTSA, Datapoint, Valero, NuStar, and other significant businesses in San Antonio's Northwest quadrant produced the Stone Oak, Elm Creek, Shavano Park, and Rogers Ranch neighborhoods—affluent enclaves with top-rated public school systems and amenities. Not far from these neighborhoods, at the foot of the Texas hill country, the Dominion is a master-planned country club community constructed in 1988. Home to many celebrities, star athletes, and wealthy Mexican nationals who have moved to the United States, it is known for its luxurious estates, beautiful golf course, and attention to security.

Nearby, the Rim and La Cantera are large shopping centers with restaurants, movie theaters, and high-end retail shops offering an array of dining, shopping, and entertainment options. Just down the highway, Six Flags Fiesta Texas, once a limestone quarry, attracts more than 500,000 locals and tourists to its 200-acre theme park every year.

Laurel Heights/Monte Vista

The first streetcar routes connected Main Plaza (downtown) to San Pedro Park and the fairgrounds to the south. By 1910, routes expanded northwards, and the new neighborhoods of Laurel Heights and Monte Vista developed on that slightly higher ground (hence the names). Early entrepreneurs like Otto Koehler, who

photo courtesy of Taddy McAllister

In a sepia-toned photograph circa 1912, some nicly dressed people sit on the porch of a ranch house at what is now 205 Terrell Road—Henry Terrell's ranch house. Below them on the hill rises Dr. Frederick Terrell's three-story home at 203 Terrell Road, designed by famed architect Alfred Giles. There is no landscaping; the tracts are dirt. Terrell Hills is being born by gentry, leaving the flood-prone flats of downtown, and like nearby Alamo Heights and Olmos Park, it will be incorporated into a city unto itself. Meanwhile, even with other houses in sight, it is an outlier of old San Antonio. Something new is in the air.

— Taddy McAllister, granddaughter of Mayor McAllister, owner of the home built by Dr. Terrell

photo by Al Rendon

The McNay Museum was the first contemporary art museum in Texas.

ran the Pearl Brewery, and Harry Landa, built elegant homes. He owned several businesses, including a milling operation on land near the small German-settled town of New Braunfels. After the death of his wife in 1947, Landa donated his Monte Vista mansion, described in 1929 by *The San Antonio Light* as "one of the South's finest homes," to the city of San Antonio for a library and children's playground. But it wasn't until 1991, when a neighborhood group formed the Landa Library Alliance, that his vision was fully honored. The Alliance partnered with the Monte Vista Historical Association and soon started yet another support group, the Landa Gardens Conservancy, in 2004. A massive fundraising campaign began; corporate citizens including the Kronkosky Foundation, the Myra Stafford Pryor Charitable Trust, the Greehey and Whitacre family foundations, SBC, H-E-B, and Valero Energy contributed. Construction began in 2007. Today, more than 100,000 people visit this unique treasure in Monte Vista each year.

"When my grandparents arrived in San Antonio from Mexico, they lived in a small house on Cherry Street on the East Side because that was the cheapest neighborhood. They started a business washing clothes for neighbors but soon found that the neighbors could not afford the luxury of that service. When my Dad was twelve years old, he rode his bicycle to the Alamo Heights neighborhood and offered laundry services to its residents. He was an entrepreneur at heart, promising potential customers that his parents would launder the first shirt for free, and if satisfied, customers could continue the service. When my Dad was in high school, he met and married my mother, and when he was twenty-one, he opened his own laundry in the more affluent Prospect Hill neighborhood on the West Side. It was ethnically mixed then, largely German and Belgian, so Dad called his new business the Prospect Hill Cleaners instead of Sosa Cleaners. He chose a location across from Crockett Elementary School, on a block that had a feed store and a five-and-dime store, and we lived in a room behind the business until we moved to a bigger house on Buena Vista Street."

Lionel Sosa, artist and founder of Sosa, Bromley, Aguilar Advertising

Jefferson/Monticello Park

To the west of Laurel Heights and Monte Vista, the Jefferson/Monticello Park area is considered an urban core neighborhood, located on the northwest border of the city's central business district. Before 1887 it was a dairy farm but when the streetcar line extended that far, its development as residential real estate opened a "new frontier." A few years after the neighborhood was founded, a dam was built on Alazan Creek to create Woodlawn Lake, eighty acres of water with a distinctive lighthouse. Later, the community initiated a Fourth of July fireworks display that takes place every year.

After World War II, many original residents moved to newer suburbs north of downtown, and the Jefferson area deteriorated. Recent decades have witnessed an influx of young professionals who like the idea of living close to downtown. While the area is undergoing an exciting rebirth, the historic landmarks remain. One of those is Jefferson High School. Erected in 1932, it is the alma mater of a long list of successful graduates including US Representative Henry B. González, Brigadier General Lillian Dunlap (the second woman to achieve that rank in the Army Nurse Corps), television journalist Jim Lehrer, former mayor Ed Garza, former mayor and US HUD Secretary Julián Castro, and his twin brother, U.S. Representative Joaquin Castro.

Also built during the Great Depression, the nearby Basilica of the National Shrine of the Little Flower is a treasury of art, artisanry, and relics. It is one of only 82 churches in the United States bearing the papal designation of "minor basilica."

Today the Jefferson neighborhood is predominantly Hispanic with a mix of modest cottages, mansions, and single and multi-family homes—all displaying a wide range of architectural styles. Traditions remain—like the sales of paletas (frozen fruit bars) by bicycle vendors—existing side by side with the modern amenities of grocery stores, restaurants, and busy retail stores.

West Side

San Antonio's West Side has been a catalyst for change and a source of the city's unique cultural history and flair. The Latino music, traditional Mexican food, and fiestas that San Antonio is famous for have been enjoyed for over one hundred years in its diverse neighborhoods. These incluse the Avenida Guadalupe district, San Juan Gardens, Stockyard district, and Prospect Hill. Our Lady of the Lake University was founded on the West Side in 1895. It was the first accredited institution of higher learning in San Antonio. The first public housing community in the city—the Alazán-Apache Courts—was built between 1939 and 1941 by the Zachry Company through the newly-established United States Housing Authority. The federal government loaned the project ninety percent of the cost; the required ten percent local contribution was raised through a bond issue.

Construction stopped briefly when slumlords demanded more compensation. First Lady Eleanor Roosevelt intervened and work restarted that summer with the demolition of more than 900 substandard structures The new buldings contained multiple single-family dwellings ranging from three to six rooms and each residence had a private bath,

Virgin Veladora, created by San Antonio artist Jesse Treviño, graces the exterior of the Guadalupe Cultural Center.

photo by Al Rendon

Artists and civic leaders Kathy and Lionel Sosa

photo by Ellen Arnold; courtesy of Lionel and Kathy Sosa

kitchen, and modern appliances. President Franklin Roosevelt attended the grand opening and by 1942 the Alazán-Apache Courts had nearly 5,000 tenants. It was considered one of the most well-maintained housing projects in the country.

The Guadalupe Cultural Arts Center was built the same year to anchor a thriving entertainment district. Today, that corner at Guadalupe and Brazos Streets is the epicenter of San Antonio's Latino culture.

> When we arrived at our new home on Monterey Street there were only a handful of Latinos on each block. Going west on our street were the families of Alex Briseno, who later became city manager; Henry Cisneros, who later became mayor and HUD Secretary, and Jesse Treviño, who became a world-famous artist. We all lived on Monterey Street.
>
> — Dr. Ricardo Romo

Nearby Kelly Air Force Base was the major employer, providing upward mobility for generations of West Side families between 1917 and the base's closure in 2001. Dr. Ricardo Romo, a journalist and the former president of the University of Texas-San Antonio (UTSA), remembers that everyone living on the West Side knew someone who worked or had worked at Kelly Field. "In the postwar decades, Kelly had one of the largest industrial workforces in the Southwest, with nearly 25,000 employees at the height of the Vietnam War. Scholars estimate that Mexican-Americans represented sixty percent of that workforce. Jobs at Kelly over its eighty-five-year existence made it possible for Mexican-Americans to live middle-class lives."

Romo's family came to San Antonio in 1916, leaving behind the Mexican Revolution and a brief sojourn in south Texas where they had been farm workers. Searching for a better future in town, the family settled on El Paso Street. Romo's grandmother, Maria Saenz Romo, worked as a successful midwife when few families could afford hospital costs and most babies were delivered at home. His father operated a "mom-and-pop" grocery store. Over the next few years, Romo's abuelita (grandmother) convinced more than three dozen family members to join her on the West Side of San Antonio, all within a few blocks of each other.

In the late 1940s, the family moved north, just across Durango Street, into the Prospect Hill neighborhood. Many of its Anglo residents were moving into newer suburbs farther to the north, and Prospect Hill was a desirable new frontier for Latinos living on the West Side. The move north across the dividing line of Durango Street was all of five blocks, but as a seven-year-old, it appeared to be one of many miles. Historically the West Side has been a powerful incubator for talent in San Antonio, producing leaders in city, state, and national government, business entrepreneurs, educators, musicians, artists, and actors. Television star Carol Burnett grew up in the Prospect Hill neighborhood; as did former Texas Secretary of State Hope Andrade; conjunto legend Flaco Jiménez; Rosita Fernandez, described by Lady Bird Johnson as the city's "First Lady of Song"; and renowned artist Jesse

Treviño, whose paintings and murals are exhibited nationwide including at the Smithsonian Museum in Washington, DC.

Another San Antonian from the West Side holds a place at the Smithsonian as well, as part of its "American Enterprise Series." Lionel Sosa, founder of the largest Hispanic advertising company in the United States, produced media campaigns for clients ranging from Church's Fried Chicken to Presidents Ronald Reagan and George Bush. He was named one of the twenty-five most influential Hispanics in the United States by *Time Magazine* in 2005. Like many Hispanic families that immigrated from Mexico to San Antonio, his grandparents arrived in the late 1920s to escape the aftermath of the Mexican Revolution.

Television star Carol Burnett grew up in the Prospect Hill neighborhood, as did former Texas Secretary of State Hope Andrade, conjunto legend Flaco Jiménez, Rosita Fernandez, described by Lady Bird Johnson as the city's 'First Lady of Song'; and renowned artist Jesse Treviño.

Decades later, Sosa watched as houses and businesses on nearly 100 acres downtown were demolished to make room for HemisFair, feeling the loss of favorite haunts like El Diamante Café, as well as sensing the positive transformation underway that impacted his future. San Antonio was changing and at times it was bittersweet. San Francisco-based artist Richard Wilson hired Sosa to create the finished, camera-ready logo art for the fair and his career in graphic design was launched. When HemisFair closed in the fall of 1968, banks and other businesses approached him to design branding materials—logos, printed materials, storefronts, even uniforms. With partners Ernest Bromley and Al Alguilar, Sosa saw the company expand to include offices in New York and Miami with revenues of more than $130 million annually. Sosa retired in 1996 to pursue a multi-faceted career as a professor at Harvard, a painter, a television film producer ("*Children of the Revolution*"), Along with his wife, artist Kathy Sosa, he was co-founder of "Yes! Our Kids Can (YOKC)". The nonprofit educational program—designed to disrupt generational poverty by creating a new mindset of success in local at-risk school districts—reached 10,000 San Antonio students in seven local school districts before the Covid-19 pandemic resulted in its closure.

But the message of potential for youth success endures in a restored cottage on the West Side that was once the home of actress Carol Burnett. In total disarray in 2011, it was scheduled for demolition until a nonprofit, American Sunrise, rescued it and transformed it into an after- school learning and literacy center appropriately named the San Antonio After School All-Stars.

San Antonio is a city of neighborhoods—a rich mosaic, each part with unique architectural treasures, places of worship, restaurants with diverse culinary tastes, festivals, and family traditions. Perhaps because neighbors have lived near each other for so long, its citizens live together well now.

San Antonio's West Side is known for its colorful murals.

photo by Al Rendon

Chapter Five:
A Confluence of Civilizations

INTEGRAL TO THE COMMUNITY CONSENSUS THAT WE HAVE DEVELOPED IN SAN ANTONIO IS A DEGREE OF MULTICULTURAL RESPECT NOT EVIDENT IN MANY CITIES. THE CONFLUENCE OF CIVILIZATIONS IS REAL HERE; IT HAS MORPHED INTO SOMETHING THAT IS RICHER AND MORE FUN THAN THE INDIVIDUAL PARTS.

— HENRY G. CISNEROS

photo by Al Rendon

The 2,600 square-foot "Confluence of Civilizations" mural was created by Mexican artist Juan O'Gorman for HemisFair; it is a San Antonio treasure that reflects its continued celebration of inclusiveness.

Even before Mexican artist Juan O'Gorman was commissioned to create the immense, 2500 square-foot mural for San Antonio's HemisFair in 1968, the city recognized that its multicultural composition was an asset to be treasured. But the mural, entitled "A Confluence of Civilizations," emblazoned across the Henry B. González Convention Center, took that appreciation of the city's diversity to a new level. It symbolized a celebration of cultures on a global level and served as a unifying message of hope for all humanity.

That message thrives today, illustrated by the spectrum of celebrations that occur throughout the year, sponsored by the many ethnic groups that settled in San Antonio over several centuries. However, for the first time since World War II, many cherished traditional events were canceled during the 2020-2021 pandemic. Others reinvented themselves through virtual experiences. With the resilience that is such a part of San Antonio, all survived and prepared for happier times. And the events calendar is packed.

In January, there is the Chinese New Year Festival of Lanterns, African Market, and the Martin Luther King Parade—the largest in the country. The San Antonio Stock Show and Rodeo, Asian Festival and Mardi Gras River Parade fill February. In March, the San Antonio River flows green for Saint Patrick's Day, and the Cajun Festival reverberates with zydeco sounds and spicy jambalaya with some early French, Caribbean, and African spooned into it. Cinco de Mayo, celebrating Mexico's defeat over the French Empire on May 5, 1862, reflects the city's deep Latino roots and a perfect time to say 'Viva Mexico' while

photo by Al Rendon

photo by Al Rendon

enjoying traditional food washed down with some tequila.

The Texas Folklife Festival happens in June at the University of Texas Institute of Texas Cultures, located on the HemisFair grounds. It

salutes the many cultures that co-exist in the Alamo City with a wide array of food, crafts, music, dance performances, vendors selling traditional handmade products, and historians portraying many characters who were part of the confluence of cultures.

Moving ahead to September, Diez y Seis de Septiembre (Sixteenth of September) kicks off Hispanic Heritage Month in the fall. The celebration begins with a re-enactment of the famous El Grito (the shout) that started Mexico's battle for independence from Spain. More than thirty other official events take place during this historic month in San Antonio.

German Oktoberfest, the Lebanese Food Festival, and Diá de Los Muertos all occur in October and November serves up Diwali, the Lighting of the River, and Luminaria.

Give San Antonians an excuse—and they will organize a party! There is ample opportunity to partake in the revelry throughout the year. The array of deep-rooted traditions—coupled with food, drink, music, and dance—offers an alphabet soup of international sensory delights. All are "quills" on that "porcupine" that poet Sidney Lanier spoke of when he visited San Antonio. (See Chapter 1). With origins in Mexico, Central and South America, the Caribbean, Western Europe, Eastern Europe, the Middle East, Africa, Asia, and Polynesia, they are evidence of the unique "DNA" of the ever-evolving Alamo City.

But no celebration is as all-inclusive and grand as Fiesta San Antonio. Every April, the city hosts its largest party of the year, attended by more than 3.5 million people, featuring more than a hundred events and generating more than $350 million in revenues, mostly for charities.

Established in 1891 to honor Texas Independence Day on April 21, it started as a simple parade to honor the heroes who fought at the famous battles of the Alamo, Goliad, and San Jacinto. Despite its historical roots in the conflict between Mexico and Texas, Ricardo Romo reminds us

Raphael Tuck & Son, Wikimedia Commons

that "today Hispanics, Anglos—and everyone else in town— come together as one united group of partygoers." And what a party it is!

In 2020, shortly before the April celebrations were scheduled to begin, the Covid-19 infection rate was climbing fast, hospitalizations and deaths were increasing. The Fiesta Commission made the difficult decision to postpone San Antonio's biggest celebration. There was hope that it could occur in the fall, but the pandemic still had the city—and the world—in its grip. Fiesta was rescheduled for 2021. A June date was chosen to be safe but in June, while a vaccine had been approved for emergency use and Covid numbers were dropping, only a partial Fiesta Week could be held. However that did not curb the enthusiasm for planning an all-out celebration come 2022.

More than 130 years ago, the first celebration was small. It evolved from descriptions of flower parades in Spain that Ellen Maury Slayden, wife of US Congressman James Slayden, witnessed during a trip to Europe with her husband. She suggested that San Antonio initiate one like it to honor the fallen Texan heroes. A small group of her friends decorated carriages, baby buggies, and bicycles and walked around the Alamo, throwing flowers at each other. It was a huge success, and other local women joined the effort in subsequent years.

Later, the first "horseless carriages" were used in the parade; and a Spring Carnival was added to the celebration, presided over by a queen.

Presently, it is the second-largest float parade in the United States, with more than a quarter of a million people from San Antonio and around the world lining the streets of downtown. They are entertained by high school, college, and military marching bands; vaqueros on horseback; antique cars, and dance troupes. Clowns and cartoon characters march alongside the mayor, county judge, other officials. Just as in the original celebration, the now dazzling floats are decorated with flowers.

What is still called Fiesta Week now extends for seventeen days.

The Battle of Flowers Parade had humble beginnings more than 100 years ago; today it is Fiesta Week's biggest event, attracting a crowd of more than 500,000.

Carol M. Highsmith, Public domain, via Wikimedia Commons

Kings and queens are chosen, daytime and nighttime parades are attended by nearly a million cheering citizens and visitors. Margaritas and German beer flow freely; cuisines ranging from tacos and bunuelos to gumbo and baked oysters provide a delicious taste of San Antonio's diversity.

The early days were less inclusive. In 1909, a group of local businessmen led by John Carrington established the Order of the Alamo to crown a queen, a princess, and 24 duchesses to "rule" over the carnival festivities created by Slayden and her friends. The queen, princess, and twelve duchesses were chosen from San Antonio—usually, daughters of Order of the Alamo members—and twelve more duchesses were selected from other cities in Texas. Like Mardi Gras in New Orleans, the "Coronation" of Fiesta royalty became an important social event, drawing in prominent families from around the state. The first queen, Eda Kampmann, was crowned in 1909.

In 1913, the Battle of Flowers Parade Association was officially chartered by the State of Texas, with membership limited to four hundred women. Its first president was Kampmann's mother. Over the decades, San Antonio's "royalty" has expanded to include monarchs from all over the city. In addition to the Order of the Alamo's Fiesta court, King Antonio presides over the Texas Cavaliers, a men's group established as a social group in 1926 to operate the Fiesta River Parade. El Rey Feo, first introduced by LULAC in 1947 and invited to join Fiesta in 1980, rules over the ten-day Fiesta de Los Reyes celebration in Market Square.

One of the most colorful events of Fiesta Week honors a traditional Mexican sport that predates the American rodeo, the charreada. It, too, selects a queen. Charreada, the national sport of Mexico, originated with the Spanish conquistadores in the sixteenth century as a dramatic show of equestrian skills. In San Antonio, the tradition has attracted a considerable following, thanks to the Asociación de Charros, which sponsors the "Day in Old Mexico Charreada" over an exciting weekend during Fiesta Week. Dashing charros in showy outfits perform amazing feats on horseback. Women charras, riding side-saddle in their

The Texas Cavaliers sponsor Fiesta Week's River Parade, presided over by King Antonio; the Rey Feo Consejo Educational Foundation elects its own king in friendly competition. Both organizations raise money to support local charities.

photo by Al Rendon

photo by Al Rendon

Adelita dresses, demonstrate intricate Escaramuzas (skirmishes) in an arena south of downtown, between the San Antonio River and Mission San José.

Since HemisFair was the catalyst for San Antonio's transformation in 1968, it is appropriate that the city's annual Fiesta celebrations begin in the new Hemisfair Park. Fireworks light up the April sky; food booths are bustling; music resonates. The party never ends.

A Taste of New Orleans is sponsored by the city's local Zulu Association at the San Antonio Sunken Gardens. Proceeds from musical performances, Cajun delicacies (would you believe alligator on a stick?), and family-friendly fun support college scholarships. Laissez le bon temps roulet is the theme throughout this two-day event.

Because everybody loves a parade, there are three of them during Fiesta Week. From the legendary Texas Cavaliers' River Parade, themed around the historic missions in 2020, to the spectacular sounds and lights of the Fiesta Flambeau night parade, to the now-massive Battle of Flowers Parade, San Antonio shows off its confluence of civilizations.

The Fiesta Flambeau Parade is the longest illuminated night parade in the United States. It evokes the spirit of Carnival in Rio, with street dancers, music, and plenty of sparkle—but a family-friendly ambiance pervades despite the late hours.

A highlight of every Flambeau is URBAN-15's always surprising parade-within-a-parade. Artists, dancers, and musicians—led by co-founders George and Catherine Cisneros—weave electronic sound, extravagant costuming, and magic into their creative and complex art performances. Their traditional and avant-garde themes epitomize San Antonio's confluence of civilizations. For more than forty-five years, they have gyrated and glittered in all sorts of venues—from parking lots, garages, and rooftops to the Smithsonian Institution in Washington, DC.

"HemisFair was our catalyst," George Cisneros remembered. "San Antonio was a player on an international stage. I was inundated with sounds, visuals, and sensibilities that were not yet a part of my vocabulary; they became part of my art."

The sounds of more traditional mariachi music are an integral part of San Antonio's soul as well. With origins in rural Mexico more than a hundred years ago, it developed as the music of people living in the country,

photo by Al Rendon

The Indian festival of Diwali (previous page), action-packed charreadas (left), and traditional Mexican dancers (below), reflect San Antonio's cultural diversity.

photo by Al Rendon

photo courtesy of the Archdiocese of San Antonio

Traditional mariachi orchestras, (above), the ballads of San Antonio's own Rick Cavender band (below), and conjunto and country western legends (page 56) are all part of San Antonio's varied music scene.

celebrating their joys and struggles. It was introduced to audiences in Mexico City at the beginning of the twentieth century. It came north with the immigrants who left their country during and after the Mexican Revolution. Today, San Antonio and Mariachi music are intertwined. Regardless of ethnicity, everyone in town can sing a stanza of some favorite ballad.

More than 10,000 people attend the annual Mariachis Vargas Extravaganza every December in San Antonio. It's the largest and longest-running mariachi music festival of its kind, organized and promoted by Cynthia Muñoz, the founder of Cynthia Muñoz Public Relations. She learned to play the guitar from the legendary Orta family of musicians. Muñoz grew up on the city's South East side. Her father, Jesse Muñoz, once worked on the famous King Ranch in south Texas and later at Kelly AFB in San Antonio. He was an early member of COPS and encouraged his daughter to celebrate her Latina culture through the music of old Mexico.

The mariachi movement in San Antonio burgeoned after the Pope allowed masses to be given in Spanish in the 1970s. Josephine and Jesse Orta's family invented a special "Mariachi Mass," and innovative priests incorporated it into those at Mission San José. It was phenomenally successful and quickly became a magnet for church attendance, attracting Catholics and Latinos and the city at large.

The movement became a part of the San Antonio Independent School District. Its superintendent, Paul Elizondo, approached Belle San Miguel, a music teacher at Lanier High School, to urge her to start a mariachi program. Elizondo (who would later serve nine terms as the Bexar County Commissioner of Precinct 2) loved music and played a mean saxophone. While studying at St. Mary's University, he formed an orchestra and served as a band director at several public schools. San Miguel's students, and their parents, reacted with enthusiasm. By the late 1970s, the mariachi school program was thriving.

San Miguel married a dashing, talented mariachi named Juan Ortiz, and the couple established Campanas de America, staging San Antonio's first Mariachi Festival in 1979. The famous Mariachis Vargas group, considered el mejor del mundo (the best in the world), traveled from Mexico to perform. San Antonio was declared "the birthplace of US mariachi music."

Both the Festival and the mariachi program in San Antonio schools flourished in the 1980s. Similar events and

photo courtesy Claire Cavender McNab

Diá de los Muertos has become a major celebration in San Antonio, originating in Mexico and honoring departed loved ones with beautiful ofrendas, parades, and costumes.

photo by Al Rendon

photos these two pages by Al Rendon

educational programs were established throughout the southwest, especially in New Mexico and Arizona.

Toward the end of the decade, musician Linda Ronstadt included the Mariachis Vargas in her Canciónes de mi Padre tour, causing an explosion of interest and excitement for the unique musical genre. Mariachi "ambassadors"—both students and professionals—delight their audiences in San Antonio and beyond, sharing their music and cultural pride. When young Sebastien De La Cruz appeared on "America's Got Talent" in 2012, he won an international following. He sang the national anthem at a Spurs basketball game during the 2013 NBA finals, creating another burst of momentum for the music. De La Cruz has pushed the music into the future with original songs and videos he created during his senior year at Wagner High School during the pandemic in 2020.

The Beethoven Meannerchor celebrates San Antonio's German heritage with the same gusto. It has been a part of the city's musical life for nearly 150 years. When Sidney Lanier attended a Meannerchor practice at the old San Antonio Casino Hall in 1873, he described it this way: "Last night at 8 o'clock came Mr. Schiedemantel, a genuine lover of music and a fine pianist, to take me to Maennerchor, which meets every Wednesday night for practice... Presently seventeen Germans were seated at the singing table. Great pipes were all afire. The leader, Herr Thielepape, an old man with a white beard and mustache, formerly mayor of the city, rapped his tuning fork vigorously, gave the chords by arpeggios of his voice, and off they swung into such a noble, old full-voiced lied (song) that imperious tears rushed to my eyes."

The Beethoven Maennerchor organization keeps that music alive at its historic German beer garden and offers educational programs about German culture and language.

Of course, country music is also a big part of San Antonio's cultural mix. Home of the "King of Country," George Strait reigns over the genre. His career spans four decades, producing a miles-long list of platinum albums and number one songs. In 2013-2014, he organized a final tour, calling it "And the Cowboy Rides Away." Accompanied by a stellar group of musical greats including Jason Aldean, Eric Church, Little Big Town, Gloria Estefan, and Billy Joel, its last concert in Arlington, Texas, broke all previous records for attendance and revenues at a single show in the United States, surpassing both the Beatles and the Rolling Stones. Fortunately for San Antonio and music lovers everywhere, he did not ride away—he is just not touring as much as he did in the past.

Other big-name country stars, like Pat Green and Tish Hinojosa, call San Antonio home. Venues like Cowboys Dance Hall, Thirsty Horse Saloon, and John T. Floore's Country Store offer boot-stomping fun for the city's ever-present cowboy culture.

Like the city's diverse music, the art scene in San Antonio is also rich

Mi Tierra Café, located in the city's downtown mercado district, twinkles with colorful lights, displays city leaders on its muraled walls, and offers the best in Mexican food and traditional mariachi music.

photo by Al Rendon

▶ Grammy-award winning Tejano musician David Lee Garza grew up in Poteet, Texas, just 30 miles south of San Antonio.

▶▶ Artist Jennifer Ling Datchuk's multi-cultural heritage is reflected in her work; she was selected as a United States Artists Fellow in 2020.

This 2019 work is titled *Live to Die*; it is constructed of customized welcome mats, slip cast porcelain, and overglaze paint.

Varied dimensions (each mat is 30.5" x 22")

▼ San Antonio musician Augie Meyer was a co-founder of the Texas Tornadoes in the 1990s, along with Tejano greats Flaco Jiménez, Freddy Fender, and Doug Sahm.

with examples of the confluence of cultures. Local artists have created a strong community that embraces diversity. From Bob "Daddy-O" Wade's iconic cowboy boots in front of Saks Fifth Avenue, juxtaposing the cowboy culture with a capacity for elegance, to Rolando Briseñõ's legendary "inverted St. Anthony" protesting in front of the Alamo, San Antonio is always open to new dialogues, especially creative ones.

Briseñõ, who grew up in the Prospect Hill neighborhood on the city's West Side, has produced installations for public spaces across the United States, including Houston's Intercontinental Airport and Trinity University's spectacular campus that overlooks San Antonio.

Jesse Amado is another product of the West Side and was the first artist selected by Artpace for a residency in 1995 within its new bright red building. Founded by Linda Pace to support local, national, and international artists, Artpace has grown into a premier contemporary art center with national stature. Ruby City, Pace's later dream for a contemporary museum, opened its doors in 2019; Lone Star Art Space added still more to San Antonio's expanding art scene.

photos by Al Rendon

San Antonio artist Jennifer Ling Datchuk is the child of a Chinese immigrant and the grandchild of Russian and Irish immigrants. Her family histories of conflict are her source of inspiration for her work. She uses an eclectic mix of materials and objects to capture the expressive power of rituals that she believes "fix, organize, soothe, and beautify our lives." Datchuk is an Assistant Professor of Studio Art at Texas State University in San Marcos. In 2020 she became a United States Artists (USA) fellow and was awarded a $50 thousand unrestricted grant from that organization. Its board chair, Ed Henry, explained that "USA believes strongly that the arts are critically important to the well-being of our communities." San Antonio agrees.

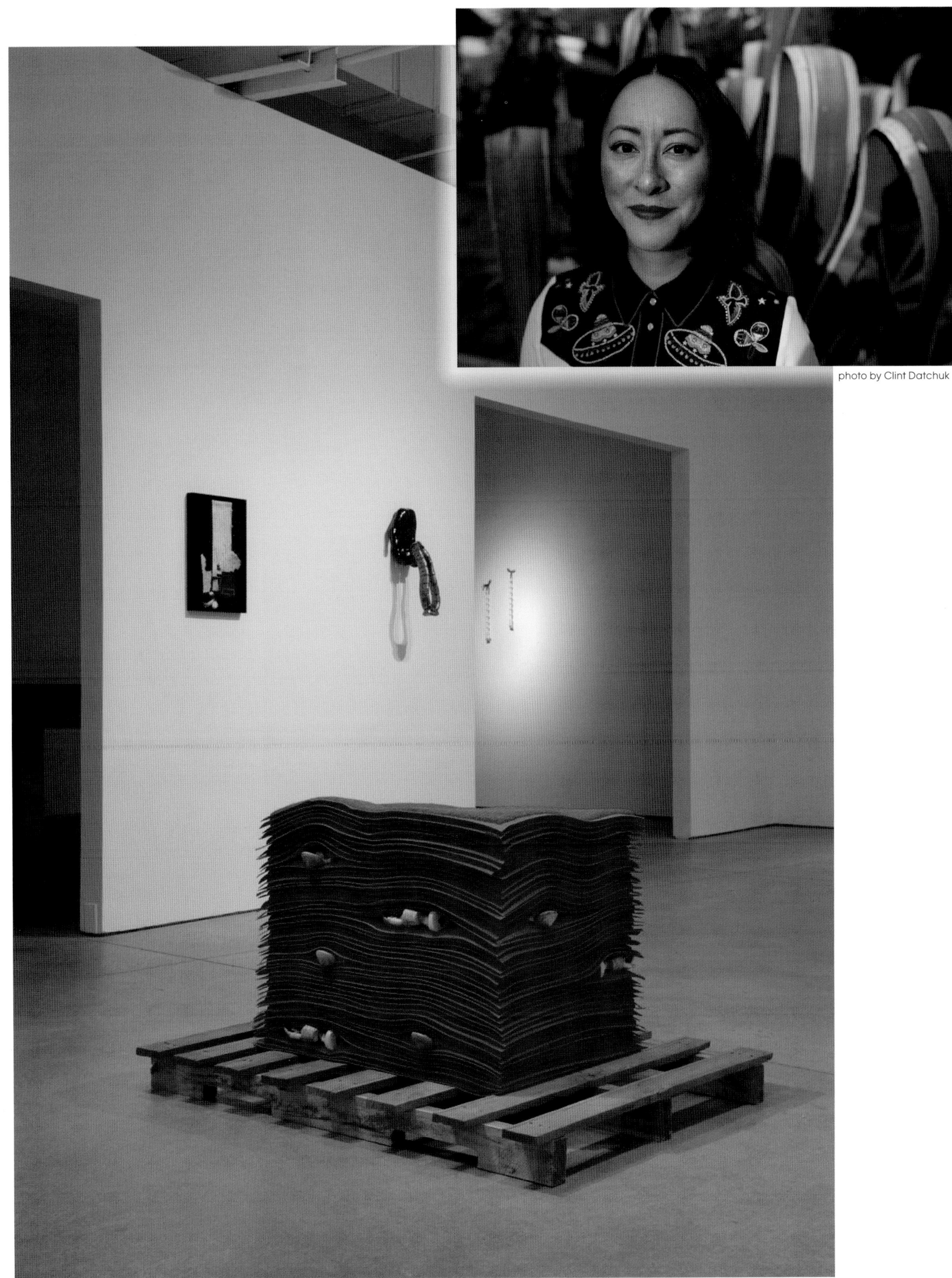

photo by Clint Datchuk

photo by David Hunter Hale

Linda Pace (1945-2007), a local artist and founder of ArtPace, envisioned a new contemporary art center she called "Ruby City." Designed by world-famous architect, Sir David Adjaye, it was built after her death by the Linda Pace Foundation and opened in 2019.

Our multicultural persona extends beyond San Antonio's festivals, music, and art; it is evident in the city's everyday life as well... especially in the food. With so many ethnic influences permeating the Alamo City, it is not surprising that food choices are plentiful and play an outsized role in defining the region. Visits to the hundreds of family-run local restaurants take diners on a tour of the world—to Africa, China, Cuba, France, Greece, India, Italy, Jamaica, Japan, Mexico, the Middle East, Thailand, and a pleathora of other exotic locales.

The legendary Mi Tierra Café in Market Square, in the heart of the city's Zona Cultural, is a love story that captures the cultural flavor of San Antonio. Pedro ("Pete") Cortez was a young man who immigrated from

photos courtesy of Ruby City

Mexico to San Antonio. He married Cruz Llanes who was born on San Pedro Creek banks at Casa Navarro. Together they bought a small café near El Mercado in 1941 for $150. It had only three tables, but the Cortez family hoped their family recipes would make it a popular breakfast spot for the farmers who came to the market early each morning. It did. Over the years, it expanded; and Pete Cortez bought nearby buildings. Always a family business, it is now run by Cortez's grandchildren. It is still open early for breakfast—in fact, it never closes. It seats more than 500 people and has become a cornerstone of Latino culture in San Antonio. La Familia Cortez was named one of San Antonio's "five families of the twentieth century", along with the Frost, Steves, Zachry, and McAllister families, in honor of their essential contributions to the city's development. Food critics describe Mi Tierra as the best Mexican food restaurant in town; from the constant crowds, it is evident that locals and tourists agree. Surrounded by pinatas and twinkling lights, year-round Christmas decorations, serenaded by mariachis, sipping a margarita, devouring a platter of nachos or enchiladas with frijoles... who could ask for más?

During the Covid-19 pandemic—when restaurants were forced to close, and many grocery stores were low on supplies—Mi Tierra converted its parking lot into an old-fashioned mercado. It offered food, staples like toilet tissue, and other high-demand supplies it had acquired in large quantities.

Other restaurants and individual chefs lent time and talent to providing food to those in need. Before the pandemic, no one imagined the joblessness or the food insecurity that challenged San Antonio, particularly those in the lowest income strata. The San Antonio Food Bank and tens of thousands of volunteers stepped forward as frontline heroes to ensure no one went hungry. Individuals, businesses, and nonprofit foundations helped meet the $6 million a week need for food and funds. Mobile, Covid-safe distribution centers in large parking lots became the norm for people needing food.

UNESCO selected San Antonio Food Bank chef Kelly Daughtey as one of its Chef Ambassadors for 2021-2023. Based at the 210,00-square-foot warehouse on the city's South side, she helps provide food for thousands of Central Texas residents every week. The site also includes forty acres of crops, a teaching garden, and a teaching kitchen. A partnership with nearby San Juan Capistrano Mission provides access to a fifty-acre indigenous crop farm that still uses historic acequias in some of its fields.

Daughtey shares the UNESCO honor with five other San Antonio chefs—Lili Bernal/ Culinary Institute of America; John Brand/Hotel Emma; David Caceres/La Panaderia; Jesse Kuykendall/Milpa at Hotel Havana; and Stephen Paprocki/Chef Cooperatives. All reflect San Antonio's extraordinary cuisines and during their term as ambassadors they will travel on educational missions to share those diverse cuisines with the world.

The global culinary experience is not new to San Antonio, nor is giving back to the community. Rosemary Kowalski and her husband began their meteoric rise in the food industry serving up Texas barbeque in a tiny San Antonio diner. Following her success as the official caterer at HemisFair, she and her family built the now-iconic RK Group, with more than 800 employees and clients worldwide. Based in San Antonio, they have continued to give back to this community by supporting philanthropic endeavors.

In 2021 the RK Group purchased the historic eighty-acre Red Berry Estate on San Antonio's East Side and transformed it into a new headquarters. Berry was a colorful Texas politician and gambler who built an elegant 14,000-square-foot mansion in 1951, equipping it with escape routes to avoid police raids. Today it is a spectacular entertainment venue, with an expansive ballroom overlooking a lake stocked with electric boats for special events. The adjoining 158,000- square-foot office and warehouse space accommodate hundreds of employees working on events across the country and internationally. It's a success story with roots in HemisFair, coupled with the Kowalski family's ongoing commitment to hard work and community involvement.

The RK Group, San Antonio's premiere catering company, opened its new headquarters at the historic Red Berry Estate in 2021. Its founder, Rosemary Kowalski began her career more than six decades ago, was a young caterer at HemisFair in 1968, and today she and her family run a company that creates events for clients all over the world.

photos courtesy of the RK Group

Chapter Six:
Lifelong Learning

EDUCATION IS THE UNIFYING THEME FOR BUILDING SAN ANTONIO'S ECONOMY AND INTEGRATING ITS DIVERSE POPULATION. WITH INNOVATIVE EARLY CHILDOOD PROGRAMS AND FIFTEEN COLLEGES AND UNIVERSITIES, AN AMBITIOUS PUBLIC LIBRARY SYSTEM, AND HIGH-TECH DIGITAL LEARNING CENTERS, SAN ANTONIO IS BUILDING A STRONG TALENT POOL FOR ITS FUTURE.

— CATHERINE NIXON COOKE

sketch by Joaquim Pedro de Sousa, 1860s, wikimedia commons

José Antonio Navarro served in the federal congress in Mexico City and as mayor of San Antonio in 1835; he urged government officials to build a university in San Antonio long before Texas became a state.

St. Mary's University was built in 1852 and is the oldest Catholic university in Texas and the American Southwest.

José Antonio Navarro, a legendary statesman and leading Mexican participant in the Texas Revolution, championed the idea of a public university in San Antonio as early as 1827. He helped craft the Constitución de Coahuila y Texas, which called for establishing a first-class university in the Mexican State of Texas. Navarro pushed for it to be built in his hometown of San Antonio. When he was elected mayor eight years later, he urged the Mexican government to focus on education in its northern frontier. Passionate about his belief in higher education, he sent his son to Harvard.

With a father from Corsica and a mother from Spain's nobility, Navarro considered himself a new breed—a Tejano who represented a blending of cultures—and he signed the Texas Declaration of Independence with Stephen F. Austin in 1836. He carried his vision for education to the New Republic, where he served as both a representative and three-term senator. Navarro and another famous Tejano named Juan Seguín both offered parcels of land they owned to San Antonio to construct a public university, but the city declined.

In 1862, the United States Congress passed the Morrill Act to donate federal public land to fund higher education. Still, no action was taken until after the Civil War, when Texas agreed to create a college. With the donation of 2,416 acres by the citizens of Brazos County to establish the first public university in the state, the Agricultural and Mechanical College of Texas (now Texas A&M University) was founded in 1866 and opened its doors to 200 students a decade later.

It would be many decades before branches of those two public universities were built in San Antonio. The University of Texas at San Antonio (UTSA) and the University of Texas Health Science Center were established in the city's Northwest quadrant in 1969. Texas A&M University-San Antonio (TAMUSA) opened on the South Side in 1999, originally located on the campus of Palo Alto Community College. It would be another ten years until a new TAMUSA campus would become a proud stand-alone presence on 700 acres of land where San Antonio's first inhabitants once lived.

The first universities in San Antonio were private, established not long after Texas joined the

photo courtesy of Institute of Texan Cultures/UTSA Special Collections

United States. These were St. Mary's University, founded in 1852 by Marianist missionaries; the University of the Incarnate Word, founded in 1881 by the Sisters of Charity of the Incarnate Word; and Our Lady of the Lake University in 1895 by the Sisters of Divine Providence, all Catholic schools. Another private university was Trinity University, founded by a Presbyterian triad in 1869. With earlier locations in Tehuacana and Waxahachie, it moved to San Antonio in 1942 becoming the city's first Protestant university. All continue to have robust campuses today and national recognition as excellent institutions of higher learning.

St. Mary's University is the oldest Catholic university in the American Southwest, established in 1852. Its School of Law and Greehey School of Business are nationally recognized for excellence. It has received additional national recognition, including the Carnegie Foundation's prestigious Community Engagement Award.

The University of the Incarnate Word's historic campus encompasses the Blue Hole, at the headwaters of the San Antonio River; George Brackenridge's original mansion; and St. Brigid's Oak, a 600-year-old tree dedicated to the Irish St. Brigid of Kildare (451-525 AD) by the Sisters of Charity of the Incarnate Word.

Our Lady of the Lake University (OLLU) began as an all-girls high school in the late 1800s; it was accredited as a four-year college in 1919 and achieved university status in 1927. Today it offers sixty undergraduate majors, fourteen master's programs, and three doctoral programs to its more than 3000 students. In 1968, it was host to the US Commission on Civil Rights Hearing on Mexican-Americans in the Southwest. Well-known graduates include civil rights activist Rosie Castro, Native American actor Jonathan Joss, former US Representative Ciro Rodriguez, and folklorist Jovita Gonzalez.

Trinity University was founded in Tehuacana, Texas, in 1869, with an enrollment of seven students. Its second location was Waxahachie; San Antonio became home to the university in 1942. Today it is ranked number one in the nation in its category as a private liberal arts university by the *Princeton Review*. More than 6,000 students enjoy undergraduate and graduate programs on its hillside campus designed by architect O'Neil Ford. US Senator John Cornyn, actress Jaclyn Smith, poet Naomi Shihab Nye, philanthropist Alice Walton, and San Antonio Mayor Ron Nirenberg are a few of Trinity University's notable graduates.

Public institutions of higher education, sometimes evolving from primary schools, were established as well. St. Philip's College on San Antonio's East Side was founded as a school for African-American children in historic downtown La Villita in 1898. James Steptoe Johnston, first bishop of the Episcopal Diocese of West Texas,

Artemisia Bowden (center, in hat), the daughter of slaves, was invited by Bishop Johnston to become the principal at St. Philip's when she was twenty-three years old. She traveled alone by train to San Antonio in 1902, converted a sewing class to an elementary school, then to a vocational school, and ultimately to a junior college in 1928. When funding from the Episcopal Church was withdrawn during the Depression, Bowden stopped taking a salary and sold beef, pork, and chickens raised on campus to keep the doors open. In 1942, the school was deeded to the San Antonio Independent School District and became part of what is now Alamo Colleges District. No longer a private institution, it was the first Alamo College to be accredited by the Southern Association of Colleges and Schools in 1951. In 1954, following the Brown vs. Board of Education Supreme Court ruling, St. Philip's began admitting white students for the first time.

"She is the school," St. Philip's president, Adena Loston, told *San Antonio Express-News* columnist Rich Marino." It was her determination, her commitment to education that made St. Philip's possible... When I talk to students, I often tell this story as an example of being a visionary, of going beyond what is expected of you."

architectural rendering courtesy of The University of Texas at San Antonio

The University of Texas at San Antonio's downtown campus is located in the historic Cattleman Square District.

established the school. Its first students were six African-American girls who enrolled in a weekend sewing class. In the early twentieth century, under the leadership of Artemisia Bowden, it became an industrial school for girls, then a high school, and finally a junior college.

Today it is part of the Alamo Community College District, with more than 12,000 students. It has the distinction of being the only school in the nation that is a historically Black and Hispanic-serving institution.

Visionaries also played a role in the establishment of Palo Alto College, assisted by a strong grassroots effort. At the first COPS convention, held in 1974, Fernando Rodriguez, Jr. introduced a resolution to pursue an institution of higher learning on San Antonio's underserved South Side. Residents in the area had grown disappointed with the distance and lack public transportation available to reach the city's new four-year public university, a branch of the University of Texas, established on the far Northwest side in 1969.

In 1983, the Texas legislature approved a charter for Palo Alto College on the South Side; its doors opened in 1985, with 231 students. Federally designated as a Hispanic Serving Institution since 2000, it currently has 10,000 students and is recognized nationally for its excellent academic programs. In 2019, Palo Alto won the Aspen Institute's prestigious Rising Star Award; and its parent organization—the Alamo College District—won what many Fortune 500 companies describe as "the Super Bowl" of awards.

The Malcolm Baldridge Quality Award from the National Institute of Standards and Technology is a "gold standard" usually bestowed on extraordinary businesses for their excellent management. In 2018, the Alamo Colleges District became the only community college system to ever win one. And in 2021, it won the $1 million Aspen Prize for Community College Excellence. There are five colleges in the Alamo College District, each located in a different area of the city—Palo Alto, St. Philip's, San Antonio College, Northeast Lakeview, and Northwest Vista. All offer workforce development programs and courses that transfer credits to four-year universities for students wishing to pursue a more advanced degree.

Efforts by LULAC and COPS to improve access to higher education for minorities resulted in a lawsuit in 1989, filed by the Mexican-American Legal Defense Fund (MALDEF) on behalf of LULAC. It claimed that Texas discriminated against Mexican-Americans living in South Texas by not providing an equitable distribution of educational opportunities. While the lawsuit was lost in court, it focused critical attention on the problem, leading the Legislature to enact the South Texas Border Initiative (STBI), which has provided higher funding levels for public universities, including UTSA and TAMUSA. The new money was the impetus needed for UTSA to move forward with plans for a long-awaited downtown campus; it allowed Texas A&M–University to plan for a campus on the South Side.

Now a presence in San Antonio for more than fifty years, UTSA has become a tier one research university, offering 225 undergraduate and graduate degrees and serving as an economic engine for the region. Its expansion in the heart of downtown has created a vibrant second campus; the university expects its enrollment to reach 45,000 students by 2028. According to a survey conducted by Hewlett Packard, its achievements range from the award-winning Carlos Alvarez College of Business—home of the number one ranked cybersecurity program in the nation, to the city's first Division I football program featuring its team, "The Roadrunners."

The University of Texas Health Science Center at San Antonio (now called UT Health San Antonio) was built on land that had been a hundred-acre dairy farm. Joe J. Nix conveyed that property in the city's Northwest quadrant to the State for a medical school in 1968. Today, it is the only tier one research university in south Texas, with schools of medicine, nursing, dentistry, other health-profession programs, and graduate programs in biomedical sciences. UT Health San Antonio offers more than sixty-five degrees, the majority being graduate or professional degrees. As part of the vast South Texas Medical Center, its 3,000 students benefit from training opportunities in more than a hundred affiliated hospitals, clinics, and health care facilities.

UT Health San Antonio is the largest health services university in South Texas, with branch locations in the border communities of Laredo and the Lower Rio Grande Valley. It contributes over a billion dollars a year to the South Texas economy and is a chief catalyst for San Antonio's $25 billion biosciences and health industry. Thanks to its excellent leadership and preparedness, the UT Health system is credited with extraordinary healthcare delivery and vaccination roll-out during the Covid-19 pandemic. As 2022 approached, it broke ground on a new $50 million medical building at UTSA's Park West campus, located in a sector of the city that is experiencing significant growth.

The Texas A&M–University System established its San Antonio branch in 1999 under the umbrella of A&M-Kingsville. Its first home was on the campus of Palo Alto College, in temporary buildings erected specifically for the new university. Once enrollment was close to reaching the required number of students for its own campus, A&M-San Antonio began to assess various sites for the new university. Dr. Maria Hernandez Ferrier, an educator who had grown up on San Antonio's West Side, was hired as the new executive director. With bachelor's and master's degrees from Our Lady of the Lake University and a doctorate from Texas A&M–College Station, she had taught in San Antonio schools and had recently served as President George H.W. Bush's deputy assistant secretary of education in Washington, DC.

Ferrier was an innovator, designing new courses and hiring faculty as she and longtime university proponents pushed forward with the dream of a new campus. In 2008, the donation of 700 acres of South Side ranchland by the Verano Land Group, a Las Vegas-based real estate development company, moved that dream towards reality. The developers envisioned a future boom on the South Side, including residential and retail projects anchored by a large, four-year university.

A crowd gathered in 2009 to break ground for the new campus; it was a victory celebration for the South Side. Community leaders, including the university's decades-long champion, Senator Frank Madla, wielded their shovels in a pasture that was part of San Antonio's earliest history, confident of the land's new future. With the skills of Kell-Muñoz

Trinity University was ranked as the 17th most international university in the world in 2020 by the Times Higher Education Rankings.

Courtesy of Bartlett Cocke General Contractors

photo courtesy of TAMUSA

Texas A&M University San Antonio encompasses more than 700 acres on the city's South Side.

Architects, campus buildings were designed to reflect the rich intersection of Spanish and indigenous styles exemplified by the early missions. The decision was made from the beginning to make the new university a "military-friendly" campus, and leadership focused on academic programs and amenities that would make a difference in the lives of the many veterans who were returning from military fronts. Ferrier was clear in her message that the university was "committed to restoring, recharging, and re-energizing our military community students as they transition into the civilian workforce."

When Ferrier retired in 2014, another visionary leader stepped up to lead the still-new university. Cynthia Teniente-Matson had spent her early childhood on the South Side before her father's civil service career took the family first to California and then to Alaska. She became the first person in her family to earn a bachelor's degree, majoring in management, at the University of Alaska-Fairbanks. Next, she earned a master's degree at UA-Anchorage, then added a doctorate to her already-impressive credentials at California State University-Fresno.

Texas A&M–San Antonio President Cynthia Teniente-Matson is, in her own words, "laser-focused on student success," the leader of a "conspiracy of high expectations."

Mick Deeds, Wikimedia Commons

The new university has grown its enrollment to more 6,500 hundred and has earned the support of some of San Antonio's most generous corporate citizens, including Bartell Zachry, Lowry Mays, Bill Greehey, Peter Holt, Carl Raba, Weisie and John Steen, Dan Allen and Peggy Hughes, Elaine Mendoza, Carlos and Malu Alvarez, and Henry Cisneros. These "Dream Makers" carry forward the goals of early visionaries like José Navarro and Juan Seguín and are helping turn Frank Madla's hopes for the South Side into realities.

The city's higher educational opportunities are plentiful and varied in structure, cost, and degree programs. In addition to the more traditional colleges and universities, there are many other innovative places to earn a degree. The Southwest School of Art, situatied on the banks of the San Antonio River in the heart of downtown, operated as the state's only independent college of art until 2022, when it announdced plans to merge with the Universtiy of Texas at San Antonio. Despite the change, SSA will retain its name and envisions building on its unique brand.

The nationally recognized Culinary Institute of America (CIA) at the historic Pearl offers associate dgrees as well as hosting an annual Latin American Food Festival in October.

San Antonio recognizes that learning can take many forms, that it begins long before a student is ready for college, and that it can and should continue long after graduation. With seventeen separate independent school districts, more than fifty private schools and charter schools, more than thirty libraries in the public library system, and the BiblioTech electronic library system, educational opportunities abound across the city.

Founded in 2013 by Tracy Wolff, a former First Lady of San Antonio and a tireless community activist, BiblioTech was the first all-digital public library in the United States. Its stated goal was to bridge the literacy and technology gaps existing within the city. During the Covid-19 pandemic, when most schools pivoted to online learning, it created internet hotspots to provide students who did not have computers and/or internet service at-home access to their classes. It also became a resource for teachers developing their new online classes, parents learning how to Zoom, and students struggling with the new education models that were part of their school year.

Two years before BiblioTech

opened its first branch library, former mayor Julián Castro convened a "Brain Power Task Force," citing solid data documenting the importance of early involvement in the education process. Two dynamic business leaders co-chaired it: Charles Butt, whose innovations at H-E-B created one of the largest private grocery chains in the country, and General Joe Robles, CEO of USAA, one of the most successful insurance companies in the nation. Other business leaders, school superintendents, and education professionals participated, identifying ways to improve early education in San Antonio. The result was a recommendation to develop a high-quality pre-kindergarten program for four-year-old children, based on research demonstrating that children who enter kindergarten prepared to learn are more likely to stay in school and attend college. In 2012, the citizens of San Antonio voted overwhelmingly to invest in its youngest generation, and Pre-K 4 SA was born. Its $47 million annual budget comes from the federal government, with $4.5 million from the city and state generated by sales tax. The program opened in 2013 with 700 children, an all-day curriculum to assist working parents, and seven partner school districts, mostly in lower-income areas of the city.

Two additional centers opened in 2014, and enrollment more than doubled.

By 2019, 2,000 children participated; every year since the program's launch, students enrolled in Pre-K 4 SA have scored above the national norm for entrance to kindergarten. It is noteworthy—even miraculous—that San Antonio took a real leap of faith with its decision to implement the program since Pre-K education has never been a part of

photo by Al Rendon

Our Lady of the Lake University was established in 1895 on the city's West Side.

BiblioTech is the first and only all-digital library in the United States, the brainchild of Tracy Wolff, one of San Antonio's most imaginative civic leaders.

photo courtesy of BiblioTech

photo by Al Rendon

The Culinary Institute of America, located at the Pearl, offers associate degrees in culinary arts and special programs for leaders and professionals in the food industry.

city government. In subsequent bond elections, citizens have continued to affirm their belief that early education will produce successful students who become contributing members of their community as adults.

Fortunately for San Antonio's future, there is a true cornucopia of educational choices today, ranging from traditional schools to surprising options, ensuring a "fit" for every child.

The Young Women's Leadership Academy, part of the San Antonio Independent School District, is the city's first public, tuition-free, all-girls elementary school. It focuses on science, technology, engineering, the arts, and math (STEAM) and adds courses in social-emotional learning and early college preparation.

The IDEA Carver Academy is a public charter school initially established by basketball great David Robinson as a private Christian school based on an expectation of student success. The formula seems to work—all fourteen IDEA charter schools in San Antonio, and the others across Texas, have reported 100% college acceptance for thirteen consecutive years. Other public charter school systems also have produced stellar results; most of the city's seventeen school districts are incorporating many of the same innovative approaches to education; private schools have done so as well. One such method is underway at the private Will Smith Zoo School, where pre-schoolers spend half of their day playing outside, mingling with crocodiles, monkeys, and other animals as well as butterflies, insects, and birds on the grounds of the San Antonio Zoo. It is the largest nature-based pre-school in the United States and the only one in the country to win the prestigious LEED Platinum Certificate from the US Green Building Council.

Undoubtedly, George Brackenridge, who donated those acres more than 150 years ago, would be delighted to see a future generation of conservationists playing and learning outside.

Affirming South African statesman Nelson Mandela's belief that "education is the most powerful weapon you can use to change the world," San Antonio is changing its future. Commencing when our youngest citizens enroll in creative pre-school programs; blossoming in the hundreds of public and private schools; booming in community colleges, vocational schools, and universities that offer top quality higher education; and never-ending as citizens explore the array of post-graduate courses, lectures, libraries, and so many other opportunities for lifelong learning.

During the Covid-19 pandemic, San Antonio's panorama of educational offerings, including museums and popular after-school programs, came up with various hybrid models to enable learning to continue. When the normally hands-on, immersive experiences of the city's oldest museum closed its doors to the public in March 2020, the creative staff sprang into action. Witte Museum President Marise McDermott explained that 28,000 field trip students already had been scheduled; both children and the museum staff were deeply disappointed. "We immediately pivoted and launched Witte Where You Are, an online series of virtual programs with InterActors, featuring characters like 'Vaquero Josh" and 'Dr. Dig', eventually producing more than fifty programs in six weeks, with more than 1 million online engagements." They did not stop there because Covid continued into 2021. Witte educators developed a "Witte Box of Wonders" that could be delivered or mailed, full of specimens, activities, supplies, and a syllabus with online support and virtual interaction allowing students a hands-on experience.

But with the reliance on online learning, educators and parents became acutely aware of the existing "digital divide" and the need to address it with new vigor going forward. In academic settings, teachers also discovered high levels of anxiety in their students; as a result, there is unanimous recognition of the need for initiatives to address mental health. Data acknowledges learning loss in 2020-2021, especially in schools with fewer resources. Studies underway will show the detailed impact of these unusual years, providing valuable insights and instigating plans for future school years. Of course, there were other non-academic lessons for San Antonio's young generation of learners during the pandemic—lessons about courage and resilience in times of adversity that will help them navigate their world for years to come.

When the 2021-2022 school year began with in-person classes, students were thrilled; most found wearing a mask in class to be a minor inconvenience that enabled them to learn and socialize in classrooms again. In November 2021, the CDC expanded access to the Covid-19 vaccine to children as young as five years old. Three hundred and thirty thousand children became eligible for the shot, and San Antonio's vaccination rate quickly exceeded the statewide percentage. "It's a level of peace of mind that's been rare during this pandemic," Mayor Ron Nirenberg told the public as he urged parents to get their children vaccinated as the end of the year approached. Clinics created child-friendly spaces with colorful posters of favorite cartoon characters, stickers, candies, and fun bandages; news stories shared photos of smiling children bravely rolling up their sleeves. San Antonians hoped that good health would persevere in the new year.

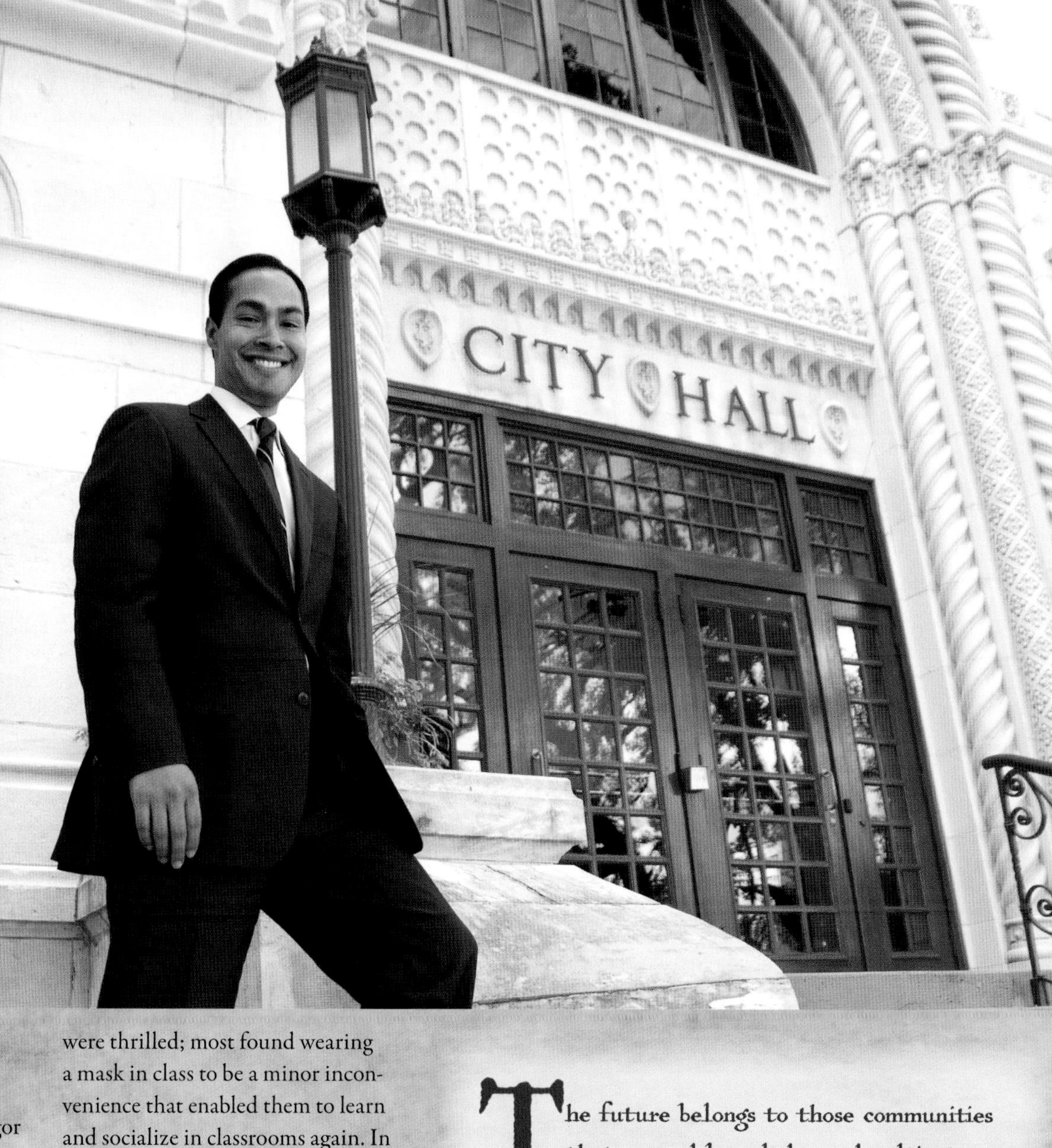

photo by Al Rendon

The future belongs to those communities that expand knowledge and cultivate brainpower.

—Julián Castro, former mayor of San Antonio and U.S. Secretary of HUD

Chapter Seven:

Nourishing the Soul

THE ORIGINS OF SAN ANTONIO ARE SPIRITUAL. IT HAS ALWAYS BEEN A PLACE WHERE PEOPLE SOUGHT PEACE, SAFETY, PROTECTION, AND HARMONY. ITS ORIGINAL NAME, 'YANAGUANA,' MEANS THE PLACE OF THE PEACEFUL WATER.

—HENRY G. CISNEROS

Nic Tengg, Wikimedia Commons

Military Plaza San Antonio Texas, c 1857

Courtesy Institute of Texan Cultures University of Texas a San Antonio

The legends and myths involving the earliest people to occupy San Antonio are elaborate and plentiful. The first residents are said to have been Payayas in search of water. They found it clean, clear and abundant in a river surrounded by lush shade trees. They settled and called it 'Yanaguana'—the place of the peaceful water.

The discovery by a Payayan scout of the source of the San Antonio River is a story ripe for retelling and sets the stage for the random appearance of the mythical blue panther. The scout, a young female, followed a bird along the route of the river and became a water spirit upon her death. That spirit took residence at Blue Hole at the headwaters of the river form time to time took on the form of the legendary blue panther.

The blue panther captures one of the city's origin myths, representing the young Payaya woman who discovered the important source of water that welcomed the First People and subsequent settlers to San Antonio.

Many centuries later, the first Spanish explorers and missionaries landed in the area, also drawn to the availability of clear water. One Spanish explorer determined in 1709 that there was enough water to supply a town. After traveling further south to San Pedro he declared it could support "not a village, but a city."

That historic river now makes its way through the seventh largest city in the United States; proving the adventurer to be correct.

The convergence of Spanish and indigenous peoples in the eighteenth century accounts for the establishment of five missions along the river, including Mission Espada which lies about twelve miles to the south.

Built by the Franciscan order, they offered sanctuary, training in successful farming techniques, and a social and religious community to the Payayas and other native peoples. Today they remain vibrant places with ongoing traditions. As a result, they were designated as a UNESCO World Heritage Site in 2015.

The Alamo (San Antonio de Valero) was built in 1718; its rich history has led to San Antonio's nickname, "The Alamo City." In 1720, Mission San José was constructed using Texas limestone and brightly colored stucco. The largest of the missions, it provided protection and community to more than 300 indigenous people. Folklore credits Pedro Huizar, a carpenter and surveyor from Spain, with carving its famous Rose Window, a lasting remnant of Spanish colonial ornamentation. Both Mission San Juan Capistrano and Mission Espada were constructed in 1731. The residents developed the fertile farmland nearby, thanks to the acequias built for irrigation. Finally, Mission Concepcion was completed

The mythic blue panther lives on.....Local artist Oscar Alvarado created the intricate mosaics for the Yanaguana Gardens at HemisFair Park as a salute to San Antonio's earliest history.

in 1755 is currently the oldest unrestored church in the United States. The missions remain repositories of what the Spaniards brought to their northern frontier—protection, food, clothing, medical care, education, and evangelism.

In 1731, a group of fifteen families from the Canary Islands established San Fernando Cathedral. The dome of the new church was the geographic center of the city, facing Main Plaza. Jim Bowie, a widely-known participant in the Battle of the Alamo (and known for his creation of the Bowie

San Fernando Cathedral, built in 1731, is the oldest and largest continuously functioning religious community in Texas.

Irid Escentt, Wikimedia Commons

corporations. Following that success, he was appointed director of the Old Spanish Missions of the Archdiocese. He was asked to do the same thing for San Antonio's crumbling landmarks; he organized a team of city leaders, raised $15 million for restoration, earning the new UNESCO status for the missions.

Father David's ministry began when he was a young priest on the West Side in the early 1970s. Immaculate Conception Church faced an illegal junkyard and dumping ground. The community had asked the city for help—without success until it enlisted the parish priest in the effort. Father David was an early supporter of COPS and a friend of its founder, Ernie Cortés, whom he credits with teaching him how to organize people to make change happen in their neighborhoods. The junkyard was demolished; the site eventually became a park adjacent to Father David's first church.

When he retired in 2019, the entire city celebrated his contributions to pastoral care that reached every corner of San Antonio. He delivered his last mass at the restored Mission Concepcion, where he reminded the standing-room-only crowd that "we can live our lives in one of two ways—as if nothing were a miracle or as if everything is a miracle."

Miracles are a big part of San Antonio's historic spirituality just as faith and hope have been sustaining elements in the city's evolution. In the 1840s, a stream of Anglo Protestants began arriving, escaping from the economic woes of Europe. They brought their own powerful civic, economic, and cultural influences, and over the next two decades, every religious denomination erected a downtown church.

The First Presbyterian Church was built in 1847 on Commerce Street, using adobe and rubble from the Alamo (purchased for fifty cents a cartload). It was the city's first Protestant church, known as the "Old

> **Our city's spirituality derives from the very founding of San Antonio as a mission—San Antonio de Valero. The concept that a church is 'missionary' means going outside of its walls, reaching out to others, looking for those most vulnerable and helping them. San Antonio de Valero did that—offering education, health care, a sense of community, as well as the Word of God.**
> **— Father David Garcia**

knife), married Ursula de Veramendi in the cathedral in 1831. Mexican General Antonio de Lopez de Santa Ana hoisted the flag announcing "no quarter" from its bell tower five years later as the famous battle began.

Today San Fernando remains at the heart of Catholic religious life in San Antonio, attracting 5,000 participants to its weekend masses, and it is the seat of the Catholic Archdiocese. When it needed restoration in 2003, Protestant and Jewish leaders joined Catholic leaders to help raise the $21 million necessary for the work.

Father David Garcia served at four parishes—including San Fernando Cathedral—during his forty-four years as a pastor in San Antonio. He was the force behind the restoration, which attracted sixty percent of its donations from non-Catholic individuals and

First Presbyterian Church was San Antonio's first Protestant church, established in an old adobe in 1846; its much larger Gothic revival structure was built in 1910.

photo courtesy of First Presbyterian

Adobe." A storm destroyed it in 1868. After several more attempts to build and maintain buildings downtown, it constructed its permanent home in 1910—a Gothic revival style church on South Alamo Street, designed by renowned architect Atlee B. Ayres.

Its congregation has grown to more than 2,200 members and it was one of eleven different congregations involved in the founding of the San Antonio Metropolitan Ministries, Inc. (SAMM). With locations throughout the city, the group provides supportive services for those experiencing homelessness. In 2020, this church-led community effort helped 356 families find a safe place to stay every night of the year.

Other early Protestant churches were established shortly after First Presbyterian's "Old Adobe" opened its doors. Travis Park Methodist held its first services in San Antonio's Courthouse before building its impressive white limestone building across from Travis Park both the church and the park were named in honor of William Barret Travis, a hero from the Batttle of the Alamo. St. John's Lutheran Church was established in 1857, with a congregation of fifteen. St. Mark's Episcopal Church was built on yet another corner of Travis Park.

The small Episcopal congregation met in various downtown halls until vestrymen hired New York architect Richard Upjohn, admired for his church projects in New England, to design a building for the fledgling congregation. The Civil War halted the construction of the new church before the walls were completed. Eventually, the building was finished in 1875. Over the years, other well-known architects made additions, including Alfred Giles; and today, St. Marks is part of the National Registry of Historic Places.

The First Baptist Church was founded in 1861 by a missionary named Reverend John Thurmond. For the first few years, worshippers met in various places, including the second floor of a downtown drugstore, until the church built its first structure across from Travis Park in 1872. Eventually, its membership grew. In 1900, with a growing membership, it moved to its current site just north of downtown, where its active congregation still worships today.

photo courtesy of the Temple

Established in 1874, Temple Beth-El is the oldest synagogue in South Texas; it moved to its current location in 1927.

In 1874, forty-four Jewish families built the city's first synagogue, Temple Beth-El, on a corner adjacent to First Baptist's original church. Like many others who emigrated to San Antonio, Jewish immigrants left economic uncertainty, political upheaval, and persecution. Julius Joske, one of those early pioneers, established a successful dry goods store on Main Plaza in 1867. Business boomed at several more stores he established and Joske's was known as "the largest store in the largest state" by the turn of the century.

Temple Beth-El experienced growth as well. By 1927, a much larger congregation necessitated the move to a larger property located in the fast-growing neighborhood of Laurel Heights, just north of downtown. Today its landmark building is considered the heart of Reform Jewish life; more than 1,000 families worship there and participate in its youth groups, educational programs, and social justice activities with city-wide outreach.

The first Orthodox Jewish synagogue in San Antonio was Agudas Achim, chartered in 1889. The congregation met in various halls downtown until it purchased property on the San Antonio River in 1893 and five years later, in 1898,

I moved from Brooklyn to San Antonio in 1970. There was a real heart to this city and I immediately found a sense of community here. Hand-in-hand with its growth and beauty, there was a sensitivity to the spirit of 'other'. A few years later, I learned firsthand what San Antonio could become from a young mayor named Henry Cisneros, when I heard him speak to a gathering of 1000 people in Denver. He was brilliant and eloquent—his message was that both diversity and unity can co-exist and can transform a city, if partnerships are formed to honor subsets of American culture working together to design the city's future.

— Rabbi Aryeh Scheinberg

photo courtesy of Sikh Dharamsal

Sikh Dharamsal is one of two Sikh temples in San Antonio.

dedicated a Moorish-style synagogue designed by architect J. Riely Gordon. Sadly, the "flood of 1921" destroyed that structure and adter many moves and several decades, the current synagogue was erected in 1992 at the corner of Huebner and Bitters Road.

Congregation Rodfei Sholom is also in the city's northwest quadrant. It was established as an Orthodox synagogue in 1912, and its name translates as "pursuers of peace and harmony." Led by Rabbi Aryeh Scheinberg for more than fifty years before his son succeeded him in 2020, its consistent message is a respect for diversity, and like San Antonio itself, it is a unique and welcoming home where everyone can feel connected.

As part of the synagogue's mission to pursue peace and harmony, coupled with a solid commitment to inclusion and social justice, Scheinberg has established meaningful relationships with the city's Latino community, focusing primarily on issues of immigration, education, and Israel. Soon after he arrived in San Antonio, he recognized affinities shared by his Jewish community and its Latino neighbors—"precious ties to family, faith, and the fact that both of our cultures came as minorities from elsewhere."

During his tenure as the spiritual leader at Rodfei Sholom, Scheinberg forged strong partnerships with San Antonio and beyond. In 2018, Israel's Minister of Foreign Affairs paid tribute to him for his leadership in changing the landscape of Jewish-Christian relations.

Today, San Antonio has thirteen mosques located throughout the city. Still, as recently as the 1980s, before the first mosques were built, Muslims held religious services at Fort Sam Houston and other military bases where many were stationed. While the Sunnis comprise the largest denomination of Islam—in San Antonio as in the rest of the world—other sects have established mosques and education centers here. They operate harmoniously, proving that their religious bond is more vital than any ethnic dissensions. The Islamic Center of San Antonio, located in the South Texas Medical Center area, is both a mosque and the home of the Islamic Academy and the recipient of a recent educational grant. The Academy provides Muslim education for children from eighteen months through the sixth grade.

But as children laugh and play and pray, prejudices about Muslims, exacerbated by the Islamic terrorist attacks on September 11, 2001, still linger in the US and, unfortunately, in San Antonio.. According to Sarwat Hussain, President of the Council on American Islamic Relations in San Antonio, "as much as San Antonio embraces diversity, many Muslims who live here feel a sense of disconnect and isolation. As the city grows, the bridge dividing Muslims and others seems to be growing too." He reports that all thirteen mosques in San Antonio regularly receive hate mail and threats. City leaders have condemned the anti-Muslim sentiment originating in recent years. Mayor Ron Nirenberg, the city council, Police Chief William McManus, and the police force all have formally registered their support of San Antonio's growing Muslim community.

Suhail Arastu is part of that community and was chosen as one of "San Antonio's Most Compelling People" by *Scene In SA* magazine in 2021. He is optimistic about San Antonio's future as an inclusive place to live. He describes San Antonio as "a compassionate city, with leadership that celebrates our diversity." He was a toddler when he moved with his parents to San Antonio, where his mother had been selected for a fellowship at Wilford Hall Medical Center in 1983. Dr. Raiqua S. Arastu, an immigrant from India, became the first woman and first foreign-born person to enter the highly competitive program. By the time she retired from the Air Force in 2001, she was a flight surgeon and a decorated lieutenant colonel. Until her death in 2019, Dr. Arastu ran a bustling private medical practice in San Antonio; was active in her mosque, Bhurhani Mosjid; contributed to education, music, and the arts in San Antonio; and traveled the world. She is remembered as a symbol of this city's confluence of civilizations.

Waheeda Kara helped establish a new Islamic gathering center, Ismaili Jamat Khana, on San Antonio's far North Side in 2014. She has seen its membership grow to more than 2,000; her description of the membership might also define San Antonio and what it hopes to be. "We have always been for peace and pluralism. We are all under one humanity."

Almost thirty years before Raiqua Arastu joined the faculty at Wilford Hall, Dr. Pemmaraju N. Rao and his wife Rani were the first

Indians—and the first Hindus—to move to San Antonio. Tom Slick recruited Rao to become one of the first scientists at Texas Biomedical Research Institute. Rao's 1956 laboratory was an un-air-conditioned room in an old ranch house west of the city; he sometimes found snakes coiled in its corners. His facilities were eventually modernized during more than fifty years of research that led to discoveries in hormone metabolism and its link to cancer. San Antonio's Indian population increased exponentially to as many as 3,000 families and the first Hindu temple was finally built in 1989 in nearby Helotes, Texas.

A smaller constituency of San Antonio's Indian population follow the Sikh religious tradition. The Sikh Center of San Antonio is a spacious gurdwara located near the Medical Center area, where members gather each week to worship. Everyone is welcomed, regardless of race, caste, gender, religion, or ethnicity—hospitality is at the heart of the Sikh tradition, along with the seva, the concept of selfless service.

Dr. Gurvinder Pal (G.P.) Singh was a 26-year-old engineer when he brought those traditions to San Antonio from northern California in 1979. He was hired by Southwest Research Institute as a senior research engineer with specialized expertise in electrical power, fossil fuels, and nuclear energy. Eventually, he became part of the faculty at UTSA.

In 1986, Singh founded Karta Technologies in his garage. Specializing in information technologies, the company expanded into health care management systems. It employed 400 people by the time he sold it to NCI, Inc. for $65 million in 2007. With four children and grandchildren born and raised in San Antonio, and several corporate and nonprofit board positions, Singh and his wife have come to love the city and "cannot imagine calling any other place home." The family helped build the Sikh Dharamsala, the gurdwara that raised more than a quarter of a million dollarsfor the San Antonio Food Bank during the covid-19 pandemic in 2020.

Kiran Kaur Bains, CEO of SA2020 and an Atlantic Fellow for Racial Equity, grew up in San Antonio and was exposed to the Sikh concept of seva at an early age by her mother. In an interview with *San Antonio Magazine* in 2021, she described volunteering in the community as a child, where she often felt that her "brown, Punjabi-speaking, turban-wearing, working-class immigrant family ... didn't quite belong in my hometown." Today she credits that experience with preparing her to become the first chief equity officer for the City of San Antonio, then president of SA2020 in 2021. She is passionate about the nonprofit's mission to build a shared "Community Vision" for San Antonio, noting that "everyone who calls San Antonio home actually belongs."

That sense—that everyone belongs—is evident in the fact that all of San Antonio's early flagship churches and synagogues still operate today. Each denomination has expanded its reach into city neighborhoods. During the past few decades, mosques, Hindu and Sikh temples, the Church of Jesus Christ of the Latter Day Saints, and many other places of worship like Community Bible Church and Fellowship Bible Church have become a part of the city's spiritual landscape. All have joined hands to address the needs of the less fortunate—-the poor, the sick, and those experiencing homelessness—recognizing that nourishment of the soul entails more than religious instruction and worship.

Non-religious, ecumenical entities have taken up the baton of human service as well.

One of the most compelling challenges in San Antonio and the nation is the dramatic increase in the number of people experiencing homelessness exacerbated by the Covid-19 pandemic. San Antonio has developed a nationally recognized model that reduced its downtown count by eighty-one percent in 2019, according to Father David Garcia. As early as 2000, downtown religious leaders of various faiths began to focus on the issue of homelessness at their regular

In 2010, Bexar County Judge Nelson Wolff, City Councilwoman Patti Radle, Valero CEO Bill Greehey, Mayor Phil Hardberger, and City Manager Sheryl Sculley (left to right) were forces behind Haven for Hope.

photo courtesy of NuStar Energy

Haven for Hope was built as a public-private partnership to tackle homelessness in San Antonio; it has become a national model and more than 30 community partners provide services.

monthly meetings. All recognized that the number of people experiencing homelessness was growing and that something had to be done.

City Councilwoman Patti Radle—a longtime champion of the city's underserved—and businessman and philanthropist Bill Greehey led the effort to engage the support of city leaders. Using data from research conducted at more than 200 shelters around the country, Haven for Hope opened its doors in San Antonio in 2010. In recent years it has been described as "a transformational campus that changes lives," delivering a one-stop array of services on its twenty-two-acre campus. After its first decade of operation, the facility reported that more than 13,000 people have transitioned from street life to living in permanent or supportive housing. Haven for Hope's 184-partner organizations provide services onsite, avoiding the challenge of requiring public transportation to reach counseling, educational programs, job training, medical assistance, and childcare.

Fortunately for San Antonio,

courtesy of jason john paul haskins through creative commons

photo by Al Rendon

photo by Al Rendon

other deeply caring organizations—faith-based, governmental, and ecumenical—contribute their talents and resources to the city's ongoing struggle to care for its unshoused population. And like all big cities, San Antonio has developed a network of organizations that deliver a wide array of human services that extend beyond providing shelter. Food banks, children's shelters, orphanages, domestic violence centers, veteran homes, and peace and justice centers are all ways that San Antonio embraces its community.

Its natural beauty—that feeling of "high touch" instead of "high tech"—offers its citizens another embrace. From a walk along the river to a backyard barbecue with neighbors, the human spirit can find solace, friendship, and celebration here.

The city's art and music also lift that spirit by the sheer beauty of places like the Japanese Tea House/Sunken Gardens and the San Antonio Botanical Center, where nature reveals its most profound gifts to the soul.

Since its earliest beginnings as a serene resting place for indigenous people, San Antonio has supported and soothed its inhabitants with the richness of its natural gifts. Today, one of the world's most spectacular linear parks meanders down a thirteen-mile stretch of the San Antonio River, where one can almost hear the echoes of the past and embrace hope for the future.

Confluence Park is situated along the San Antonio River near Mission Concepcion, surrounded by nature, offering a mix of both peaceful contemplation and exciting educational programming.

photo courtesy of San Antonio River Foundation

Chapter Eight: A City That Heals

A CITY THAT HEALS IS A NOBLE THING. COMPASSIONATE CARE HAS BEEN A PART OF SAN ANTONIO'S SPIRIT SINCE ITS EARLIEST DAYS AS A CITY. IN MODERN TIMES, IT HAS DEVELOPED STATE-OF-THE-ART BIOSCIENCE, MEDICAL, AND TECHNOLOGY INDUSTRIES THAT INCLUDE THE NATION'S LEADING BURN AND TRAUMA CARE CENTER AND RESEARCH FACILITIES THAT ARE FINDING NEW PATHWAYS TO FIGHT INFECTIOUS DISEASES.

—-CATHERINE NIXON COOKE

photo by Charles Martin Wender, courtesy of San Antonio Medical Foundation

The South Texas Medical Center consists of 900 acres of medical-related facilities on the city's northwest side.

Just a little more than five decades ago, as HemisFair was closing its gates, the first buildings for a new medical school were being constructed on what had been a dairy farm in northwest San Antonio. Before 1968, San Antonio was the largest city in the United States without a medical school, although city leaders had been pushing for one for decades. As early as the 1940s, when polio, diphtheria, and smallpox were still rampant, concerned citizens began to recognize the need for improved health care in San Antonio, raising their voices to ask for more accessible and affordable hospitals and clinics. Local physicians, business leaders, and the city council were part of the chorus, noting that a modern city needs to focus on economic development and quality of life, recognizing that providing for good health is an essential part of that. They began to lobby for a state-supported medical school in San Antonio.

Of course, long before there were hospital systems, there were healers. Some of the eliest were French nuns who came to San Antonio during a cholera outbreak in 1869. They established the Santa Rosa Infirmary in a two-story adobe building in the heart of downtown San Antonio. It was the city's first hospital; the Sisters learned to speak English and were taught to perform medical procedures by a handful of semi-trained country doctors who lived here.

San Antonio's first hospital was the Santa Rosa Infirmary, established in 1912.

The Infirmary outgrew its small adobe within a few years and moved to a larger site at San Saba and Houston Street, near Market Square. In 1912, it was renamed the Santa Rosa Hospital, delivering Catholic-based nonprofit healthcare to a growing city. In 1999, the Sisters of Charity of San Antonio joined the Sisters of Charity in Houston to form the CHRISTUS Health Care System. In 2012, the Santa Rosa Hospital became The Children's Hospital of San Antonio, the city's first freestanding children's hospital in its history.

In 1903, thirty physician members of the newly established Bexar County Medical Society partnered with the business community to organize San Antonio Associated Charities. Recognizing that the fast-growing city needed more health care facilities, they raised the money to build a four-story hospital on Dallas Street, just north of downtown. Named the Physicians' and Surgeons' Hospital, it would eventually morphed into a part of the Baptist Hospital System.

The Robert B. Green Hospital was built in 1917 due to a population boom. With World War I underway, thousands of troops were stationed here and many refugees from the Mexican Revolution were pouring into the city. Recognizing that a downtown charity hospital was badly needed, the City of San Antonio and Bexar County each contributed a quarter of a million dollars to build one. It opened just in time to treat victims of the deadly influenza epidemic of 1918.

The hospital was named for Robert B. Green, who led an illustrious life in public service, championing financial and political reform in San Antonio and Bexar County at the turn of the century. Green was born in San Antonio in 1865 and attended the German-English School and graduated from the Agriculture and Mechanical College of Texas (now Texas A&M University). He worked as a lawyer, served as the youngest federal judge in the United States and was elected to the Texas Senate. Finally, he served as Bexar County Judge until he died in 1907.

A few decades later, a respected property developer, Joseph M. Nix, built another significant health facility in San Antonio. When the 23-story Nix Hospital opened in 1930, it was the tallest hospital in the United States. Touted as the country's first "medical mall," it had doctors' offices located in the same building as the hospital. It included 200 patient rooms with private baths. In the heart of downtown, it served patients from every neighborhood. Like the Majestic Theatre and Municipal Auditorium, both just a few blocks away and built just before the Great Depression, its gothic architectural style added glamor to the city skyline. Postcards described it as "one of America's most beautiful hospitals." It closed in 2019, and more than 90 years later, developers are working on repurposing it as a hotel.

In the early to mid-20th century, the downtown hospitals—the Santa Rosa, Baptist, Robert B. Green, and Nix—were thriving. They were busy and full, expanding to meet San Antonio's growth. When the polio epidemic struck San Antonio in the mid-1940s, many victims spent time in the modern "iron lung" machines at the Robert B. Green Hospital.

No one anticipated that a few decades later, a new medical center—miles away from the city center—would attract patients from downtown or that financial problems at the iconic Nix Medical Center would lead to its closure and sale to a hotel chain in 2019.

As the city's only charity hospital, the Robert B. Green depended on physicians from the private hospitals to volunteer their time. Patient loads increased; the availability of doctors decreased. By the 1950s, the Robert B. Green experienced financial problems and closed some of its programs.

To save the charity hospital, in 1955, Bexar County voters overwhelmingly approved the creation of a new Bexar County Hospital District and a new property tax to fund it. One of the first hospital districts in Texas, it constructed Bexar County Hospital, which would become the South Texas Medical Center in 1968.

The city's long campaign for the medical center was often frustrating and tumultuous. Early attempts by the city council to get a proposal for a state-supported medical school approved by the Texas Legislature failed. In 1947, a group of private citizens took matters into their own hands. The San Antonio Medical Foundation was chartered as a nonprofit corporation; its mission was to make the dream of a local medical school a reality. Its first trustees were business and civic leaders with proven records of getting things done—General John M. Bennett, chairman of the National Bank of Commerce; Melrose Holmgreen, President of Alamo Iron Works; AJ "Jack" Lewis, founder of Jefferson Bank; Tom Slick, oilman and founder of Texas Biomedical Research Institute and Southwest Research Institute; Albert Steves III, owner of Steves Lumber Company; Mrs. Edgar Tobin (Margaret), philanthropist; and W.B. Tuttle, CEO of San Antonio's energy company and chairman of the San Antonio Chamber of Commerce. Attorney Wilbur L. Matthews' book, *History of the San Antonio Medical Foundation and South Texas Medical Center*, written in 1982, details the fifteen-year struggle. It is a dramatic

Texas Governor Price Daniel signed legislation to create a medical school in San Antonio in 1959.

photo courtesy of San Antonio Medical Foundation

MarkTSnow, wikimedia commons

Brooke Army Medical Center began as a 12-bed hospital in 1879; in 1938 a new hospital was built at Fort Sam Houston in time to take care of World War II casualties (above). Today Brooke Army Medical Center/BAMC (below) houses numerous medical facilities including the Center for the Intrepid.

story, fraught with contention about the right site for the medical complex. Some trustees pushed for a downtown location near the Robert B. Green; others were certain that northwest San Antonio, with its vast, undeveloped acres, was a better site. The battle finally was decided—in 1959; the Texas Legislature authorized the Board of Regents of the University of Texas to establish a medical school in San Antonio. In 1961, the Nix dairy farm in northwest San Antonio was approved as the site by the Board of Regents.

Today the South Texas Medical Center covers more than 700 acres and includes 45 medically-related institutions, separate medical, nursing, and dental schools, and five specialty facilities. All the city's major hospital systems have a presence there; some also have specialty clinics, outpatient facilities, rehabilitation centers, and an array of diverse medical services throughout San Antonio and its outskirts. In 2020, healthcare and biosciences comprised one of the city's largest industries, employing one-sixth of the workforce—more than 160 thousand people—with an estimated annual economic impact of more than 40 billion dollars. It was put to the test when the Covid-19 virus challenged the world in early 2020, with infections climbing to 324 thousand in Bexar County over the next two years. There can be no underestimation of the tragedies that affected people who lost families and friends, businesses that could not survive or are still struggling to do so, and the fear that most citizens had never experienced in their lifetimes. But San Antonio's position as a city that heals was never more apparent as the health care industry took care of the sick; the research laboratories searched for vaccines and treatments and the deep-rooted resilience and sense of community held firm.

CHRISTUS Santa Rosa is San Antonio's oldest health care system. It operates five full-service hospitals

throughout the city, including several in its giant complex in the South Texas Medical Center. Its Children's Hospital, located on its original downtown site, is adorned with a Jesse Treviño mural that reflects the healing spirit that has been at the health system's core since the Sisters of Charity established their first infirmary.

The Baptist Health System has evolved from one of the city's first hospitals, constructed in 1903 in downtown San Antonio. Today it operates six full-care hospitals, a specialized children's hospital, a network of cancer care facilities, rehabilitation centers, and clinics. Its newest branch, Mission Trails Baptist Hospital, is located on the city's far south side.

The Methodist Healthcare System began as the Methodist Hospital, chartered in San Antonio in 1955, anticipating the city's successful bid for a supported medical school. It was built in 1963, pioneering the way on the site in northwest San Antonio that eventually became the massive South Texas Medical Center. Today it includes nine acute care facilities and a network of specialty clinics and rehabilitation centers. It is the second-largest private employer in San Antonio, with eleven thousand employees and 2700 physicians. In 2021 it broke ground for a new 150 million dollar hospital on the city's West Side, with completion expected in 2023.

University Health System was established in 1968, in conjunction with the new South Texas Medical Center. Following Methodist hospital's lead, the Bexar County Hospital District built a new county hospital in 1965, near the site designated for the long-awaited medical school. When the medical school became a reality, the hospital was renamed University Hospital; and it became part of the new University Health System. It has become a nationally recognized teaching hospital during the last five decades and will complete construction of a new twelve-story Women's and Children's Tower in 2022. In March 2021, UT Health President William Heinrich announced the virtual groundbreaking of a new Multispecialty & Research Hospital as "a 430 million dollar investment that will advance healthcare through nationally leading medicine, innovative technologies, and scientific breakthroughs." Other components of the University Health System include: the city's original charity hospital downtown, now operating as the Robert B. Green Children's Hospital; thirteen neighborhood clinics; a network of outpatient health care centers; and the Texas Diabetes Institute, located on San Antonio's West Side but accessible to the entire metro area.

The Institute is wholly dedicated to the prevention and treatment of diabetes and is the largest and most comprehensive center of its kind in the United States. County Commissioner Paul Elizondo was its stalwart champion. After nearly a decade of planning, it became operational in 1999. Today, the 153 thousand square-foot facility houses a patient clinic, pharmacy, state-of-the-art research laboratories, hyperbaric chambers, and outpatient renal dialysis stations. It even incorporates a public vegetable garden with guides who explain healthy food choices.

Directed and staffed by specialists in a disease that is currently the seventh leading cause of death in the United States, it embraces a human, holistic approach to prevention and treatment. It includes bilingual patient education and recognizes that

photo courtesy of University Health

University Health System is the public hospital district for the San Antonio metropolitan area and is owned and operated by Bexar County.

photo courtesy of Texas Biomedical Research Institute

Dr. Larry Schlesinger is an internationally recognized authority on infectious diseases and serves as President/CEO of Texas Biomedical Research Institute.

family and community support are critical parts of healing.

Recognition extends beyond the city's modern healing centers. San Antonio is increasingly described as a national center for life science research and technology. Collaborations with military medical centers, Texas Research and Technology Foundation, BioMed SA, Texas Biomedical Research Institute, Southwest Research Institute, and others are catapulting the city's ability to heal to new levels.

After two years of development, a recent collaboration opened its doors to San Antonio's underserved East Side in 2020 as an incubator for life science startups. VelocityTX is the "innovation superhub" spearheaded by the Texas Research and Technology Foundation. In 2021, it received four million dollars in the latest rounds of CARES Act funding to expand its bioscience labs. Stem cell manufacturer GenCare, a subsidiary of BioBridge Global, is the anchor tenant. As part of the new superhub, it will have the capacity to multiply its production capacity nearly six times, which would make it one of only a few large-scale manufacturers of stem cells in the United States. Other tenants of VelocityTX include: MedCognition, which develops augmented-reality training for emergency professionals; Sports Sonar, a sports-tech startup that moved to San Antonio from Costa Rica; Cancer Insight, a clinical research organization; and Emtora Biosciences, which develops a pharmaceutical agent being used to fight cancer in clinical studies. According to TRTF CEO Randy Harig, the new incubator has the potential to kick off a revitalization boom in this historically overlooked part of San Antonio, much the way the development of Pearl and Geekdom have done in other parts of the city.

BioMed SA has been promoting the health care and bioscience sectors in San Antonio for fifteen years. Supported partly by the city, it has fostered meaningful industry partnerships and helped boost the health care/biosciences annual economic impact on San Antonio to more than 40 billion dollars. Ann Stevens, who retired in 2019 after serving as executive director since the organization began its work, has seen firsthand the exciting progress in the health care and bioscience sector that made it the largest industry in the city. She is quick to point out the importance

▼ In 2022 construction of University HealthSystem's new Women's and Children's Hospital got underway, with completion expected in 2023.

▼▼ UT Health San Antonio's new Multispecialty Research Hospital broke ground in 2022 and will focus on the treatment of complex diseases.

architectural rendering courtesy of University Health

architectural rendering courtesy of UT Health

of military medicine in San Antonio and the many collaborations that have resulted from its presence since the city's earliest days.

Military medicine arrived in San Antonio a century before the courageous Sisters of Charity opened their infirmary. In the mid-1700s, Spanish soldiers established a thirty-bed hospital at the Alamo, staffed by one doctor, one nurse, and a cook to care for patients. When Texas forces established their garrison at the mission during their fight for independence from Mexico, they also had a small hospital inside the walls. A few decades later, soldiers pitched medical tents not far from the Alamo during the Civil War.

After the war, the US government set up a new military hospital in a two-story house downtown.

When Fort Sam Houston began operating as an Army post in 1876, a small medical dispensary with twelve beds was constructed on the grounds. Over the next few decades, it was replaced several times with slightly larger station hospitals; and from 1929 until 1933, Brigadier General Roger Brooke, a tuberculosis specialist, commanded a hospital that accommodated eighty-four patients. In the years following the stock market crash, construction began on a new Station Hospital; and in 1937, the 3 million-dollar project was completed. With 418 beds, an impressive brick and stone façade, tile and terrazzo floors, and an ornate stone entrance, the new hospital was as modern as any in the nation.

It would need those facilities and even more beds once World War II began in 1941. The Station Hospital immediately converted a nearby barracks into additional patient wards. A few years later, it converted another into a convalescent facility for many wounded soldiers returning from the war.

In 1942, the Station Hospital was renamed Brooke General Hospital in honor of its former commander. During the next 75-plus years, the extraordinary growth in military medicine transformed it into one of the most extensive and impressive facilities of its kind in the world.

Today the hospital operates as Brooke Army Medical Center (BAMC); with 425 beds and (that can be expanded to more than 600, if needed). It is the Department of Defense's largest facility and the only civilian-military Level One Trauma Center in the United States. BAMC is responsible for administrative and clinical oversight of all Army health care facilities in San Antonio, including the Center for the Intrepid, located next door to the military hospital. The four-story, 65 thousand square-foot center was initially built to provide the country's best burn and trauma care. Officially dedicated in 2007, with US Senators John McCain and Hillary Clinton in attendance, more than 600 thousand private citizens contributed to the Intrepid Fallen Heroes Fund to assist financing in order to build it.

photo courtesy of TRTF/VelocityTX

J. Randolph "Randy" Harig is CEO of the Texas Research & Technology Foundation, the parent company of VelocityTX, an innovation district on San Antonio's East Side that focuses on bioscience.

Its state-of-the-art rehabilitation for amputees and burn victims was designed for veterans returning from wars in Iraq and Afghanistan. Today, it provides care for any military personnel who sustained injuries in either combat or noncombat. It is a tremendous source of pride in San Antonio, recognized worldwide for its excellence, and a symbol of the city's commitment to men and women of the military.

BAMC's reach stretches beyond San Antonio—it conducts medical-readiness exercises in developing countries around the world. Its physicians perform complex operations in extreme situations where state-of-the-art facilities such as those in San Antonio do not exist. It operates as a Level One Trauma Center and it took on additional patients during the Covid-19 pandemic to help ease the ever-increasing burden on the local healthcare system. In coordination with the city's trauma system in 2020 and 2021, it received all inter-facility transfers of injured patients who required a higher level of care from twenty-two counties across Southwest Texas. This critical collaboration freed up community hospital beds for critically ill Covid patients.

The United States Air Force's largest medical wing—the 59th Medical Wing—is in San Antonio. It comprises seven medical groups across the city. Three are located at the new Wilford Hall Ambulatory Surgical Center, all part of Joint Base-San Antonio-Lackland.

Following the base closures in 2005, the "joint base" idea provided an innovative solution for creating cooperative medical facilities at Fort Sam Houston (JBSA-Fort Sam Houston), Lackland (JBSA-Lackland), and Randolph (JBSA-Randolph). The 59th MDW operates the program with a 271 million dollar annual budget and a staff of more than 8000 military, civilian, and contract personnel. It is home to the Critical Care Transport Team Pilot Unit and the Defense Department's largest blood donor center and dental facility. Its extracorporeal membrane oxygenator (ECMO), a portable

CHRISTUS Santa Rosa Health System converted its downtown hospital to the Children's Hospital of San Antonio in 2012. Overland Partners designed its beautiful exterior; West Side artist Jesse Treviño's iconic mural reflects the hospital's commitment to hope, renewal, and quality care.

photo courtesy of Bartlett Cocke General Contractors

▶ U.S. Air Force airmen from the 37th and 59th Air Wing at Lackland evacuated hospital patients from Beaumont, Texas, as Hurricane Ike approached in 2008; military medicine is an important part of San Antonio's healthcare system.

▼ The Center for the Intrepid was established in 2007 as a rehabilitation facility for United States servicemen and women and their families.

heart-lung bypass machine for newborns, was developed at Wilford Hall in 1972. The program moved to BAMC in 2011 and expanded to include adult patients suffering from severe cardiopulmonary failure. Today it remains the only program of its kind within the Department of Defense; its presence at BAMC gives it the unique capability of global air transport. In 2013, the military's first transatlantic ECMO treatment of a patient took place on a near 12-hour nonstop flight from Germany to San Antonio on a C-17 Globemaster III transport plane.

U.S. Air Force photo by Staff Sgt. Chris Willis, wikimedia commons

U.S. Air Force wikimedia commons

Army, Air Force, and Navy physicians, nurses, technicians, and managers all work together in this life-saving work. The Austere Surgical Team, created at JBSA in the mid-1990s, is another emergency care practice with a global reach. Comprised of six highly trained personnel capable of deploying to any disaster region to perform necessary surgery, it proved invaluable after the Oklahoma City bombings in 1995, during Hurricane Maria in Puerto Rico in 2017, and most recently, in war zones in the Middle East.

In February 2020, 235 American evacuees from China's Hubei province, the epicenter of the Covid-19 outbreak, were brought to the base for two weeks of quarantine. Of those, eleven tested positive and were sent to a local hospital for treatment. In March, 200-plus people arrived from the Covid-contaminated Grand Princess Cruise Ship liner for quarantine at Lackland. The Center for Disease Control chose Lackland because of its large lodging capacity and proximity to high-quality medical facilities like the Texas Center for Infectious Disease. The arrival of the evacuees alarmed the citizens of San Antonio—it produced the first inkling of perceived danger from a global pandemic, something that had not been experienced since the Spanish Flu of 1918, more than a hundred years ago. The CDC and local officials at Metro Health attempted to soothe the

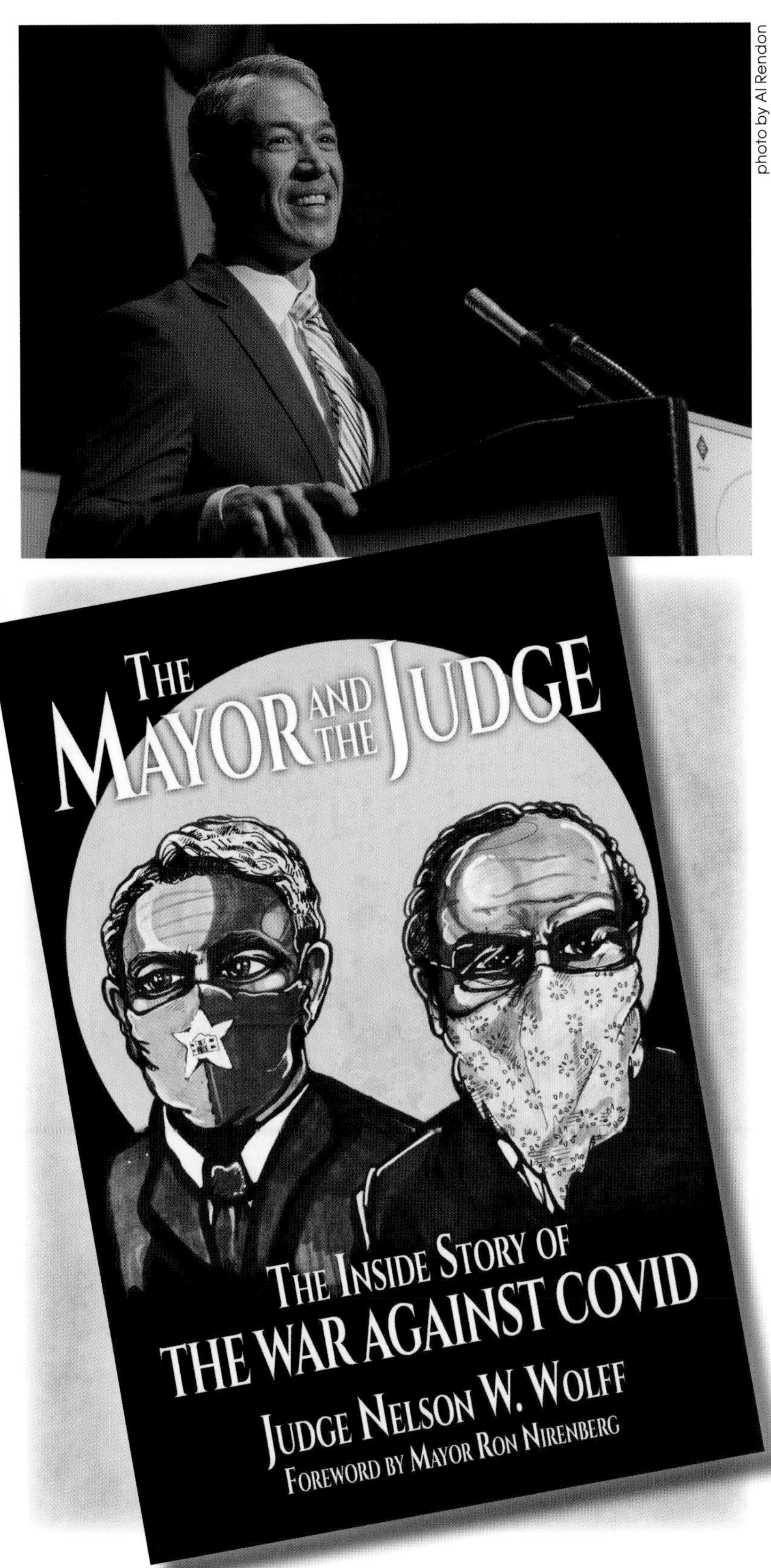

photo by Al Rendon

photo by Al Rendon

San Antonio Mayor Ron Nirenberg (left) and Bexar County Judge Nelson Wolff (right) led the San Antonio community through the Covid-19 pandemic.

public.Eventually, those quarantined at Lackland returned to their homes across the United States. But as Covid-19 infection rates began to climb around the country and the world, San Antonio watched with alarm.

Mayor Ron Nirenberg and County Judge Nelson Wolff began nightly briefings on local television. *The San Antonio Report* created a special daily update online, appropriately called "*The Curve*," written and edited by JJ Velásquez. The diverse hospital systems collaborated to deliver treatment. San Antonio did not run out of beds, intensive care units, or ventilators even at the pandemic's peak. When vaccines were first cleared for use in January of 2021, there were long lines at large venues like shopping malls and the Alamodome. As the vaccines became more plentiful, local pharmacies expanded the process. By late April 2022, 69 percent of those eligible had been vaccinated in San Antono and Bexar County, but more than 569,000 had contracted the virus, and 6,177 had died.

That resilience is a cornerstone of San Antonio. The partnership of military medicine and our state-of-the-art civilian health care systems makes the city even more robust, providing some of the best medical care in the world. Collaborations among biotechnology research laboratories led to the development of "miracles" like artificial skin for treating burns and the invention of the life-saving fluids administered by EMTs. Partnerships with infectious disease research facilities have produced vaccines for against deadly diseases like Hepatitis C and tuberculosis. The preparedness and dedication of medical systems and personnel enabled San Antonio to battle the Covid-19 pandemic in 2020-21 and proceed with myriad expansion plans that will meet the needs of a growing city.

Chapter Nine:
Essentials for a Modern City

WATER, POWER, PUBLIC HOUSING AND TRANSPORTATION, ROADS AND HIGHWAYS, WASTE DISPOSAL, AND PUBLIC SAFETY PROVIDE OUR CITY'S INFRASTRUCTURE. STILL, THERE ARE OTHER ESSENTIALS AS WELL—A SENSE OF CARING AND COMFORT, WELL-BEING AND WONDER, IN A PLACE THAT STRIVES FOR THE BEST QUALITY OF LIFE FOR ITS CITIZENS.

—CATHERINE NIXON COOKE

photo courtesy of crownridge01, mlhradio, creative commons

photo courtesy of Steve Miller via Creative Commons

The Edwards Aquifer is the major source of water for San Antonio and is one of the most prolific aquifers on the planet.

For thousands of years, the clear waters from bubbling springs, slow-moving creeks, and the San Antonio River carried the hopes and dreams of those who settled along those ancient waterways. Fed by one of the world's most prolific artesian aquifers, the modern aspirations of the seventh-largest city in the nation are buoyed by its waters. The Edwards Aquifer underlies the Edwards Plateau, a vast semi-arid region in central Texas that encompasses nearly 24 million acres with sloping hills, deep caves, and a wide array of plant species and animals. Bounded by the Balcones Fault and Colorado River to the south and east, the Llano Uplift to the north, and the Pecos River and Chihuahuan Desert to the west, the entire plateau covers more than 38,000 square miles—larger than the dozen smallest US states. Thanks to this rare blessing of nature, the Edwards Aquifer provides drinking water to more than two million people. It is the primary water supply for agriculture and industry throughout the region, enabling San Antonio and other cities in the region to grow and prosper without the need to develop other water resources for more than two centuries.

Early Spanish settlers and indigenous artisans built the San Pedro acequia to capture the clear artesian water and until 1836, it was reserved for drinking, cooking, and irrigation. Once regulations were relaxed, entrepreneurial business people found new uses for the city's prized resource. They established the San Antonio

Gas Company in 1860 and used the water from San Pedro Creek to power their enterprise, converting tree resin into gas for the first lights on Main Plaza. San Antonio was one of the first cities west of the Mississippi River to have streetlights.

When a severe cholera epidemic struck San Antonio in 1866, city leaders began to consider proposals for improving the safety and quality of the water supply. A decade passed before J.B. LaCoste was awarded a contract to provide clean water to San Antonio. He built a pumphouse near the headwaters of the San Antonio River on land that belonged to another entrepreneur, George Brackenridge. The pump used water pressure to lift water to a reservoir that is now the San Antonio Botanical Gardens site. In 1883, Brackenridge acquired LaCoste's system and created his privately-owned San Antonio Water Works, providing the first running water to homes in Government Hill and neighborhoods being developed at the end of the nineteenth century. By 1900, all the water was obtained from clear and sparkling artesian wells linked directly to the distribution system.

Today, San Antonio boasts the most extensive aquifer-based water system in the United States, thanks to the Edwards Aquifer and its hidden world of underground lakes. Because freshwater from the Edwards Aquifer is "recharged", or percolated, by the limestone formations of its surrounding plateau, San Antonio has never needed to rely on treated water from surface reservoirs as other Texas cities do. The San Antonio Water System (SAWS) cleans and maintains 12,000 miles of water and sewer mains, and its desalination plant converts groundwater into twelve million gallons of drinking water every day.

But aquifer water availability is vulnerable to drought periods, and as water demands increased by the city's growing population, SAWS took essential steps for the future. It built its Aquifer Storage and Recovery Facility in south Bexar County, utilized

San Antonio's water supply comes from the Edwards Aquifer; historically the city has appreciated that unique blessing; George Brackenridge and his sister Mary Eleanor built the first waterworks in 1877.

Zereshk wikimedia commons

during the 2011-2014 drought. The Vista Ridge Pipeline project is now buying additional groundwater from the Carrizo and Simsboro aquifers in Burleson County. Voters approved the controversial $930 million project in 2016. The 142-mile pipeline was completed in 2020. The pipeline is six feet in diameter, and can bring more than 16 billion gallons of water a year to San Antonio—an increase of 20 percent in the city's water supply, enough to provide water for 162,000 new families.

Conservation programs also are part of the water company's strategy for the years ahead. Irrigation improvements, encouragement of low-water-use plants, and yard-watering restrictions during dry periods already have affected water usage. SAWS estimates that in 2070, total water demand will be 74,000 acre-feet less than its 2012 figure, despite the increased demands of the fast-growing city. Unlike many other cities across the United States, San Antonio is secure in its water supply, which adds to its appeal as a desirable place to live.

Also fueling San Antonio's growth is an abundance of reasonably priced energy provided by CPS Energy, the largest municipally-owned gas and electric utility in the United States. From its humble beginnings as the San Antonio Gas Company on the banks of San Pedro Creek, it has provided the city with steady and affordable power for 160 years. Visionary city leaders convinced the City of San Antonio to purchase the privately-held company in 1942. CPS contributes 14 percent of its annual gross revenues to San Antonio's operating budget—resulting in lower property taxes for citizens by contributing more than $300 million to the city budget annually. Over its long history, the utility has adapted to changing energy sources and environmental concerns. From coal and natural gas to nuclear energy and renewables, CPS continues to deliver reliable power to San Antonio, increasing the city's ability to attract new businesses and sustaining its growing population. Although more than 1000 company-owned railroad cars still transport coal from Wyoming to CPS power plants, large quantities of wind and sunshine in Texas are harnessed by the utility, making renewable energy a rapidly increasing percentage of its total energy production. In 2021, San Antonio was ranked fifth in the nation for solar energy production. It received roughly twenty-two percent of its total energy from renewables, making it the second-highest in the state for renewables, just behind Austin. CPS Energy CEO Paula Gold-Williams describes the company as "nimble," ready to power San Antonio and its dreams into the future, with a goal of 40 percent renewable energy by 2040.

Water and power in San Antonio are two essentials that San Antonio has enjoyed without worrying about shortages that plague many other cities. However, the historic winter storm that struck in February 2021 disrupted that claim in a dramatic way. Texas is one of the few states to have a power grid of its own, operated by the Electric Reliability Council of Texas (ERCOT). The grid was pushed to the edge of collapse by the unprecedented arctic blast. Later investigations revealed that ERCOT had not invested in the upgrades necessary for extreme weather events. Local power companies were helpless; millions of Texans were left without electricity during the frigid conditions that lasted nearly a week. In San Antonio, many were without water since the San Antonio Water System (SAWS) depends on electricity to operate its pumps. Tragically, six people died during the disaster, and there were immense losses to local businesses and human well-being. Although CPS Energy and SAWS employees worked around the clock to restore the essentials of power and water, the utility companies were highly criticized by the media and the citizens they serve. San Antonio and other Texas cities are working to formulate better safety plans for the future of their grid and delivery systems that will prevent this from happening again. San Antonio already has devised thoughtful strategies for future power and water consumption, looking ahead at changing needs as the population increases.

Public transportation also has evolved into an award-winning part of San Antonio's infrastructure, and it has a long history in the city. In the 1800s, several privately-owned companies provided mule-drawn transportation for travel from Main Plaza to restful destinations like San Pedro Park and the Hot Wells spa and "distant" neighborhoods just a few miles from the center of town.

The San Antonio Edison Company was chartered in 1899 to establish an electric streetcar line replacing mule-driven carriages. Within a year, San Antonio was described as "a forest of poles" as several small independent electric companies strung their wires with abandon and five different private companies offered mass transportation.

In 1900, the five companies were consolidated into the San Antonio Traction Company, a subsidiary of City Public Service Company, the predecessor of CPS Energy. In 1921 it manufactured its first motorized buses, and in 1933, San Antonio became the largest city in the United States to convert from streetcars to buses. When the City purchased the utility in 1942, the transportation department was sold to the privately-owned Smith, Young, Tower Corporation, and the San Antonio Transit Company was born. San Antonio became the first city in the world to offer air-conditioned bus service in 1947.

Mass transportation in San Antonio became publicly owned in 1959 when the city bought the company from the Smith, Young, Tower Corporation and renamed it the San Antonio Transit System. It became the first regional transit authority in the nation in 1978 when voters approved the establishment of the VIA Metropolitan Transit Authority. Today, VIA services fourteen member cities and the unincorporated areas of Bexar County. Its fleet of 479 compressed natural gas (CNG) buses covers more than 90 routes, with more than 7200 bus stops throughout the city and its suburbs. VIA Primo offers frequent daily service from Centro Plaza in the heart of downtown and its terminal on the East Side to its South Texas Medical

Center Transit Center and UTSA offer Wi-Fi and provide bike racks on the buses. More Primo routes are planned and "next-generation" stations that light up at night to increase safety for passengers and future use of Transit Signal Priority that would enable buses to change

photo courtesy of Institute of Texan Cultures/UTSA Special Collections

In 1889 the city's mule-drawn transportation system was replaced by electric streetcars operated by the San Antonio Edison Company. Today the VIA Metropolitan Transit system carries more than 100,000 riders a day.

San Antonio is committed to renewable energy; in 2022 San Antonio was ranked No. 1 in Texas for solar power by the Environment Texas Research and Policy Center.

photo courtesy of CPS Energy

Alexander Jones wikimedia commons

traffic lights to stay on schedule. Today, more than 150 thousand passengers ride VIA buses daily, and the company has a workforce of more than 2000 employees. While consistently recognized as one of the best public transit systems in the state by the Texas Transit Association, VIA acknowledges that it faces challenges. With an additional million people and 500 thousand more vehicles expected in San Antonio by 2040, complex transportation issues must be addressed to meet the mobility needs that the future will most certainly create.

In 2018, the city and county initiated working groups of leaders from every civic sector of San Antonio to focus on future mobility needs. The result from dozens of community town halls—under the working title ConnectSA—is a framework for building and financing regional mobility improvements including sidewalks, hiking trails, bicycle and scooter paths, streets and freeways, and new systems of advanced rapid transit to crisscross the city. A series of elections will be scheduled over the next 20 years to seek voter approval to "future proof" the region's mobility. Hope Andrade, a former member of the Texas Transportation Commission, states it directly, "If we are going to grow by another million people by 2025, we need to have solid plans."

Mobility is not the only challenge that accompanies San Antonio's continuing growth. Safety plays a "yin-yang" role in the equation. Data proves that new residents are attracted to safe cities, yet as cities become larger, crime rates increase. Police Chief William McManus describes San Antonio as "one of the safest large cities in the nation," noting that 89 percent of its neighborhoods have seen a decrease in violent crime for the past few years, and 73 percent of neighborhoods have seen a reduction in property crime.

Law enforcement in San Antonio began more than 300 years ago, with the alguacils (constables) of the Villa de San Antonio de Bexar in 1718. The Texas Rangers and City Marshals replaced them. In 1873, Marshal John Dobbin transformed his lawmen into a more organized police department. Two years later, San Antonio officers were issued standard uniforms, a shield, and were required to conceal their guns under their coats.

Today, the San Antonio Police Department employs 2400 officers

Alexander Jones wikimedia commons

and explores modern technologies to keep the city safe. Like other big cities in the US, San Antonio is considering using robotic cameras, handheld lasers, automatic license plate recognition, thermal imaging, and even GPS vehicle pursuit darts which would enable police officers to track a fleeing suspect without a high-speed chase.

John Naisbitt, the bestselling author of more than twenty books, including *Megatrends*, reminds us that "whenever a new technology is introduced into society, there must be a counterbalancing human response—that is, high touch—or the technology is rejected. We must remember to learn to balance the material wonders of technology with the spiritual demands of our human race." San Antonio has done that well. It also has recognized that more than high-tech water, power, transportation, and safety systems are essential to a city's well-being, heeding the advice of the ancient healer, Hippocrates, who wrote that "nature itself is the best physician." Throughout history, poets and naturalists have described and documented the importance of the natural world as we create more and more constructed environments. San Antonio has become a metropolis without sacrificing its trees, waterways, and wide-open spaces. Parks, botanical gardens, bird sanctuaries, walking and bicycle trails, and quiet creeks can be found throughout the city, recognizing them as essentials for the health and happiness of a modern citizenry.

On San Antonio's South Side, a 600-acre lake is surrounded by more than 500 acres of wetlands, ponds, and upland habitat. In partnership with the City of San Antonio, the San Antonio Water System (SAWS) converted a waste-water reservoir into the Mitchell Lake Audubon Center. In this haven, both humans and nature can enjoy clear, clean water.

Many of the city's green spaces are named in honor of former mayors. Perhaps they realize more than anyone the need to escape to nature for much-needed stress relief. John Muir encouraged us all to "allow nature's peace to flow into you as sunshine flows into trees," and there are some beautiful places to do that in and around San Antonio.

On the city's northwest side, Phil Hardberger Park is located near Salado Creek on what was once a dairy farm. Its 311 acres of walking trails, two dog parks, picnic facilities, and basketball courts offer recreation and relaxation to visitors and their four-legged friends. It is named in honor of former San Antonio mayor Phil Hardberger, whose love of exploration and nature made him a powerful champion of the city's San Antonio River Improvements Project during his tenure from 2005 until 2009.

Former mayor Howard Peak was also a strong proponent of the river extension project, although it was only in the planning stages during his tenure from 1997 until 2001. After he left office, he continued to work on the San Antonio River Oversight Committee with another former mayor, Lila Cockrell. They were essential supporters as Hardberger pushed the project through with the critical assistance of Bexar County Judge (and former mayor) Nelson Wolff. The Howard W. Peak Greenway Trail System, one of the city's newest outdoor experiences, evolved from Peak's vision of building a ring of hike and bike trails around the creeks and waterways of San Antonio. Today that "ring" is nearly 70 miles long; and more than 40 significant trailheads branch off from it, connecting neighborhoods to Salado Creek and Leon Creek on the northside, to Alazan, Apache, San

Pedro, and other creeks on the West Side, and dozens of other parks around the city.

Just as it did during the city's earliest existence, the San Antonio River provides a beautiful, green respite from the heat and the trials of life in a growing metropolis. For more than five decades, plans for enhancing and extending the city's treasured waterway were discussed and debated. In 1998 a concerted community effort to revitalize the river began when Bexar County, the City of San Antonio, and the San Antonio River Authority created the San Antonio River Oversight Committee. Co-chaired by former mayor Lila Cockrell and architect Irby Hightower, the committee included 22 civic and neighborhood leaders. It was charged with completing construction of a thirteen-mile linear park that would stretch from near the river's headwaters to the city's southernmost mission, Mission San Francisco de Espada. The nonprofit San Antonio River Foundation was created to raise private funds for the amenities, landscaping, and artwork that would be so critical to the massive project's success.

The linear park is formed by three segments, each with unique attractions and opportunities for recreation and relaxation. The first and oldest segment is the two-mile River Walk, designed in the 1930s. It had been neglected until improvements and additions made during HemisFair in 1968 gave it the boost it needed to join the Alamo as one of the two most-visited places in Texas. Hotels, restaurants, bars, music venues, and retail shops line the river banks, and colorful barges provide a scenic way to see downtown San Antonio.

The first phase of the new extension project, the Museum Reach, was designed by Ford, Powell & Carson Architects and built by Zachry Construction. Completed in 2009, it is a four-mile segment of the river that goes north from downtown, connecting the River Walk to

photos by Al Rendon

photo courtesy of the San Antonio River Foundation

the San Antonio Museum of Art, the new Pearl development, and the Witte Museum in Brackenridge Park. It includes a lock-and-dam system that lifts the colorful barges nine feet, enabling them to carry passengers upriver. For walkers, there are beautifully landscaped sidewalks and overlooks.

Sculptures created by renowned artists have transformed the automobile underpasses, and other artful surprises appear in planted flower beds along the way. Restaurants in the museums and at Pearl are as diverse as the city itself—-ranging from tasty Mexican street food at La Gloria to the elegant fare at Supper, located in Hotel Emma.

The third segment of the $384 million project is a seven-mile extension from the downtown River Walk to Mission Espada, San Antonio's southernmost mission. Appropriately named the Mission Reach, it offers spectacular walking trails, bicycle rentals, and a restored natural habitat where birds and butterflies abound. The new Confluence Park is an architectural wonder located at the start of the trails, where the San Antonio River and San Pedro Creek flow together. It has received numerous awards for its design, created by Lake-Flato Architects, including one from the prestigious American Institute of Architects in 2019. It has been recognized nationally for its unique outdoor classrooms, where schoolchildren learn about the river, its surrounding habitat, and the critical importance of conservation in the 21st century.

Frates Seeligson, director of the San Antonio River Foundation, states its value clearly, "Confluence Park belongs to everyone in San Antonio; it is a place where our city's diverse stories converge, where we revel in the river's natural beauty and honor our past, and where we re-imagine our future."

The Mission Reach trail ends at Mission Espada, just yards from the spectacular *Arbol de Vida: Memorias y Voces de la Tierra* (*Tree of Life: Memories and Voices of the Land*) created by Latina artist Margarita Cabrera. The 700 clay sculptures that adorn the steel tree were made by the people of San Antonio. Each reflects a story related to the rich traditions of the sculptors.

San Antonio's story is one of confluences; its past is constantly reflected in the present and will most assuredly influence the years ahead. What's old becomes new again. Former mayor Julián Castro describes San Antonio as "what the country will look like in the future." Inclusion, celebration, health, and recreation are all part of that future.

The San Antonio River is a waterway and walkway with art adorning its Museum Reach to the north, a vibrant social scene downtown, and restored habitat along the Mission Reach to the south, ending at Mission Espada and the spectacular Arból de Vida (Tree of Life) by artist Maria Cabrera.

Chapter Ten:
Into the Future

RARELY IN THE ANNALS OF URBAN HISTORY HAS A CITY INTENTIONALLY CHOSEN TO REDIRECT ITS PATH AND THEN WILLED ITSELF TO CHANGE SO PROFOUNDLY. AS A RESULT, MORE SAN ANTONIANS ARE CONFIDENT, PROSPERING, AND HAPPY IN THE PLACE THEY LOVE. LOOKING AHEAD, WE MUST STAY ON COURSE, IMPROVE OUR PERFORMANCE, ELEVATE OUR SIGHTS, AND MOST IMPORTANTLY, CONTINUE TO LISTEN TO EACH OTHER AND WORK TOGETHER.

—-HENRY G. CISNEROS

photos by Al Rendon

San Antonio's continued growth is inevitable. The city's "preparedness" is one driver of that growth—ample water and energy, a good freeway system, improved mobility, a commitment to education, an increasingly skilled workforce, a responsive and aggressive approach to economic development, and a strong focus on the quality of life. Our inclusiveness is also a key to our success. We have learned to live and work together in San Antonio, and we will continue to do so.

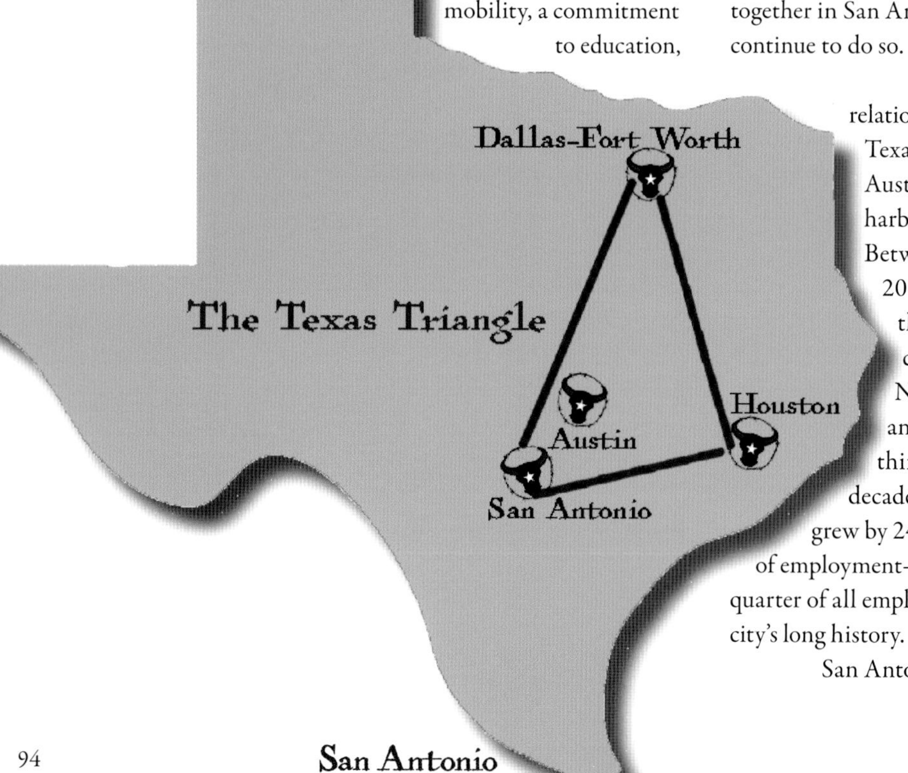

Our unique relationship with other Texas cities—especially Austin—is another harbinger of growth. Between 2007 and 2017, Austin was the fastest-growing city in the U.S.; Nashville was next, and San Antonio was third. During that decade, San Antonio grew by 24 percent in terms of employment—in other words, a quarter of all employment during the city's long history.

San Antonio and Austin are just 70 miles apart; when you have cities ranked No. 7 and No. 11 in the country so close to each other, an extraordinary dynamic occurs. If the economies of San Antonio and Austin were to be combined, the result would equal the economy of the nation of Egypt. The region is on track to be one mega-metro by 2030.

Beyond the fast-developing San Antonio-Austin corridor, other major Texas cities are part of a more extensive partnership of productivity and growth. It's been described as the "Texas Triangle"—with Dallas/Fort Worth to the north, Houston/Galveston to the east, and San Antonio/Austin to the west. While almost every state has several major cities, not many have developed the relationships that Texas has. "The Texas Triangle" creates one of the most dramatic opportunities for growth and progress in the world.

As San Antonio moves into the future, its growth will need to be managed, harnessed, and made to work for everyone. With a historically high poverty rate in San Antonio, ways must be found to bring marginalized people into the mainstream—that means creating more entry-level jobs and getting jobs that offer advancement and upward mobility. San Antonio must become a matchmaker between industries it wants to nurture and develop and the people trained to work in them.

Jenna Saucedo-Herrera is President and CEO of greater:SATX, which existed as the San Antonio Economic Development Foundation until its name changed in 2021. She joined EDF in 2016 and has worked hard to keep that "popcorn popper" producing what the city needs as it moves into the future. A graduate of St. Mary's University and vice president of public affairs and brand management at CPS Energy before assuming the leadership of EDF, Saucedo-Herrera has added bold new strategies to the almost 50-year-old organization. "We've been around for a while," she told the *San Antonio Express-News* in January 2020, "but we were primarily just recruiting companies from out of market. Fast

photo by Al Rendon

San Antonio tends to do well even in times that the country is down. We want to continue to build an economy that grows regardless of cycles. As Red McCombs told me when I was mayor, 'We need to get the popcorn popping so fast you can't keep the lid on it'.

— Henry G. Cisneros

HENRY B. GONZÁLEZ CONVENTION CENTER

photo by Al Rendon

▲ With rapid growth between San Antonio and Austin, futurists suggest that the corridor may someday create one combined metropolis.

▶ The Tundra truck has been manufactured in Toyota's large plant on the South Side since 2006 and NaviStar's move to San Antonio in 2022 created more manufacturing jobs for the city.

▼ Jenna Saucedo-Herrera is CEO of greater:SATX and is driving economic development for San Antonio and nearby regions.

forward to 2016, and we knew that if we were going to position ourselves to recruit and retain organizations, we needed to focus on workforce and availability. So we integrated SA Works into our operation in 2017; in 2018, we acquired the Free Trade Alliance."

In 2021, after working on more than 100 projects and seeing the creation of more than 20,000 jobs and revenues of $2 billion, EDF wanted a name that reflected that achievement and captured its future vision. Saucedo explained that "we felt we had evolved past our previous name as we integrated more businesses and expanded our service territory to represent broader San Antonio and neighboring regions. The greater:SATX name reflects our much bigger reach."

In addition to increased territory, incentives play a big role in San Antonio's economic development strategy. Saucedo-Herrera lists "authenticity," quality of place, competitive cost of living, and workforce as the most compelling ways to lure businesses to the city. Financial incentives—in the form of property tax exemptions, fee waivers, energy discounts—also were part of San Antonio's appeal to two new companies that will add to the city's growing manufacturing industry. Navistar, a leading manufacturer of commercial trucks and buses, is building a new $250 million plant on the South Side, bringing approximately 600 new jobs to the area. Aisin AW has begun construction on a new plant in Cibolo, along the San Antonio-Austin corridor. The company will manufacture both automatic and hybrid automobile transmissions used by car manufacturers worldwide. greater:SATX estimates that it will result in 900 new jobs by 2023. And Navistar is already adding suppliers, as is Tesla.

"We invest a lot more money as a community in workforce development and education than we do in financial incentives," Saucedo-Herrera said. She believes that strategy will be significantly more effective in the long run, noting that "schools are beginning to align with skill-set workforce training and with supply and demand. You can go to Alamo Community College and get a two-year certification to work at Toyota or Aisin and make $100,000 a year. And careers in technology—not your grandfather's technology!—produce good salaries. All of this is a pathway to breaking generational poverty in San Antonio."

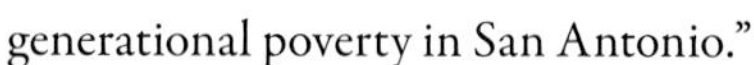

Nanzig wikimedia commons

Pointing out that 70 percent of jobs created around the U.S. are in local businesses, she stressed the importance of nurturing San Antonio's existing companies. "During the pandemic, San Antonio ranked fourth across the entire county in job retention," Saucedo-Herrera reported, "but looking at economic health indicators, we are trailing behind Austin and Houston. We need to concentrate on our people, on developing a talented workforce, for San Antonio to be relevant around the world."

As San Antonio moves forward, it recognizes that educational attainment is a challenge. But with programs like Pre-K 4-SA, the city is positioning its youngest citizens to believe

photo courtesy of greater:SATX

they are an essential part of that future and prepare for it. Later in the educational process, the city's institutions of higher learning are developing professional certifications in addition to the more traditional four-year degrees.

In 2019, *The Rivard Report* (now *The San Antonio Report*) partnered with local television station KSAT to establish *Bexar Facts* to ensure citizens' voices were heard as the city grew. Charged with gathering and sharing fact-based data on issues, attitudes, and trends shaping the greater San Antonio area, the new organization's first community-wide poll was conducted in 2020. Among the 65 topics on the survey, participants were asked to prioritize sales tax funding choices for various infrastructure proposals. Protection of the Edwards Aquifer received the highest support, followed by the continuation of Pre-K 4-SA and adopting the VIA Metropolitan District's new expansion plan. While other cities have had surveys of this kind in place for years, this was San Antonio's first-ever community data-gathering and polling service—a modern example of the city's commitment to inclusion and an innovative way for every citizen's voice to be heard.

A few decades ago, inclusion was a new idea. Born during HemisFair, it gathered momentum through more equitable representation in city government and citizens' groups like COPS. Over more than four decades, it has changed San Antonio into a city where people listen to each other and work together.

> In 1986, Mayor Henry Cisneros formed a Martin Luther King Commission in San Antonio, in anticipation of organizing the city's first MLK March the following January. He appointed me as the chair. As the event approached, Blanquita Cullum, who worked for VIA, suggested adding a bus to the parade, to honor Rosa Parks. I loved the idea; and we convinced Rosa Parks to come to San Antonio for that first celebration. Today the march is one of the biggest in the country.
>
> —Aaronetta Pierce

Aaronetta Pierce attended college in Nashville; in 1964, she moved with her husband to San Antonio, where he completed his medical residency at Fort Sam Houston. Following his residency, the young couple traveled through Europe, visiting landmarks and viewing art at many of the classical European galleries and museums.

When they returned to San Antonio, Dr. Joseph Pierce became an early investor in the basketball team that became the San Antonio Spurs in 1974. "San Antonio was the first city in the United States to purchase an ABA team (it later became an NBA team) with African-American investors involved," his wife recalled.

In the early 1980s, Aaronetta Pierce became involved in the city's nascent art scene as a docent at the new San Antonio Museum of Art. Leading a group of students through the 19th-century portrait gallery at the museum, Pierce fielded a poignant question from a little girl who asked her why there were no Black people in any of the paintings. She recalls, "I was surprised by her observation and began to think about that." When she joined the museum board a few years later, she was instrumental in bringing the first exhibit featuring African-American artists to San Antonio. "That little girl's voice, along with my own rich cultural background, compelled me to suggest to the board that it was significantly important to consider a future exhibit that included some African-American artists." After the meeting, another board member—one of the city's most generous philanthropists, Betty Coates Maddux—took Pierce and the museum director aside and told them if they could locate an exhibit, she would fund it. They enlisted with seven other national museums to bring "Hidden Heritage," an exhibition organized by the Bellevue Art Museum and the Art Museum Association of America, to San Antonio. Pierce had brought about significant change to the community. She is not unaware that racism persists and exists in San Antonio, despite its respect for diversity. As the city moves towards the future, she hopes that San Antonians will embrace that diversity even more courageously. She quotes her late friend. the poet Maya Angelou, saying, "without courage, you can't practice any of the other virtues."

The importance of game-changers like Pierce and philanthropists like

Aaronetta Pierce is a civic leader and longtime advocate of inclusiveness. She was instrumental in bringing the first African-American art exhibit to San Antonio in the 1980s, and she organized the first Martin Luther King March in 1986.

photo by Al Rendon

San Antonio sponsors the second-largest Martin Luther King March in the United States.

Maddux cannot be underestimated. Today, the philanthropic sector remains a crucial part of San Antonio's identity—its impacts are evident in past achievements in current endeavors. They will be essential in the years ahead.

Since 1964, the San Antonio Area Foundation has distributed millions of dollars in grants and scholarships to educate youth, protect the environment, protect animals, fund research and provide services for people who live in and around San Antonio. The community foundation handles more than 500 charitable funds established by individuals, families, and corporations.

In 2015, a gift of $605 million from the estate of a local cinema businessman and real estate entrepreneur John L. Santikos established the John L. Santikos Charitable Foundation Fund at SAAF. It was the largest in the foundation's history, increasing its total assets to almost a billion dollars.

Private family foundations are numerous in San Antonio, established by successful citizens—sometimes multiple generations—wanting to give back to their city. The five most significant are the East Foundation, Bessie Mae and Albert Kronkosky Foundation, Mays Family Foundation, Kleberg Foundation, and Greehey Family Foundation.

Others on the long list include the George Brackenridge Foundation, Brown Foundation, Charles Butt Foundation, Cameron Foundation, Coates Foundation, Goldsbury Foundation, Gordon Hartman Family

The historic Lone Star Brewery was repurposed into the San Antonio Museum of Art, where exhibits showcase the art and cultures around the world.

photo by Al Rendon

Foundation, Holt Foundation, McCombs Foundation, Najim Family Foundation, Susan Naylor Foundation, Minnie Stevens Piper Foundation, Muriel Siebert Foundation, Russell Hill Rogers Foundation, Smothers Foundation, Steves Family Foundation, William Knox Holt Foundation, Zachry Foundation, and many more.

Businesses including CPS Energy, Frost Bank, H-E-B, NuStar, USAA, and Valero have established foundations to manage their corporate contributions to the community. Many companies host events that raise millions of charitable dollars annually.

The Valero Texas Open and Valero Benefit for Children raised $16 million in 2020, despite the challenges of the Covid-19 pandemic. Since their inception, they have contributed more than $196 million, making Valero one of the top corporate donors in the country. The city's more than 1,500 nonprofit organizations host an array of luncheons, award ceremonies, special performances, Fiesta Week parades, and gala evenings to raise money for an equally large collection of worthy causes.

In 2005, local homebuilder Gordon Hartman and wife Maggie established a family foundation to pursue their dream of helping children and adults with special needs. Inspired by their daughter, Morgan, born with cognitive and physical challenges, they created Morgan's Wonderland, the world's first Ultra-Accessible™ family fun park in 2010, and Morgan's Inspiration Island, a splash park in 2017. Toyota assumed a sponsorship role in what has become an action-packed, fun-filled example of San Antonio's spirit of inclusiveness.

After the historic and devastating winter storm in 2021, the Hartmans and Morgan's Wonderland Inclusion Foundation launched a "Let's Help SA" fund to assist those most in need. It raised $3 million in record time and distributed it to SAMMinistries, Haven for Hope, and the San Antonio Food Bank.

San Antonio is also a city where innovation fuels new strategies for the future. Some of its most creative leaders continue to come up with ideas to harness that innovation. In 2016, a committee led by H-E-B's chairman and CEO, Charles Butt, other H-E-B executives, industry leaders, school superintendents, and workforce development experts proposed a new idea for education in San Antonio. The Centers for Applied Science and Technology (CAST) were envisioned as technology-focused magnet high schools that would prepare students for the new workforce Saucedo-Herrera described. Butt and H-E-B provided the startup funds to create a network of partners and to open the first CAST-Tech school in 2017, on the old campus of Fox Tech High School downtown. Partners included the San Antonio Independent School District (SAISD), a core group of local employers, San Antonio College, UTSA, and Tech Bloc, an alliance of technology leaders.

The first campus offered a curriculum to prepare students for careers in coding, cybersecurity, gaming, and entrepreneurship, providing two years of college credit and industrial certificates and a high school degree. In 2018 and 2019, two more CAST-Tech campuses were added. One is near the Toyota plant and focuses on engineering, manufacturing, power, and energy; the other is on the Brooks City Base campus, emphasizing medicine, public health, and biosciences.

Graham Weston, the billionaire co-founder of the San Antonio-based cloud computing company Rackspace, is another creative local entrepreneur who believes education and innovation are crucial to the city's future. In 1999, he met three Trinity University students searching for someone to invest in their business proposal to rent computer servers to businesses in conjunction with their leasing of new office space. Recognizing the mammoth potential of the burgeoning internet and the demands for web hosting that it would produce, he invested, and Rackspace was born. Weston became CEO of the new company. It employed 15 people. By 2006, when he became executive chairman, more than 1,200 "rackers" worked for what had become a global company. After the sale of Rackspace in 2016, he established Weston Urban, a real estate development

In 2021, UTSA's downtown campus broke ground on its new $90 million School of Data Science and National Security Collaboration Center.

photo by Al Rendon

company that is reinventing downtown San Antonio. Part of the effort includes building a thriving new tech district anchored by Geekdom and helping to fund a massive expansion of the University of Texas-San Antonio's downtown campus, where a new school of data science will feed more tech workers into the area.

"UTSA is building the best data science program in the world," he said when he announced his pledge to contribute $15 million to the university. "It will train the smartest students in the field and make them the hottest commodity in the

"My personal mission is to create constructive environments for startups and entrepreneurs to flourish in the San Antonio area. I'm drawn to big, transformative ideas. It's the reason I helped found Rackspace, Geekdom, and the 80/20 Foundation. I'm passionate about issues of entrepreneurship, specifically, how cities can build and maintain fertile environments for young entrepreneurs to learn the skills they need to create the next wave of innovation."

— Graham Weston

workforce. We hope that as UTSA creates them, the biggest employers in the world will come to downtown San Antonio to recruit their workforce.

"My personal mission is to create constructive environments for startups and entrepreneurs to flourish in the San Antonio area. I'm drawn to big, transformative ideas. It's the reason I helped found Rackspace, Geekdom, and the 80/20 Foundation. I'm passionate about issues of entrepreneurship, specifically, how cities can build and maintain fertile environments for young entrepreneurs to learn the skills they need to create the next wave of innovation."

During Weston's years at Rackspace, he discovered that it was often difficult to lure top recruits to San Antonio. When one of the founders of Webmail informed him that the company had chosen to relocate to Austin because San Antonio "did not have a scene for developers and was not a place where entrepreneurship thrives," he contacted former mayor Julián Castro to share his concern. A decade later, that has changed thanks to the hard work of many. In 2011, the establishment of Geekdom by Weston and co-founder Nick Longo was a significant catalyst for that change.

Today it is a bustling 45,000 square-foot co-worker space in the heart of downtown, recognized as one of the top three facilities of its kind in the United States and the largest in Texas. Touted as "The Place Where Startups Are Born," Longo has described it as being "like a gym membership for bright minds to explore ideas

photo by Al Rendon

in entrepreneurship, technology, leadership and creativity and to take them to the next level."

Lorenzo Gomez III served as its CEO for a few years before founding Geekdom Media, a collaborative spin-off that produces podcasts and e-books. He grew up in one of the city's tough South Side neighborhoods; his technology skills earned him an entry-level job at Rackspace despite his lack of advanced education. He worked closely with Weston and today helps others get the training and support they need to pursue careers in the tech industry. Gomez has participated in Weston's 80/20 Foundation, which awards startup grants to technology entrepreneurs. He is an essential member of Tech Bloc, officially described as "a tech ecosystem that is producing new jobs and generating millions of dollars in economic impact."

Co-founded by Lew Moorman and David Heard, the idea for Tech Bloc was born during an informal meeting at Rackspace, where Moorman, Heard, and Gomez were lamenting San Antonio's temporary loss of Uber, Lyft, and rideshare. They were concerned that the city was backsliding, especially when compared to places like Austin, Nashville, and Oklahoma City. They brainstormed about how they might energize the tech community. Three months later, they hosted a rally at Pearl that attracted more than 1,000 participants.

Moorman credits former mayor Julián Castro with "putting a stake in the ground for both downtown development and education when he was mayor," but recalls that the momentum stalled when Castro moved to Washington, DC, to become HUD Secretary in 2014. "I was worried that we had lost track of where we were going; that San Antonio was not ambitious enough about its future," he admitted. "When Ivy Taylor stepped in as mayor, all of us in the tech community urged her not to let San Antonio slip behind other cities that were charging ahead. Our city had lost Uber and Lyft, and those setting public policy seemed to think

Opposite page: Graham Weston is a major force behind San Antonio's march into the future. Weston Urban built the Frost Tower in 2019 and several other big downtown developments are underway.

David Heard (left) and Lew Moorman (right) are leaders in San Antonio's technology boom.

The cloud-computing company Rackspace Technology converted an old shopping mall into a quirky, colorful headquarters in 2008.

▲ photos courtesy of Rackspace Technology ▶

Lorenzo Gomez III is CEO of Geekdom Media, and a major force in the city's technology revolution.

that San Antonio's future success was a given. Success is never a given. That's when David and I formed Tech Bloc, and Mayor Taylor got behind what needed to be done, especially with her support for the CAST Tech school. Our economy still is not as dynamic as it needs to be, but I am optimistic we can change that if we play our cards right."

Two years after Moorman left his position as president of Rackspace in 2013, he and Ed Byrne co-founded Scaleworks. This technology equity fund buys remotely situated companies and brings them to San Antonio. Its offices in the historic Savoy building reflect the unique mix of past and future that constitute a vital part of the city's character.

The technology companies that Scaleworks has brought to San Antonio have been varied; some have been sold but still operate here. All have grown, which means the city's skilled workforce is growing, too. Moorman lists Mailgun and Chargify as two of his favorite Scaleworks success stories. Mailgun began as a small startup in Austin, with 12 employees, focusing on developing transactional email systems. Its clients are companies that sell (almost anything) online; its systems email a near-immediate receipt to the buyer. When Scaleworks bought Mailgun in 2016, the company moved to San Antonio, and in just five years, as online shopping exploded, its revenues did, too. Its workforce grew to nearly 200 people.

Dallas Mavericks owner Mark Cuban was an early investor in Chargify, a small company with 25 employees—all working remotely—developing systems for recurring billing. Scaleworks purchased the company and moved it to San Antonio. Its revenues have increased from $4 million to almost $20 million, employing close to 100 people in its downtown office.

Like Moorman, Weston is optimistic about San Antonio's future. He describes it as "the best city in Texas for opportunity," noting that young people are the fastest-growing component of its large population. But he recognizes the challenges—including historically lower than average wages and too many jobs that do not require advanced skills and are easily replaceable. "We all know that skills drive wages," he says, "and our city is in a great position to develop skilled workers through its educational pipeline. We've got the wind at our back to make this happen."

As San Antonio's young population participates in an array of innovative educational opportunities, it is positioning itself and the community for success. "Today, a young resident can go through the San Antonio Independent School system, attend UTSA, and go to work for Tesla," Weston says with a grin. "If we produce 50 graduates a year, with expertise in data or cybersecurity, every one of them will get a good job at some tech company somewhere in the United States. If UTSA, Texas A&M–San Antonio, and other universities here are graduating 5000 data scientists a year, those tech companies will move to San Antonio."

Something unexpected and unwelcomed moved to San Antonio in 2020 and lingered through 2022. Covid-19 arrived as a murderous visitor, and over the next 22 months, there were 324,000 cases of the virus in Bexar County during its dark presence here. In addition to the tragic cost in human lives and staggering impact on economies worldwide, it exerted a grim power over our psyches.

"I was all in favor of San Antonio's lockdown down during the spring of 2020," Weston says," and I believe Mayor Ron Nirenberg and Bexar County Judge Nelson Wolff did a great job keeping our citizens informed and compliant in terms of social distancing and wearing masks." Thanks to the city's outstanding medical facilities, San Antonio maintained more than 70 percent of capacity in terms of hospital beds and ventilators, unlike many other large cities in the country.

Local businesses, schools, and other organizations all worked together. They provided help ranging from paid leave for employees to online learning for hundreds of thousands of students, from donations to the Food Bank to manufacturing face masks, even relief from utility bills and mortgage payments. San Antonio's resilience was evident in full force.

In January 2021, pharmaceutical giants Moderna and Pfizer announced vaccines that required two doses, followed by Johnson & Johnson's development of a one-dose vaccine in late February. The Center for Disease Control approved them for emergency use, prioritizing people over 65 or with underlying medical conditions. In San Antonio, the University Health System led the way in designing a complex and massive distribution effort, and citizens flocked to large venues like Wonderland shopping mall and the Alamodome to receive their free vaccines. The city worked hard to ensure that vaccines were accessible to everyone. By the end of 2021, San Antonio exceeded most cities in Texas in vaccinations.

Weston thinks the pandemic will have a lasting impact on how San Antonio and the world lives. He suggests, "in the world of the future, we will have to live with a certain level of risk, and that we'll need to protect our most vulnerable populations, just as we have protected them from influenza and pneumonia for decades. We have incorporated some of the practices of remote working that dominated our lives during 2020 and 2021. That trend was already in motion; it seems to be morphing into some new balance between remote work and face-to-face business. Maybe people will work remotely for a few days a week and come into the office a few days a week—think of the impact on commuting time, on gasoline, and even on clothing. But most importantly, San Antonio's momentum is building again; and its citizens and businesses have emerged even more cognizant of the need to work together... and to innovate."

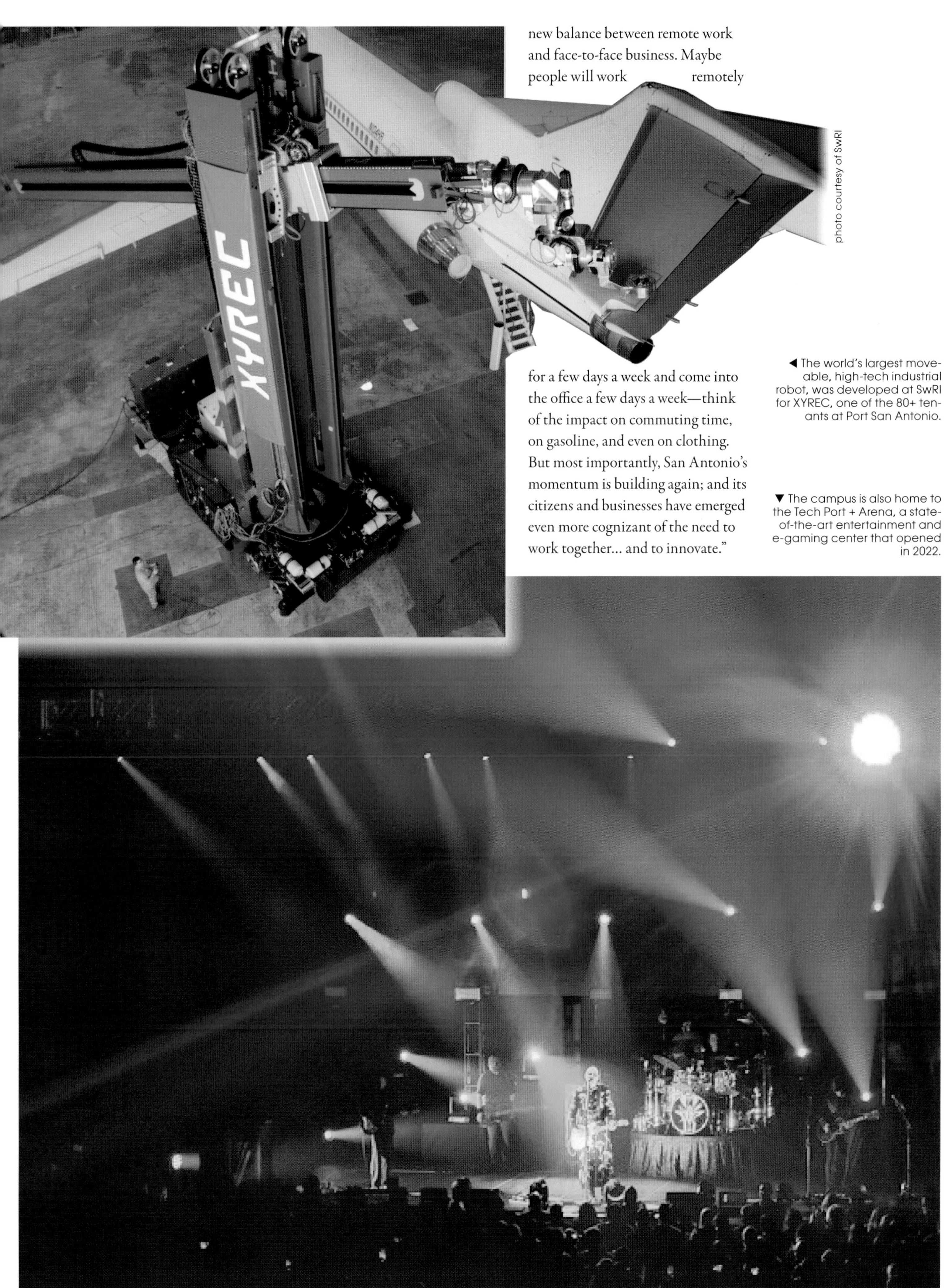

photo courtesy of SwRI

◀ The world's largest moveable, high-tech industrial robot, was developed at SwRI for XYREC, one of the 80+ tenants at Port San Antonio.

▼ The campus is also home to the Tech Port + Arena, a state-of-the-art entertainment and e-gaming center that opened in 2022.

photo courtesy of Port San Antonio

photos courtesy of LocalSprout

The experiment in urban farming known as LocalSprout is located on San Antonio's East Side. It sponsors wide-ranging agricultural projects and products like the edible landscaping (pictured at top) and (above) the sandwich prepared by Wild Barley, a wood-fired sourdough bagel food truck parked at Broadway News.

Innovation is underway. Described as one of the most technologically advanced entertainment and esports facilities in the world, the new 130,000 square-foot Tech Port Center + Arena opened in April 2022 and a sellout crowd rocked out to the music of Smashing Pumpkins. Its state-of-the-art LAN gaming center offers high tech fun; it also serves as an action-packed conduit for recruiting talent for aerospace, cybersecurity, robotics, and even military missions. There is a bigger story behind the neon-lit steel and glass facility that sponsored some of the largest post-Covid events in 2022—a story that takes place on its 1,900-acre "innovation campus" known as Port San Antonio.

Located seven miles southwest of downtown, Port San Antonio is one of South Texas's fastest-growing economic engines, housing more than 80 technology-oriented businesses and 14,000 employees, with a regional economic impact of $5.8 billion annually. Tenants include Boeing, the North American headquarters for XYREC, where the world's largest movable, laser-technology, industrial robot was developed, and the new headquarters for DeLorean Motor Company, which produced the famous gull-wing automobile featured in the 1985 film, *Back to the Future*, and is now focusing on new electric car designs.

Port San Antonio's CEO, Jim Perschbach, believes the future is all about systematically integrating new technologies into the way we live, and in the last two years, Port San Antonio has added 3,500 new jobs that are doing just that. In addition to the innovative technologies being developed by the wide array of tenants on the campus, Perschbach is also proud of Port San Antonio's youth programs and their creative approaches to STEM learning—including drone races, access to NASA experts through programs at its Science and Technology Museum, and cybersecurity gaming competitions at the new arena. More than 10,000 students participated in programs last year, representing a growing technology talent bank for San Antonio.

Along with high tech advances, high touch is essential to the city's growth, and it is especially evident downtown. The ultra-chic Thompson Hotel, positioned on the River Walk, with a spectacular rooftop bar that is perfect for socializing and stargazing, opened in 2021. The Artista, another new lifestyle and art-centric boutique hotel along the river, is under development, designed by the local architectural firm, CREO; it is scheduled to open in 2023. It is described as "an experiential encounter with the artistic, cultural, and maker communities," and promises to embrace the city's special persona.

Kris Feldmann, principal designer at CREO, was selected as one of San Antonio's "40 Under 40" leaders by the San Antonio Business Journal in 2020, and he echoes Weston's belief in the city's future. "There is a tremendous opportunity to raise your hand and get involved here," Feldmann said. "City officials are more accessible here than in many other cities, and that really increases the odds of impacting the trajectory of San Antonio."

Part of that trajectory includes the firm's vision for its Essex Modern City project, in development on an eight-acre site on the city's near East Side. Envisioned as a walkable community, with vertical and horizontal farms which will grow produce for restaurants on property, a bustling mercado where artisans will sell their wares and a center for local arts and entertainment. "It's a big dream," Feldmann acknowledges, "but remember, architects are optimists when it comes to the story of the future."

Another social experiment that already has become a part of that story is Soilworks. Co-founded by Moorman and Byrne as a Benefit or "B-Corporation" in June 2020, it focuses on regenerative agriculture, investing in and buying companies that support this new industry. Data show that consumers want healthier food without chemicals and synthetics. In 2020 General Mills committed 1 million acres of its farmland to regenerative agriculture. Moorman and Byrne believe that the changes ahead for the food industry will be as explosive as the cloud computing revolution was more than a decade ago.

Food and agriculture are also the focus of 30-year-old entrepreneur Mitch Hagney. A graduate of Trinity University and a former member of the school's award-winning debate team, he co-founded LocalSprout in 2014 with the backing of Rackspace co-founder, Pat Condon, another Trinity alumnus. With a mission to embed food production into the built environment of cities, the company started with a small hydroponic garden as an experiment in urban farming. Today its crops are sold to restaurants all over town. Its 16,000 square-foot food hub on the city's East Side—powered by a rooftop solar array—has expanded to house 20 companies. Hagney describes them as "food trucks, fermenters, chili queens, coffee roasters, pitmasters, butchers, juicers, bakers, caterers, creameries, ranchers, and farmers—a culinary community that exemplifies the new San Antonio."

Not far from LocalSprout, another example of the new San Antonio is unfolding. Texas Research and Technology Foundation has completed its Master Plan for the new Urban Innovation District, encompassing 80 acres on San Antonio's near East Side, with an additional 90 acres of influence area. At its core, existing developments—including VelocityTX, the G.J. Sutton Redevelopment, and Merchant's Ice Campus—already are bolstering the city's growing bioscience ecosystem. According to TRTF's CEO, Randy Harig, inclusivity of surrounding residents and businesses are key parts of the bold vision, which includes new public spaces, improved transportation corridors, and well-designed low density residential development, in addition to new opportunities for collaboration between the science and technology sectors.

photos courtesy of CREO Architects

Several similar innovation districts have been built around the U.S. in recent years—in St. Louis, Winston-Salem, and Indianapolis—and their cities are reporting increased entrepreneurship and inclusive growth. San Antonio's Innovation District estimates that more than 10,000 jobs will be created within 20 years, with an economic impact of $3.2 billion. It's a big dream as the city moves into the future.

Siblings Peter J. Holt and Corinna Holt Richter (above) are CEO and President of HOLT CAT and major shareholders of the San Antonio Spurs; both are building the city's future, both figuratively and literally.

◀ Kris Feldmann (bottom left) is principal designer at CREO Architects. He has targeted the artistic, cultural and maker communities as the audience for the new Artista Hotel, in development on the downtown River Walk.

As every quadrant of the city feels San Antonio's momentum—South Side, East Side, West Side, and North Side—construction and infrastructure projects are booming. At its headquarters in southeast San Antonio, HOLT CAT's fleet of heavy construction machinery is in constant use. Today the company sells, services, and rents equipment for diverse industries—earthmoving, mining, industrial, petroleum, and agriculture—that are building our modern world. HOLT CAT's recent solar energy acquisitions have further diversified the company that is now led by a new generation of a historic family.

In 1883, an innovative young man named Benjamin Holt moved west from New Hampshire by covered wagon, using his skills as a wheelwright to repair the axles and broken frames of the wagons on the rough journey to California. He and

photo by Scott Ball

Spurs and Sports Entertainment, assisted by the Spurs Coyote, broke ground on its new $500 million human performance center, "The Rock" in 2022.

his brother bought land for farming in California's Central Valley but soon discovered that the fields were predominantly peat soil and difficult to plow. Holt had always been mechanical. To meet the challenges of the soft ground, he invented, patented, and manufactured the first practical tractor. Its design was used a few years later to produce the first US Army tanks for World War I. In 1925, the Caterpillar trademark was established. Today the company's operations span the globe, with its largest franchise in San Antonio.

In June 2022, Caterpillar announced it move its Illinois world headquarters to the Dallas suburb of Irving, adding to the Texas Triangle.

Holt's great-great-granchildren, Peter J. Holt and Corinna Holt Richter, serve as CEO and President of HOLT CAT, having succeeded their father, Peter M. Holt, when he retired in 2017. Together they oversee more than 2,600 employees and annual revenues of nearly $900 million. They also took over their parents' controlling interest in the Spurs, and recently added Michael Dell, the founder of Dell Technologies, and Airbnb co-founder Joe Gebbia as investors.

Both siblings are champions of the arts, education, medical research, and many philanthropic causes; they are part of the increasing number of civic-minded millennials who are shaping San Antonio's future. Just as young men and women pushed for HemisFair in the 1960s, confident that it would transform a provincial city into an international hub, a new generation is pushing for another transformation.

"I am focusing on the present and the near future," former Texas Secretary of State Hope Andrade says, "and I'm leaving the longterm to the next generation. I am so proud to

see that San Antonio now has a growing group of young visionary leaders. People like Marina Gonzalez at the Hispanic Chamber of Commerce and Cristina Aldrete at the Northside Chamber are laser-focused on this city's forward momentum."

Bob Rivard is equally enthusiastic about the generational shift. He suggests that while HemisFair could transform San Antonio more than 50 years ago, today's agent of change is technology and digital inclusion. He describes the work of Brian Dillard, a third-generation native of San Antonio and the chief sustainability officer for the city and Emily Binet Royall, the Smart City coordinator. Together they are charged with closing the digital divide and positioning San Antonio to be equipped with what is needed for success in the 21st century and beyond.

It is projected that Bexar County's population will increase by almost 20 percent by 2030. The IH-35 corridor north toward Austin will be a single stretch of metropolis, which is why Holt and others are pushing for the creation of a high-speed rail. With a gleam in his eye, Rivard predicts "San Antonio will even see the day when a high-speed train connects it to Mexico." He lists three potent ingredients he believes create "the secret sauce" for San Antonio's success—a strong collaboration between government, academia, and the private sector—the realization that diversity is a strength—and lots of civic engagement and activism.

The city is producing that special sauce, charging ahead with gusto, and working hard to put the gloom of the Covid-19 pandemic behind it. A glance at the weekly *San Antonio Business Journal* confirms Red McCombs' observation that it's hard to keep up with all the new businesses and projects. Plans for an improved and expanded international airport is gaining momentum. Weston Urban's $107 million, 32-story luxury apartment building downtown is scheduled for completion in 2023. The Rock at La Cantera, the $510 million human performance center and mixed-use development on the city's northwest side will be the new home of the Spurs... and so much more. It will encompass a state-of-the art athletic training facility, a research institute, medical office space, and 500,000 square feet of restaurant, retail, and commercial space, with 22-acres of adjoining green space.

Spurs Sports & Entertainment CEO R.C. Buford was joined by Holt, Richter, basketball legends David Robinson and Sean Elliott, the Spurs Coyote mascot, city and county officials, and a crowd of supporters when shovels moved the first ground in 2022 . Buford told *The San Antonio Report* that the inspiration behind the center came from Andy Walshe, an expert in the field of elite human performance. The Rock's bold plan to "understand how people become extraordinary at a level we've never had before."

San Antonio shares that bold plan. It is a noble thing to build an extraordinary city; that is San Antonio's mission.

Texas Research and Technology Foundation has created the master plan for its Urban Innovation District, an 80-acre site (outlined in the rendering) that will help grow the booming bioscience ecosystem that is so much a part of San Antonio's future.

image courtesy of Texas Research and Technology Foundation/VelocityTX

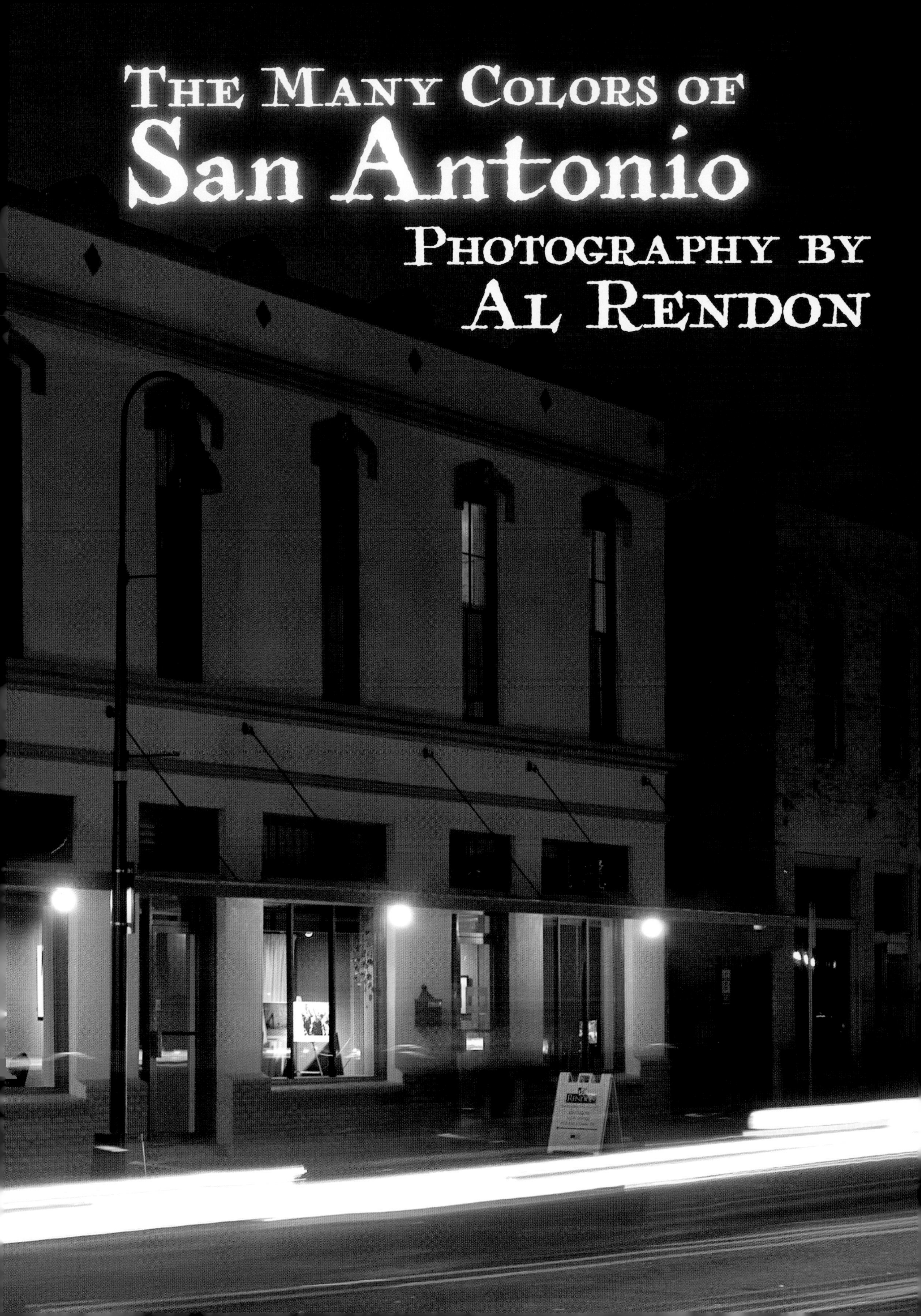
THE MANY COLORS OF
San Antonio
PHOTOGRAPHY BY
AL RENDON

San Antonio is a kaleidoscope of colors and cultures.

Gentle hues of sand-colored limestone, murky shades of blue-green river, vibrant bursts of neon pinks, purples, orange, turquoise and gold of fiestas and festivals create a unique city where 1.5 million people work, play, build and celebrate together.

Children swinging with abandon in a downtown playground, a reveler feeling the joy in Southtown, and the curator of the permanent art collection at the University of Texas San Antonio, Arturo Almeida (right)—all reflect the colorful energy that is San Antonio.

The *Asociación de Charros de San Antonio* was founded in 1947 to honor the culture of *charreria,* considered by some to be the national sport of Mexico. While western rodeos emphasize the speed of their cowboys, *charros* are primarily judged on their finesse on horseback and flourishes with the rope.

The *Jaripeo* is a dramatic display of Mexican bull-riding; in the past, the charro rode the bull until its collapse, but today the ride lasts until the animal tires and becomes docile. Is there such a thing as a docile bull?

Silk, satin, ruffles and sequins adorn the traditional *China Poblana* dress worn on Cinco de Mayo, especially in the city of Puebla, where Mexico declared victory over the French on May 5, 1862. It's popular in San Antonio as well, where the city's Mexican heritage is celebrated on numerous historic holidays throughout the year.

34

Bejeweled with color, Order of the Alamo duchesses ride in the Battle of Flowers Parade every year during Fiesta Week. It's become a tradition for crowds to shout, "Show us your shoes!" and the young women oblige, often displaying cowboy boots or more outlandish footwear.

Photo page 118
Enrique Rendon, father of the photographer featured in this photo journal, was a master woodcarver who learned the trade as a boy in Nuevo Laredo, Mexico. He passed away in 2015 at the age of 98.

Photo page 119
Sandra Cisneros is an award-winning author who was a writer-in-residence at Our Lady of the Lake University. Famous for her bright purple house in San Antonio, her books include *The House on Mango Street*, *Caramelo*, and *A House of My Own*, winner of the PEN Literary Award for creative nonfiction. A recipient of a prestigious MacArthur Foundation Genius Grant in 1995, Cisneros lived most of her life in San Antonio before moving to Mexico in 2013. This portrait of award-winning author Sandra Cisneros hangs in the National Portrait Gallery in Washington, DC.

Photo page 120
Artist Vincent Valdez was born in San Antonio. His artwork focuses on themes of social justice, memory, and under-examined historical narratives and has been exhibited at the Houston Museum of Fine Arts, the Ford Foundation, the Los Angeles County Museum of Art, and the National Portrait Gallery.

Photo page 121
Artist Oscar Alvarado has created mosaics all over San Antonio, including the Blue Panther for the Yanaguana Garden at Hemisfair; his wife S.T. Shimi is a performing artist, well-known for her association with the avant-garde Jump Start Theater.

Selena Quintanilla-Pérez was considered the "Queen of Tejano Music" until her untimely death in 1995. Her contributions to music, fashion, and style made her one of the most celebrated Mexican-American entertainers of the late 20th century, and she remains an icon today. This portrait hangs in the Houston Museum of Fine Arts.

Tomás Ybarra Frausto (standing) is an author, Chicano art scholar, and former professor at Stanford University. His research materials from 1965-2004 are housed at the Smithsonian Institute in Washington DC. He is pictured here with his partner, Dudley Brooks (seated).

Artist Cruz Ortiz created a portrait of Tomás Ybarra Frausto (previous page) that hangs in the Smithsonian's National Portrait Gallery; he is pictured with his wife, Olivia, the founder of Burnt Nopal.

Twin brothers Julián and Joaquin Castro grew up on San Antonio's West Side; both attended Stanford University and Harvard Law School and are important political leaders. Julián Castro (front) served as mayor of San Antonio from 2009 to 2014 and as U.S. secretary of Housing and Urban Development during the Obama administration. Joaquin Castro has served as a U.S. Congressman since 2013.

◀ Carl Rodriguez is a founding member of the San Antonio Charro Association (see page 112), which was the first in the United States to be accredited by the Mexican government. The organization sponsors the last events during Fiesta Week— "A Day in Old Mexico" and a Charreada that attract more than 3000 people each year

▶ Henry Brun is an award-winning jazz artist who founded the popular Latin Playerz.

San Antonio's restaurants offer the diverse cuisines expected in this international city. Dominico Ciccarelli runs family-owned La Foccacia in Southtown, one of the first restaurants established in what is now a bustling destination for foodies.

A touch of France can be found wherever Damien Watel opens his doors. Bistro Vatel in Olmos Park was a favorite for more than a decade; its popular successor is the sleek, tres chic, Bistro09 in Alamo Heights.

◀ Isaac Alvarez Cardenas, also known as "Papa Bear", is a member of the Tap Pilam Coahuiltecan Nation and the founder of the National Compadres Network.

▶ A long tradition in Mexico and Central America, honoring loved ones and friends who have passed away, *Dia de los Muertos* is celebrated in San Antonio with parties, parades, and beautifully decorated altars in late October-early November. Azul Barrientos, musician and ambassadress for Visit San Antonio, channels the Day of the Dead's immortal icon, *La Catrina*, with spectacular make-up and traditional dress; sugar skulls, candles, and ofrendas add to the magic of the day.

The Torch of Friendship stands tall in downtown San Antonio, a gift to the city from Los Empresarios, a local organization of Mexican businesses.

Located in Brackenridge Park, the San Antonio Zoo is a 50+ acre home to more than 3,500 animals and 750 species. Established in 1914 by George Brackenridge, its first animals—bison, deer, monkeys, and African lions—roamed free on the land Brackenridge purchased and deeded to the city. Today it is nationally recognized for its huge array of birds, mammals, reptiles, and fish, its creation of appropriate habitats, its breeding programs for endangered species, including the black rhino, and its new Will Smith Zoo School.

▲ Alligators at the Zoo provide drama to visitors of every age while carefree fish swim in the clear waters below.

▶ Another type of fish were created by artist Donald Lipski for the Museum Reach of the San Antonio River's bridge décor, with the San Antonio Museum of Art in the distance.

Historic theaters like the Majestic, Empire (pictured this page), and Guadalupe (opposite page) have been restored and modernized, but have kept their original façades.

GUADALUPE
S Brazos
900
800
REFUTE JULY 23
LA ESQUINITA
AUG 5 6
FALL EXHIBITION OPENING RECEPTION AUG 12
DANIELA
AND JENELLA ESPARZA

Artist David Zamora Casos creates some of the most spectacular altars and *ofrendas* for San Antonio's annual Dia de los Muertos celebration.

300
SAN ANTONIO
300
SAN ANTONIO

SAN ANTONIO
BREW'G. ASS'N.

MARIACHI
PLAZA

202
PRODUCE ROW
Los Pueblitos

Colorful barges serve as river taxis, meandering past hotels, restaurants, and the San Antonio Museum of Art; they turn around at the Pearl to return to the heart of downtown. Not far from the downtown center, El Mercado bustles with some of the city's best Mexican food and colorful gift stores. And sometimes, wherever one might be in San Antonio, the roar of the Thunderbirds is heard as planes streak through the sky; San Antoio is, after all, Military City USA.

PEARL
PRIDE

RICAN EATERY

Various Farmer's Markets around town pulse with energy—in addition to fresh produce, some feature local butchers, bakers, and candle makers, as well as booths with souvenirs, and music.

▶▲ *Raspas and Aguas Fresca*, both made with sweet juices, are part of San Antonio's food story, and Artist Jesse Treviño's mural.

▶ *La Popular Bakery* carries a message that says it all: *Familia y Cultura Es Vida* (Family and Culture is Life).

Mango

LA POPULAR BAKERY
y Cultura
...Es VIDA

Unlike many cities built mostly of steel and glass, San Antonio is "high touch." The natural world is an integral part of its downtown district, where fountains and parks complement historic landmarks. Biking and walking trails stretch along 13 miles of the San Antonio River, bordered by bluebonnets and shade trees, offering a respite from a fast-paced, high-tech world.

LEAL
14

Phil Hardberger served as San Antonio's mayor from 2005-2009; he was a major force behind the downtown River Walk's expansion into a 13-mile linear park stretching from the Pearl development to Mission Espada. He remains a stalwart proponent of conservation and education and Phil Hardberger Park, named in his honor, delivers both—with 330 acres of flora and fauna and walking trails—a natural oasis in an urban setting, with striking sculptures by Ann Wallace.

Every spring, fields on the outskirts of San Antonio are bejeweled with bluebonnets. They stretch along the roads and highways leading to the Texas hill country, eastward toward Houston, and south toward Mexico. In 1914, renowned artist Julian Onderdonk, whose paintings of bluebonnets are in galleries and private collections around the world, said "I like the bluebonnet because a field of this Texas flower seems just to have burst from the ground and it trembles subtly, making it very beautiful."

Mission San José, built in 1720 along the banks of the river, is one of five missions in San Antonio; all have been declared a UNESCO Heritage Site. Legend has it that a noted Spanish sculptor named Pedro Huizar carved the mission's beautiful Rose Window in honor of his sweetheart, Rosa, who died in a shipwreck on her journey to the new world.

Fiesta Week in San Antonio now stretches for ten full days of events—it is the city's biggest party. One of many "royals" who presides over the week is El Rey Feo, chosen by the Rey Feo Consejo Educational Foundation, established in 1982 to raise funds for scholarships. In 2022, restaurant-owner Augustine "Augie" Cortez (pictured) wore this special crown.

From just after Thanksgiving through the December and New Year's holidays, the San Antonio River is awash with twinkling lights, a glittering waterway that dazzles the eye.

Appointed by Pope Benedict XVI, Archbishop Gustavo Garcia-Siller has served as the Archbishop of the Archdiocese of San Antonio since 2010. He grew up in Mexico, the oldest of 15 children, and first came to the United States in 1980 to minister to migrant workers in California. He fosters a strong spirit of inclusiveness at San Fernando Cathedral—the same spirit that is the very essence of modern San Antonio. The annual Martin Luther King March (opposite page) advocates racial and social justice and is the second largest gathering of its kind in the country. Diwali, the ancient Hindu festival of lights (pages 180-181) celebrates the triumph of good over evil. San Antonio is a confluence of colors and cultures.

BELIEVE
Celebrating the Dream of
Martin Luther King Jr.
MY HEB
UNCONDITIONAL
LOVE
and
JUSTICE
DR. MARTIN LUTHER KING JR.

Confluences abound in San Antonio's architecture and art. The award-winning Confluence Park (opposite page) sits at the convergence of the San Antonio River and San Pedro Creek, and the many ecotypes of South Texas come together here in a living laboratory for visiting school children. There is a sacred feel to its pavilion, constructed of concrete "petals"—just as there is to ancient Buddhas exhibited at the San Antonio Museum of art (above), and carved angels on the walls of Mission San José (pictured at right).

Arte es Vida is an expression heard often in San Antonio—"art is life." The local art scene is diverse and growing almost as fast as the city itself. Renamed The Contemporary at Blue Star in 2022 (opposite page and below), this Southtown art mecca is housed in what was once a cold storage warehouse. Its exhibits feature local, national, and international artists, sharing global perspectives that encourage understanding, empathy, change and action.

(right) Alex Rubio, artist-in-residence and student mentor at the Contemporary at Blue Star, guides its MOSAIC program. He recently worked with his students on 10 murals throughout San Antonio and created *Aqua*, a public art piece in San Pedro Creek Culture Park.

The McNay Art Museum was the first contemporary art museum in Texas; today it describes itself as "San Antonio's place of belonging," and recent efforts to expand its diversity have created a growing community of supporters from all parts of the city. The original historic building was the home of the museum's founder, Marion Koogler McNay; in 2008, French

architect Jean-Paul Viguier designed a 45,000-square-foot expansion, creating new galleries, a sculpture garden, and classrooms for educational programs.

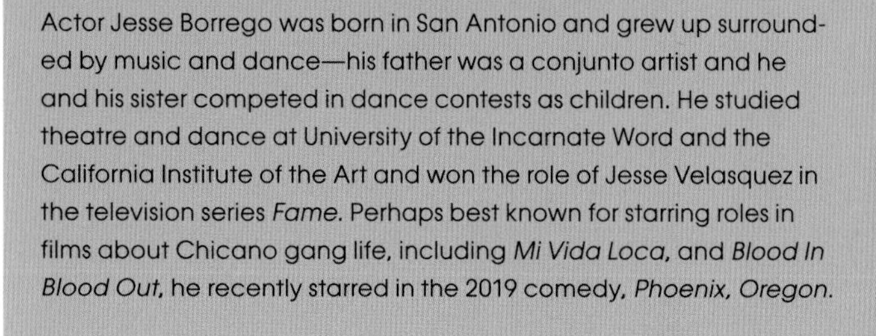

Actor Jesse Borrego was born in San Antonio and grew up surrounded by music and dance—his father was a conjunto artist and he and his sister competed in dance contests as children. He studied theatre and dance at University of the Incarnate Word and the California Institute of the Art and won the role of Jesse Velasquez in the television series *Fame*. Perhaps best known for starring roles in films about Chicano gang life, including *Mi Vida Loca*, and *Blood In Blood Out*, he recently starred in the 2019 comedy, *Phoenix, Oregon*.

Kathy Sosa is a visual artist, author, and educator; her recent works include murals for San Pedro Creek Culture Park, *Revolutionary Women of Texas and Mexico* (published in 2020), and Faces, a series of contemporary portraits of San Antonians. She received national recognition for her traveling exhibition, *Huipiles: A Celebration*, which debuted at the Smithsonian Latino Center in Washington, DC., and she and her husband, Lionel Sosa created the award-winning documentary, *Children of the Revolution*, for PBS television.

Artist Franco Mondini-Ruíz was born in San Antonio and embraces his Mexican-Italian roots, crediting them with his diverse approaches to art. Today he moves between homes in San Antonio and New York, working on installation art, performance art, painting, sculpture, and short stories, including his award-winning collection, *Pink: Tex-Mex Fairy Tales.*

Gini Garcia is a glass blower, designer, and founder of Garcia Art Glass. Her commissions include public institutions, private corporations, and individuals. Clients range from huge companies like AT&T and Warner Brothers to hundreds of devoted private collectors in San Antonio and far beyond. Garcia is the recipient of a Citation of Honor from the American Institute of Architects for her contributions to the built environment in the State of Texas, the highest award it bestows on a non-architect.

MINI TACOS · RASPAS · NACHOS · Corn CUPS · Tortas
COLD DRINKS
PALETAS
RECUERDO
95.1 FM

Juan Tejeda is the co-founder of the Tejano Conjunto Festival, a week-long celebration that takes place in May at the Guadalupe Cultural Center and Rosedale Park. Colorful food wagons (opposite page) offer frozen paletas and tacos; accordions, guitars, and trumpets blare their joyful music and dancers of all ages move to the beat of local and visiting performers like Los Texmaniacs and Conjunto Hall of Famers, Felipe Pérez, Linda Escobar, and Flaco Jiménez.

Acknowledgments

In 2019, when J. Robert Towery, publisher of CityInk/Urban Renaissance Books, invited us to write a "modern history" about the city we love, we accepted with alacrity, confident we could capture San Antonio's unique character and tell its story in time for the holidays the following year. The unwelcome arrival of the Covid-19 pandemic proved us wrong. Including that still-evolving chapter of San Antonio's history was unfortunately essential, so the project stretched into 2022. What resulted is a powerful story of resilience and resurgence. San Antonio's inclusiveness and respect for the diverse voices of our city are ingrained in its character, fueling its mission to remain one of the best places to live in America. The San Antonio Chamber of Commerce also fuels that mission, and we appreciated its important support as we researched and wrote *San Antonio: City on a Mission*.

We are grateful to so many friends and colleagues who shared memories and insights about San Antonio's past, current trajectory, and dreams for the future. The Hon. Hope Andrade, Andres Andujar, Mike Bacon, George Cisneros, Pete Cortez, Jr., Kris Feldmann, Father David Garcia, Paula Gold-Williams, Lorenzo Gomez, Connie Gonzalez, Adam Hamilton, Tuesdae Knight, Anne Krause, Dr. Cynthia Teniente-Matson, Red McCombs, Marise McDermott, Lew Moorman, Cynthia Muñoz, Mayor Ron Nirenberg, Richard Perez, Aaronetta Pierce, Robert Rivard, Dr. Ricardo Romo, Jenna Saucedo-Herrera, Rabbi Aryeh Scheinberg, Dr. Larry Schlesinger, Frates Seeligson, Jr., Suzy Thomas, Lionel Sosa, J.J. Velasquez, Graham Weston, and Judge Nelson Wolff provided important insights that are scattered throughout the book.

The San Antonio Report, *San Antonio Business Journal*, and *San Antonio Express-News* were much appreciated sources for both historic and current information, and so many individuals and organizations generously shared photographs for the editorial section of the book and are credited there.

Al Rendon's photographs in *The Many Colors of San Antonio* section illustrate the multi-faceted beauty of our city, its people, and its spirit. CityInk editor Ardith Bradshaw came up with the book's title and its clever play on words reminds us of both our past—our five historic missions are now a UNESCO World Heritage Site—and captures San Antonio's modern mission to create a vibrant future that is high touch as well as high tech.

David Hendricks, former business editor of the *San Antonio Express-News*, contributed his important fact-checking and copy-editing skills to our manuscript. Claudia Vasquez, Lucrecia Cross, and Sylvia Arce assisted us in setting up interviews and organizing our work.

Finally, a special thank you goes to our spouses, Mary Alice Cisneros and Geary Atherton. Both grew up in San Antonio, experienced HemisFair's impact on our city as teenagers, and today are dedicated community builders who made important contributions to this story.

Henry G. Cisneros
Catherine Nixon Cooke

skyline photo by Al Rendon

Special Supporters

The creators of *San Antonio—City on a Mission* express special thanks to the following entities whose patronage has been instrumental in its publication:

The McCombs Foundation

Muriel Siebert Foundation

Weston Ventures, Inc.

William Knox Holt Foundation

Profiles in Excellence

Biographies of the organizations whose generous support of this work made it possible. Listed alphabetically below, they appear in the book in the order in which the entities were founded in San Antonio.

CPS Energy

One Team

CPS Energy powers the fastest growing city in the nation (May 2022 U.S. Census Bureau report) with the skills and talent of 3,000 dedicated employees who live, work and play in the community they serve, and move as one team.

The utility's story began in 1860 as gas lights illuminated San Antonio when it barely numbered 8,000 residents. Electric lights brightened the U.S. Post Office on Alamo Plaza 22 years later.

For more than 160 years, CPS Energy has energized the Alamo City under one name or another. In a competitive play that outmaneuvered another entity, the City of San Antonio purchased the utility in October 1942 for $34 million. CPS Energy grew to become the nation's largest municipally owned energy utility providing both electric and natural gas service to 897,000 and 377,000 customers, respectively, in Greater San Antonio. The utility has since returned more than $8 billion in revenues to the City for its initial investment.

Diversity of Energy Sources

Learning from the natural gas crisis of the 1970s when gas was its only source of energy, CPS Energy steadily diversified its fleet of power plants. Diversity helps balance reliability, affordability, and sustainability. Today, the utility uses natural gas, nuclear, coal, wind, solar and landfill gas as energy sources.

In 2012, CPS Energy created partnerships with local, national and international companies to build a solar ecosystem in San Antonio. A decade later, hundreds of San Antonians are employed at OCI Solar Power, Mission Solar Energy and Sun Action Trackers.

Equally impressive, the addition of 500 megawatts (MW) of clean energy—enough to power 100,000 South Texas homes—catapulted CPS Energy into being the leader of solar power in Texas and fifth in the nation. Nearly 1,100 MW of wind power also makes the utility a leader in that renewable energy space as well - 2nd in Texas. Using these diverse forms of energy, CPS Energy's talented team of energy professionals perform the unique role of providing safe, reliable and cost-competitive power to Greater San Antonio.

Powering the Future

There's no settling for achievements of the past for the people who power the 7th largest city in the nation. In May 2022, CPS Energy announced it inked a deal for the largest single solar site in its history.

The contract for 300 MW is part of a larger strategy to add a total of 900 MW of solar, 50 MW of battery storage and 500 MW of firming capacity, or ready-around-the-clock power generation. That quest ties into an even larger plan to replace power from existing aging natural gas plants and to eventually replace a total of 3,000 MW of fossil fuels, including the final two coal units. In true fashion of a public power utility, CPS Energy is engaging community-rooted committees, customers, stakeholders and its Board of Trustees in the visionary plan for powering Greater San Antonio.

Innovative options for San Antonio's energy future are either already in the works or being explored. A pilot project is analyzing energy storage using geomechanical pumped storage technology. Geothermal solutions are being considered for future pilot projects as the community prepares for an influx of one million more residents in the next 20 to 30 years.

These solutions will help CPS Energy fulfill its commitment of full carbon neutrality by 2050 as we act as one team with the City of San Antonio on a community-wide Climate Action and Adaptation Plan.

STEPping it Up

Supplying the community's power needs is not only about the electric or gas lines feeding energy into homes. CPS Energy strongly believes in supporting its cus-

tomers with the absolute cheapest form of energy - the kind that's not used.

In 2009, the utility launched an unusual move that defies the logic of a traditional business model. It committed $849 million towards empowering residential and business customers to use less of its product. The goal was to save 771 MW, or the equivalent of a large power plant, by 2020. That would avoid building another $1 billion-plus facility while also lowering emissions.

The highly innovative Save for Tomorrow Energy Plan (STEP), which has won close to 20 awards, provided rebates and incentives for customers to pursue energy efficiency and conservation solutions. An array of offerings included home weatherization, smart thermostats, rooftop solar, and commercial lighting.

STEP surpassed the 771 MW goal a year early and under budget. By the Spring of 2022, close to 1,000 MW was saved as customers put into place measures that also lowered their bills.

Through STEP, the local solar industry solidified itself and nearly 30,000 solar systems went up on rooftops. That progress along with 552 MW in solar farms lifted San Antonio to Solar Superstar status as designated by the Environment Texas Research & Policy Center.

A Spirit of Giving and Excellence

As a community-owned utility, CPS Energy gives with the heart of one team. Employee and retiree giving to United Way hits the $1 million mark yearly. The CPS Energy team can be seen again helping non-profits and various organizations that make a difference for San Antonians as the community emerges from the COVID-19 pandemic and volunteerism ramps up.

CPS Energy leadership is proud of the work its 3,000 employees do in fulfilling the company's commitment to its customers. While there is certainly work to do to regain customer trust following the catastrophic failure of the Texas state electric grid in February 2021, recognitions and awards in the first half of 2022 speak volumes:

- COVID-19 Response and Recovery of the Year – Finalist, Disaster Recovery Institute International
- Safety Award of Excellence – Third Place, American Public Power Association
- Top 100 Fleets (#23), NAFA Fleet Management Association
- Our Driving Concern Texas Employer Traffic Safety Award, National Safety Council & Texas Department of Transportation
- Shining City – Solar Super Star – Top U.S. City for Solar Energy (#5), Environment Texas Research & Policy Center
- Shining City – Solar Super Star – San Antonio is #1 in Texas for Solar

- Capacity, Environment Texas Research & Policy Center
- System Operational Achievement Recognition (SOAR) – Bronze, American Public Gas Association

Two leading industry organizations, CS Week and Chartwell, also recognized CPS Energy for its Customer Outreach Resource Effort (CORE). Through CORE, CPS Energy proactively contacted close to 100,000 customers starting in June 2020 to check in on their wellbeing during the global pandemic. This includes both outbound calls to customers and most recently a block walking door to door campaign.

CORE connected customers with more than $55 million in bill assistance by Spring 2022 along with resources available through local governments and community agencies. This empathetic and personable outreach, in tandem with the utility's full-year suspension of service disconnections, provided timely and meaningful assistance to customers in need.

"Our employees are passionate about our customers and community," said Interim President & CEO Rudy D. Garza. "Along with a compassionate personal touch, we contribute an average of $1 million a day back to our city as a public power utility. Everything we do provides value back to our community, as we strive to provide the most reliable, affordable and resilient service to our community every day."

Dedicated to the Communities We Serve

If a financial institution can be judged by the awards it has garnered in serving its residential and commercial customers, Frost Bank can truly be viewed as a leader in its field. For 13 consecutive years, Frost has received the highest customer satisfaction awards in the J.D. Power U.S. Retail Banking Satisfaction Study.

The bank is also the recipient of the nation's highest number of Greenwich Excellence and Best Brand Awards for six consecutive years. Frost has been named to *Forbes* magazine's lists of the World's Best Banks, the Best Banks in America, and the Best Banks in Texas.

The banking sector, like most others in our economy, was adversely affected by the worldwide Covid-19 pandemic that rocked the world from 2020-2022. However, at a time when many other financial services companies were scaling back and shuttering branches, Frost expanded in fast-growing areas around Texas – nearly doubling the number of locations in the Houston area and planning to triple its number in the Dallas area.

"We're working to ensure that we're taking care not only of our customers, but our employees and our communities as well," stated Phil Green, the Chairman and CEO of Frost Bank. "Frost was a founding member of the corporate partners for racial equity here in San Antonio, and statewide we announced that we had raised our minimum pay to $20 per hour. Steps like these show our commitment to our communities and to being a force for good in people's everyday lives."

▼ The original Frost Bank in downtown San Antonio, about 1868

▼▼ Frost Tower, the headquarters building in downtown San Antonio

Building on a Proud Past

T.C. Frost had been living in other areas around Texas before settling in San Antonio where he and his brother opened a mercantile business there in the 1860s. One of the things they did to help sheep ranchers in the area was to store wool in their warehouse and extend credit to the ranchers. When prices rose, the ranchers could sell their wool and pay back the mercantile business. Around 1868, T.C. Frost decided to concentrate on banking and founded Frost Bank. The Frost family and San Antonio have been synonymous ever since.

▲ Phil Green, Frost Chairman and CEO

Frost Bank has grown over the years to become the largest bank with operations solely in Texas, and is one of the 50 largest banks in the United States. The bank's operations are in the metropolitan areas around San Antonio, Austin, Houston, Dallas, Fort Worth, Corpus Christi, the Rio Grande Valley, and Midland and Odessa. In recent years Frost has opened financial centers in Victoria, Bryan, and College Station.

Frost's banking customers include consumers, small businesses, and large corporations. Frost also has extensive operations in insurance and investments. The bank's customers are served by more than 4,700 Frost professionals.

In 2019, Frost's corporate headquarters opened in the new Frost Tower, a 22-story skyscraper in the heart of the community it calls home. Regional headquarters are also located in other parts of Texas, with more than 150 financial centers across the state.

Embracing the Technology of the Future

Since its inception, Frost has taken great pride in adopting the latest technological innovations that have transformed the financial services industry. The bank's unwavering focus on providing the highest level of service to its customers led to Frost surviving the Great Depression when more than 5,000 U.S. banks closed. In 1963, Frost entered the computer age with its IBM 1401 computer. The bank also survived the Texas banking collapse of the 1980s, along with the real estate market crash, becoming the largest Texas bank to do so without federal assistance or a takeover. Online banking service was introduced in 2000, along with operations at more than 1,200 ATMs (the state's largest network). Plus, Frost launched its app for iPhone® and Android™ devices and its introduction of industry-leading debit card alerts in 2014. The bank's 24/7 customer service phone line rounds out the impressive list of innovations for which Frost is known.

Personal services range from banking, checking, and savings and money market CDs to personal loans, gift cards, and private banking. Insurance and investment services are also available.

Business customers enjoy tailor-made attention to everything from loans and financing, retirement services, and capital markets to employee benefits, health care analytics, and retirement services.

A Good Corporate Citizen

Giving back to the communities it serves has been part of Frost's corporate culture since T.C. Frost first opened his business. During the pandemic, while many Frost employees were working remotely, Frost processed 32,000 emergency loans for more than $3 billion under the federal government's Paycheck Protection Program. Setting up systems to process, approve, and later forgive these loans, which became known by the initials PPP, was a massive effort for Frost. But those PPP loans helped keep countless Texas workers on the job and kept their employers afloat.

When Frost celebrated its 150th anniversary in 2018, it did so by committing to at least 150 charitable acts in the local communities. By the time the anniversary year had ended, Frost volunteers had far surpassed 150 charitable acts, committing to just under 11,000 hours in the process.

"Our success has been possible because of our dedicated employees and our commitment to providing unsurpassed financial services," Phil Green adds. "Our team at Frost is our true competitive advantage, and I'm proud of them for all their accomplishments."

▲ In 2018 Frost celebrated 150 years of service to Texans by performing 150 Acts of Kindness across the state. Pictured is the San Antonio team working with the San Antonio Food Bank for their Stuff-the-Truck drive.

▼ Garden Oaks Financial Center

Steves & Sons, Inc.

Welcoming Families Home Since 1866

FROM A GERMAN IMMIGRANT RIDING ACROSS CENTRAL TEXAS ON HORSEBACK—GOLD IN HIS SADDLE BAGS, SEARCHING FOR LUMBER—TO ONE OF THE TOP THREE DOOR MANUFACTURERS IN THE UNITED STATES TODAY, STEVES & SONS IS A TRUE AMERICAN SUCCESS STORY. EDWARD STEVES CAME TO THE U.S. AT AGE 20 AND SETTLED IN COMFORT, Texas where he met and married his wife, Johanna Kloepper, in 1857. Edward moved his family to New Braunfels to undertake a carpentry apprenticeship and then started his own lumber yard in 1866. In the same year, Johanna convinced Edward to move his business to San Antonio. She would later be called Mother of the Texas Lumber Industry.

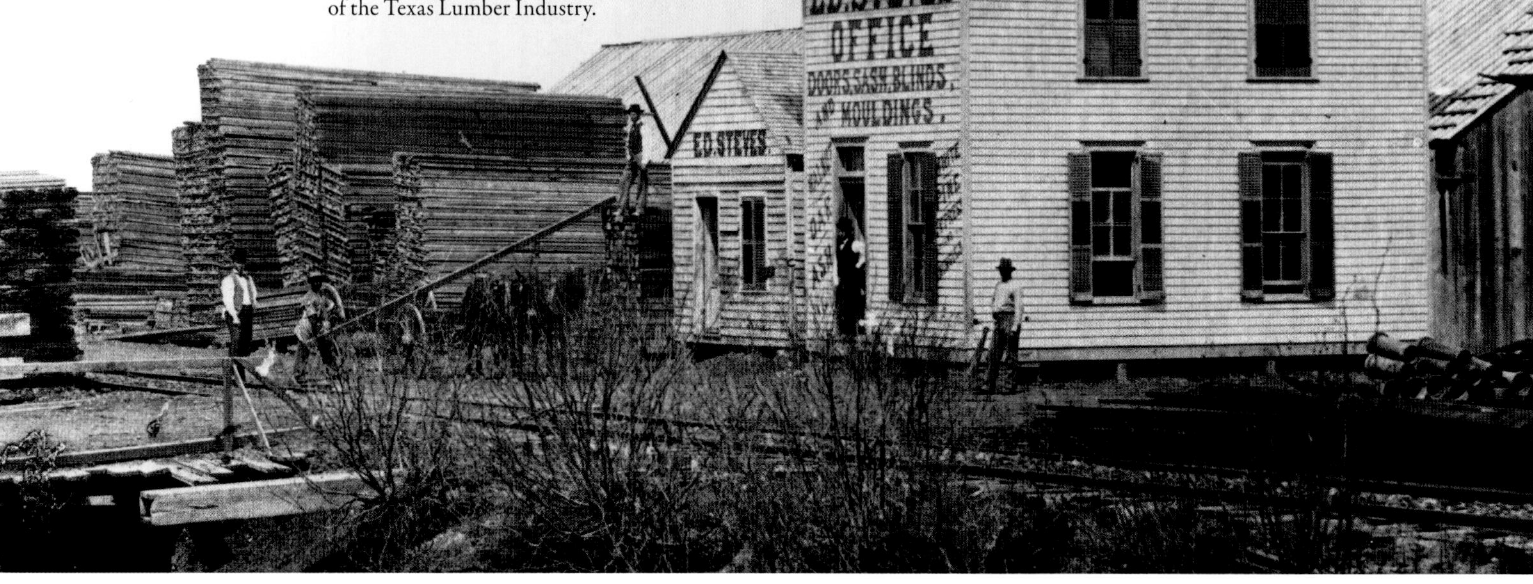

Edward opened branches along the railroad to San Antonio, including this office near Sunset Railroad Depot.

Ed Steves & Sons Lumber Yard blossomed in San Antonio with the help of Edward and Johanna's three sons: Edward, Jr., Albert, and Earnest. The Steves instilled in their family the value of creating a business to thrive for generations to come. Their visionary philosophy was to supply what is needed today, stay ahead, and be ready to supply what is needed tomorrow.

Planning to expand his business, Edward opened branches along the railroad to San Antonio. At San Antonio's train station's Grand Opening in 1877, Edward Steves stood with the mayor to usher in a new era of commerce and transportation. In the 1890s, Edward began building doors and window and stair components to support the changing market from adobe construction to a framed style construction. He reconstructed his business to fit the needs of the community and in 1912, became Steves Sash and Door Company. The company was the largest millwork operation in the southwest by 1916 and in 1941 became Steves & Sons, Inc.

Today, you still see the mark of Steves & Sons on the great city of San Antonio. At the Historic Pearl Building, you find wooden beams adorned with "Ed Steves Lumber"; at San Fernando Cathedral, you look to the ceiling and find "hundreds of Steves doors delicately hand-painted and placed as panels, fulfilling my grandfather's commitment [to restore the ceiling of the cathedral]," said Steves & Sons Vice President Gloria Steves Dilley.

The "Ed Steves & Sons Lumberyard" on East Commerce Street was part of the initial operations.

During World War I, the millwork operation shifted production to aircraft propellers for the newly established Army Air Corp.

Growing Steves & Sons

In San Antonio alone, Steves & Sons used the last 156 years to grow to five local locations with approximately 900 employees along with a recent 100,000 square foot expansion. In 1971, Steves opened its first manufacturing plant outside Texas in Lebanon, Tennessee and in 1983, the plant in Richmond, Virginia launched. Steves & Sons is growing every day, including two new facilities in Ashburn, Georgia and Brigham City, Utah. With over 1,000,000 total square feet of space and 1,500 team members, Steves plans to reach at least 2000 team members with the opening of the Georgia and Utah manufacturing operations.

With the phenomenal expansion of business, reviews from served communities have been overwhelmingly positive. When asked about Steves & Sons' investment in the Turner County community, Governor Brian P. Kemp said Georgia was "thrilled to welcome Steves & Sons" and that it would be the "largest economic investment [the county] has witnessed in decades."

The expansion outside Texas is thanks to the leadership of CEO Edward Steves and President and COO Sam Bell Steves II, the fifth generation of Steves family in management. The sixth generation is currently in leadership: Sam Bell Steves III "Tres", Vice President and General Manager of the San Antonio Door Plant, Gloria Steves Dilley, Vice President, Marshall T. Steves II, General Manager of Logistics, and Paul G. Allen, Vice President of Sales. When asked how they learned to lead such an established company, Tres Steves said: "My grandfather taught everybody how to run the business, but my grandmother taught us how to keep the business. Legacy and stewardship were really important to her."

While maintaining state-of-the-art, high-volume operations, Steves & Sons manufactures stylish interior and exterior doors. Jobber wholesalers sell to building supply companies and lumber yards for end use in residential and business construction. High-quality doors are sold across the continental U.S. to the public through The Home Depot, McCoy's, Detering, and more. The Home Depot designated Steves Doors as its Millwork Partner of the Year three times, and Environmental Partner of the Year once. Today, the company stocks 323 Home Depot stores.

A Family Helping Families

The Steves family have always accepted their success along with a duty to their community and country. During World War I, the operation shifted production to aircraft propellers for the Army Air Corp. In 1943, the company received a Maritime Commission M Award from the U.S. Government for excellent production of joinery for Liberty ships during World War II. After the war, all profits from Steves Sash & Door were returned to the government to help the country get restarted.

In more recent history, Steves stepped up after Hurricane Harvey devastated Houston in 2017. "[Steves & Sons is] a fantastic partner," noted Marc Becker, The Home Depot's Vice-President of Merchandising. "When [the hurricane] hit, they were ready to rebuild... They helped The Home Depot put a community back together." Steves also frequently gives doors to Habitat for Humanity and partners with Unicorn Centers in San Antonio to provide jobs and teach vocational skills to the physically and developmentally disabled. Additional charitable donations go to San Antonio organizations like Construction Careers Academy, Boys & Girls Club, Texas Biomedical Forum, the DoSeum, and many others.

After years of reducing manufacturing waste and developing practices which limit harm to the environment, Steves & Sons received the 2021 Pinnacle Award for excellence in sustainability from ReWorks-SA, the highest award the City of San Antonio gives a business. Steves & Sons always strives to honor their great legacy by helping communities flourish.

Interior door sizer utilized in Steves & Sons' high-volume operations.

Steves family leadership. From left Edward Steves, Sam Bell Steves II, Gloria Steves Dilley, Sam Bell "Tres" Steves III, Marshall Steves III, Paul Allen

Fourth, fifth, sixth and seventh generations of Steves & Sons ownership

The Voice of Business in the San Antonio Region

IN 1894, THE EFFECTS OF THE NATIONWIDE ECONOMIC DEPRESSION KNOWN AS THE "PANIC OF 1893" HAD REACHED SAN ANTONIO. AS A RESULT, THERE WERE MANY PEOPLE IN THE LOCAL COMMUNITY WHO WERE LOOKING FOR AN ORGANIZATION TO FOSTER COMMERCIAL DEVELOPMENT. AN OPINION PRINTED IN *THE SAN ANTONIO DAILY EXPRESS* AT THAT TIME would unwittingly become the cornerstone on which was founded the San Antonio Chamber of Commerce. "The ways and means of forming the organization, be it old or new, matters not, for it is not the organization that will accomplish the desired results, but it is the effort of the members working together under the banner thus unfurled for the world to see."

The San Antonio Semi-Weekly Express echoed those comments when it wrote, "More can be accomplished by an organized body of energetic workers in one week than will result from a scattering of efforts in a month."

The visionaries of that day accepted the challenge of creating an organization that would focus on promoting commercial development in the San Antonio Region. The Business Men's Club of San Antonio was established in 1894 and has morphed over the years into the San Antonio Chamber of Commerce. The dream of the founders continues today as the largest business advocacy organization in the San Antonio Region.

The members of the Chamber have made and continue to make an enormous impact on local business, military development, transportation, workforce development, water resources, sports industry, international trade, and much more. And while the volunteer business

photo courtesy of the US Air Force

▲ LSA 46 class during an immersive experience into the journey of military life, its challenges, and its contribution to the fabric of our nation and our communities.

▶ In 1911, the Chamber started the Fiesta Association, which is now known as the Fiesta San Antonio Commission, that manages, organizes, and runs the annual hugely popular cultural festival "Fiesta" each April. The Chamber's team enjoys visits from Fiesta royalty each year.

leaders who founded the organization have long passed, their legacy and vision of business as a force for good continue to drive the work of the Chamber.

A Vital Role in Economic and Cultural Development

The San Antonio Chamber of Commerce is the largest Chamber of Commerce in the region, representing 500,000 employees in the San Antonio area. In addition, the Chamber is part of the Metro 8 Chambers, covering the business sectors of Texas' eight largest metropolitan areas: Arlington, Austin, Corpus Christi, Dallas, El Paso, Fort Worth, Houston, and San Antonio. Collectively, the Metro 8 chambers serve more than 20,000 Texas companies and employ a large portion of the Texas workforce.

With more than 1,650 members, the San Antonio Chamber of Commerce is the largest and most influential pro-business organization in the region. As the primary voice of business in the city, the Chamber mobilizes members to promote and drive important initiatives that benefit San Antonio.

The Chamber's success has always centered on its ability to bring together members and leaders from all areas of San Antonio to address the region's issues and unique challenges. That network is large and the relationships forged with influencers are deep. The Chamber also serves as a resource to connect its members to business growth through numerous events, sponsorships, and networking opportunities.

Examples of the Chamber's success are many. The organization has incubated and spun off some of San Antonio's must successful and impactful organizations, including greater:SATX, the Fiesta San Antonio Commission, the San Antonio Medical Foundation, San Antonio Mobility Coalition (SAMCo), and San Antonio Sports, to name a few.

Throughout its history, the Chamber has had an enormous impact on military development in the Alamo City. Before San Antonio was coined Military City USA, the Chamber was building connections between the business community and local military organizations and supporting military missions accomplished here.

Back in the 1920's, the Chamber led efforts to locate Kelly Air Force Base and Brooks Air Force Base in San Antonio and developed and carried out a plan to purchase land for Randolph Air Force Base, now Joint Base Randolph. Then, in 1988, the Chamber helped secure funding for the new 450-bed Brooke Army Medical Center hospital, which has now grown into the San Antonio Military Medical Center located at Join Base Fort Sam Houston.

The Chamber also worked closely with Senator Kay Bailey Hutchison during the 2005 round of base closures to ensure more than 3,000 new jobs and over $2 billion in new construction at Ft. Sam Houston alone.

In addition, the Chamber has advocated for policy and regulatory change at City Hall, in Austin, and in Washington D.C., and it has tackled tough issues to keep San Antonio moving forward.

Impacting People as Well as Business

"For 127 years, the San Antonio Chamber of Commerce has been serving our members and the business community in San Antonio with a goal of enhancing the quality of life in the Alamo City," stated Richard Perez, the Chamber's President and CEO. "With an attitude of collaboration, service, and excellence, the Chamber advocates for the San Antonio business community and supports important policy, infrastructure, and civic initiatives. We are the voice of the business community and have a unique ability to focus the energy of business leaders and community members on key issues that make a difference."

That difference is being felt through numerous people-focused initiatives, among them are:

- Leadership San Antonio that helps to identify community leaders in the area.
- Serving as a Pacesetter organization for the annual United Way Campaign.
- SA to DC which annually leads hundreds of business, elected, and community leaders on a fly-in to Washington DC to meet with members of Congress and government officials.
- The Chamber is proud to lead San Antonio's participation in the Best Place for Working Parents® initiative.

▲ The San Antonio Chamber of Commerce building, located at 602 East Commerce Street in the heart of downtown San Antonio, was built in 1967 to house the administrative function of the 1968 World's Fair.

◀▲ Every year, the Chamber leads SA to DC, where a group of business, elected, and community travel to Washington DC to advocate for the needs of the San Antonio region. From 2022 SA to DC (left to right): Chamber President & CEO Richard Perez; Chamber Chair of the Board Phil Green, Chairman and Chief Executive Officer of Cullen/Frost Bankers, Inc. and Frost Bank; Robert L. Santos, Director, U.S. Census Bureau; Mayor Ron Nirenberg; former Mayor and Chamber Chair Henry Cisneros.

Our Lady of the Lake University

Preparing Graduates to Transform Their Communities, Families, and Professions

Our Lady of the Lake University (OLLU) is a coeducational, comprehensive Catholic university serving more than 3,100 undergraduate and graduate students. OLLU offers academic programs in online formats and in three different locations across Texas (San Antonio, Houston, and the Rio Grande Valley)

with its main campus located in San Antonio.

The university offers programs in traditional liberal arts and sciences, education, counseling psychology, communication disorders, social work, leadership studies, cybersecurity, and business.

The Birth of a Dream

OLLU was founded in 1895 by the Sisters of the Congregation of Divine Providence, a religious order begun in 18th century Lorraine, France. Mayor Henry Elmendorf had offered the sisters a gift of land on the West Side of San Antonio. Mother Florence Walter, the superior general of the Sisters of Divine Providence at that time, looked out over the land and said, "This is the place. Someday, upon this land will stand a beautiful Gothic chapel with twin spires pointing up to the blue Texas sky."

Her vision moved toward reality on August 14, 1895, when ground was broken for the construction of the Main Building and marked the beginning of what is now Our Lady of the Lake University.

The Dream Becomes Reality

Mother Walter's prophesy was fulfilled. Today, OLLU's main campus includes 32 buildings spread across 72 acres approximately three miles from downtown San Antonio. Facilities include classroom and administrative buildings, five residence halls, the Sister Elizabeth Anne Sueltenfuss Library, wellness and recreation facilities, and athletic fields and facilities. And the beautiful Gothic chapel she envisioned is identified by the soaring steeple of the Sacred Heart Chapel.

OLLU is accredited by the Southern Association of Colleges and Schools Commission on Colleges (SACSCOC). A robust offering of more than 90 undergraduate majors and minors, master's, and doctoral degrees are offered to traditional undergraduate students; non-traditional (adult) undergraduate and transfer students; and graduate students at the master's and doctoral level. The University is recognized as having the most affordable tuition among private, Catholic universities in Texas.

OLLU stands on the social justice heritage handed down by the founders. The Sisters have a history of serving the underserved and keeping inclusion and equity at the forefront of all they do. OLLU takes pride in having been the springboard for many important initiatives, among them:

- In 1968, OLLU hosted the U.S. Commission on Civil Rights Hearings on Mexican Americans in the Southwest.
- The Hispanic Association of Colleges and Universities was formed on OLLU campus in 1986.
- The first school of social work in Texas, the Worden School, was created on the OLLU campus.
- "OLLU specializes in equipping today's college-going population to lead and serve in their career fields and communities," stated Diane E. Melby, EdD, President. "We provide an education that gives students the wings to rise above. Leadership and community service are integrated into all OLLU programs at every level. OLLU elevates all of San Antonio and South Texas through higher education with a higher purpose."

San Antonio Board of Realtors®

The Voice of Real Estate in South Texas

For more than a century, the San Antonio Board of REALTORS® (SABOR) has been the primary resource when it comes to finding a REALTOR® and buying and selling a home in the San Antonio area. As the largest professional trade organization in San Antonio and the third largest REALTOR® association in Texas, SABOR today represents over 15,000 REALTORS® and affiliate members. SABOR is one of over 1,600 local boards and 54 state and territory organizations of REALTORS® nationwide that make up the National Association of REALTORS® (NAR).

For most people, the process of buying and selling a home occurs only a few times during the course of a lifetime. For that reason, it is critical to select a real estate professional with the skills and expertise to assist in navigating those often-confusing waters. The REALTOR® designation denotes business competence, high standards, that they are a member of the National Association of REALTORS® and abide by its strict Code of Ethics.

REALTORS® close numerous transactions each year and have unmatched expertise and insight. They offer invaluable assistance in numerous ways, including helping to determine a prospective homeowner's buying power. They also have access to many resources to assist in the buying and selling process. Among SABOR's signature features is the Multiple Listing Service (MLS) to members who select its access as part of their membership. The MLS creates connections between REALTOR® and clients looking to either buy or sell their properties and serves as the main platform on which those who make transactions happen come together. Since its formation in 1952, MLS has been protecting market information and enforcing rules that govern market participation. This allows REALTORS® to do their jobs with a confidence that would not otherwise exist.

A Tradition of Service

SABOR as it exists today is a far cry from the 22 members of San Antonio's real estate community who met for lunch at the St. Anthony Hotel in 1910. They felt that the city would benefit from a collective membership of REALTORS®. That meeting led to the formation of what was known as the San Antonio Real Estate Exchange. Six years later, SABOR officially adopted the term REALTOR® as the designation for active broker members. That same year, SABOR was granted membership in the National Association of Real Estate Boards.

SABOR's jurisdiction today covers Atascosa, Bexar, Frio, Karnes, Kendall, La Salle, McMullen, Medina, Uvalde, and Wilson counties.

SABOR members take great pride in their involvement in the communities they serve. They have been successful in local advocacy efforts, having received the Mark Lehman Governmental Affairs Achievement Award. At the national level, SABOR was awarded the 2020 Silver Global Achievement Program Award by the National Association of REALTORS®.

photo by AL Rendon

Transforming the South San Antonio Region

The San Antonio community known today as Brooks has traveled a long road since 1917 when the area was established as Brooks Field, an Army Air Corps installation that would provide advanced flight training for young cadets. In those days, pilots in their biplane aircraft would chase jackrabbits through

a field of grass until they knew they were going fast enough to pull the stick back to go airborne.

From that inauspicious birth, Brooks morphed into Brooks Air Force Base and, in 2001 by an act of the U.S. Congress, the State of Texas, and the City of San Antonio, into its present mission of serving as a catalyst of economic development that continues to enhance opportunities for those who live, work, learn, play, and stay there. The name was officially changed in 2017 to Brooks to align with the identity as an up-and-coming community with a vision as big as Texas. Today, Brooks serves as a redevelopment hub supporting the southeast corridor of San Antonio. It is governed by a board to ensure that it acts in the interest of the entire city in attracting investors and businesses which transform not only the southeast region, but the greater San Antonio economy.

Mission Accomplished!

In its history of redeveloping the former Air Force base, Brooks has attracted more than 50 businesses accounting for 3,200 jobs by 2022. That translates into over $818 million in development to date with $310 million currently underway. The 1,308-acre campus is expected to be home to approximately 5,000 jobs by 2025.

Brooks continues to honor its Air Force history while ushering in a new age of regional growth and prosperity. Its vision is to be a world-class region, honoring the area's rich and vibrant history and encompassing transformative investments which contribute to San Antonio's overall success. Brooks actively seeks out marquee employers from around the world that amplify its mission, vision, and values.

"Brooks has been woven into the southeast San Antonio community since its days as an active Air Force base," stated Leo Gomez, Brooks' President and CEO. "It's our duty to honor the history of Brooks Air Force Base, the rich culture of the South Side, and to fulfill a promise to the region through our vision. One where hard-working families can build better lives for their children and support some of the most innovative companies in the world."

In fulfilling its mission, Brooks has received numerous awards, including San Antonio Business Journal's "Business of the Year" in 2018. Its nonprofit philanthropic arm, Brooks Gives Back (BGB), serves as the vehicle by which all members of the Brooks community may invest in non-profit initiatives impacting people in the neighborhoods surrounding Brooks.

"We are honored to be here to support and facilitate this regional prosperity, and proud to share the legacy of Brooks with the world," Gomez added.

University Health

A Tradition of Leadership Driven by Values

As the only locally owned and operated health system in San Antonio and Bexar County, University Health takes to heart its responsibility to serve the health needs of the community not only today, but well into the future. Upwards of 9,000 University Health professionals focus every day on the system's mission of improving the good health of the community through high-quality compassionate patient care, innovation, education, and discovery.

▼ University Hospital today is the most preferred hospital in San Antonio, according to the NRC Health Market Insights consumer study 2021-2022.

University Health operates as a separate political entity – the Bexar County Hospital District. It is a nationally recognized academic health system, including a comprehensive care hospital and network of more than two dozen health centers across the community, offering everything from preventive health and primary care to urgent care and outpatient surgery.

This broad network is connected through a single electronic health records platform, enabling all members of a patient's health care team to have a complete picture of their patients' health, medications, and needs. Through MyChart, it also allows patients to see test results, schedule appointments, refill medications, and even message their doctors from a secure app on their smart phones.

University Health is the primary teaching partner for UT Health San Antonio, ensuring patients can access advanced care for even the most complex issues, helping to advance the practice of medicine through research and new discoveries, and training the next generation of health care professionals for our community.

An Auspicious Beginning

University Health's roots date back to 1917, the year the United States entered the war that had been raging in Europe for three years. The City of San Antonio and Bexar County opened Robert B. Green Memorial Hospital, named after a county judge and state senator. The new facility, lauded as "one of the best and most modern institutions of its kind in the southwest," would quickly encounter numerous challenges.

What was called the "Spanish flu" pandemic was sweeping the world and claiming hundreds of thousands of lives. The hospital opened just in time to care for victims of the pandemic. At the same time, World War I had resulted in a shortage of doctors and hospital staff members, as many were called to the battlefields, along with higher costs of supplies.

The hospital weathered that storm and, over the next several decades, the downtown hospital filled an enormous need caring for the sick and training doctors and nurses. Inconsistent funding, however, threatened its mission and resulted in intermittent closures of many of its programs.

Supporting a commitment to care for everyone, regardless of their ability to pay, Bexar County voters overwhelmingly approved the creation of the Bexar County Hospital District and a tax on property to fund it in 1955, making it one of the first hospital districts in Texas and stabilizing the Green's finances.

Today this downtown campus is no longer an inpatient hospital but serves as

▼ The historic Robert B. Green Memorial Hospital opened in 1917.

▼ The University Health Texas Diabetes Institute, home to many of the world's leading diabetes experts, offers healing and hope with specialists available for every diabetes-related complication, a community outreach team, a comprehensive diabetes education program, and researchers relentlessly working toward finding a cure.

University Health's hub for all ambulatory care, including primary care, specialists, urgent care, lab services, radiology, and outpatient surgery.

A New Generation of Care

In the early years of the hospital district, it was clear that a new teaching hospital was necessary to attract a medical school to San Antonio. In December 1965, ground was broken for the $15 million Bexar County Hospital in the South Texas Medical Center. Construction of the University of Texas Medical School at San Antonio — now called UT Health San Antonio — began soon after. The medical school and Bexar County Hospital were both completed in 1968, affirming University Health's role in providing the most advanced care and teaching future generations of health care professionals.

In 1994, the Bexar County Hospital District began doing business as University Health System and the Bexar County Hospital became University Hospital to create a stronger public association with its academic mission. At the same time, the Hospital District began to expand into the community, with new neighborhood health centers providing family doctors and outpatient care close to where people lived.

Today, University Hospital is South Texas' only Level I Trauma Center for both adults and pediatric patients. Certified by the American College of Surgeons Committee on Trauma, surgeons and specialists experienced to care for all types of critical injuries are in the hospital around the clock, every day, to provide immediate and often lifesaving care.

University Hospital is also home to the University Health Transplant Institute, one of the nation's leading centers for organ transplantation, including one of the largest living-donor liver transplant programs in the country. Patients in need of liver, kidney, and lung transplantation come to University from all over the country because of this team's expertise and excellent patient outcomes.

Community First Health Plans was established in 1995 by University Health specifically to provide health care coverage to the citizens of Bexar and its seven surrounding counties. As the only locally owned and managed non-profit health plan in the area, Community First's commitment to its members is to provide great health care benefits backed by outstanding service.

In 1999, the health system created Community Medicine Associates, a non-profit primary care physician group. The practice group was renamed University Medicine Associates (UMA) in 2016 and is today the region's largest nonprofit provider practice in San Antonio. UMA providers are employed by University Health and provide primary and specialized care at University Health locations.

Also in 1999, on the site of the former Lutheran General Hospital in the heart of San Antonio's West Side, University Health opened the Texas Diabetes Institute — a one-stop center for diabetes care, prevention, education, and discovery, where some of the leading diabetes researchers in the nation work to find new and better ways to treat the disease and make those discoveries available to patients.

Responding to the COVID-19 Pandemic

University Health was on the forefront of the community's response to the COVID-19 pandemic. In March of 2020, the team rapidly stood up testing for community health care workers and first responders to help reduce the spread of the virus among those on the front lines. When the specific liquid compound needed to transport test samples to the lab were nearly impossible to procure because of the overwhelming worldwide need, the pharmacy team sourced the raw materials and created its own viral

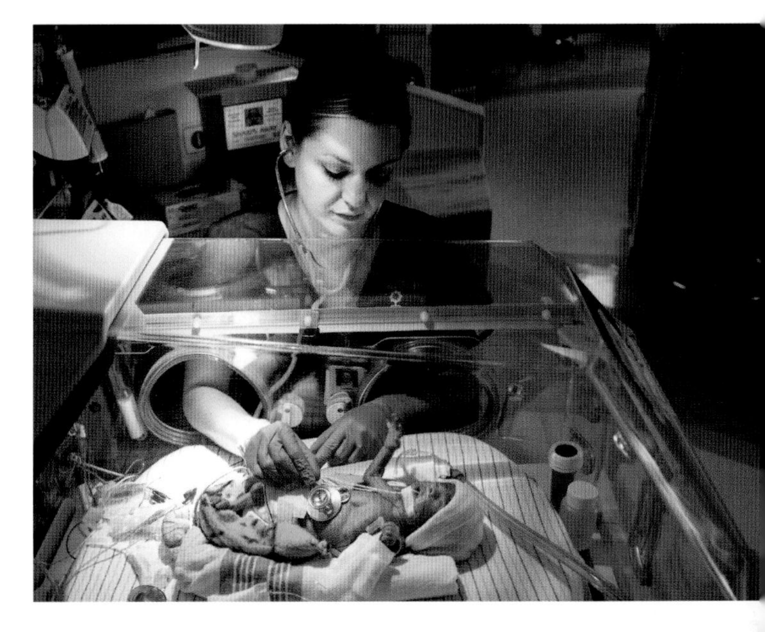

▲ University Hospital is home to both a Level IV Maternity Center and Neonatal Intensive Care Unit, the most advanced levels. These designations, by the State of Texas, mean families can rely on these teams to have all the experts and technologies in the hospital around-the-clock, to care for complex pregnancies, and for babies born too soon or with serious medical conditions.

▼ The University Health Women's & Children's Hospital will open in the Summer of 2023. It will be the first hospital in San Antonio dedicated exclusively to the unique needs of women, babies, and children with complex medical needs.

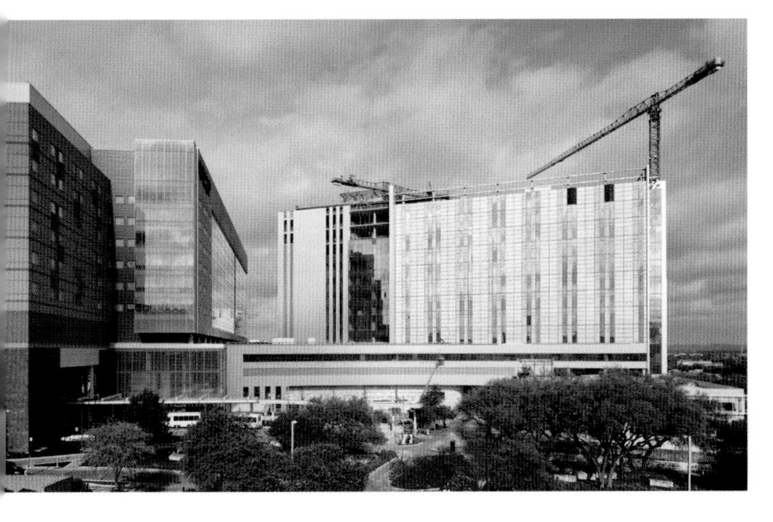

▶▼ The Dr. Robert L.M. Hilliard Center on San Antonio's East Side is named for a pioneering San Antonio obstetrician who delivered more than 14,000 babies and served numerous community leadership roles. Dr. Hilliard was a flight surgeon with the U.S. Air Force before completing his obstetrics and gynecology residency at the Robert B. Green Memorial Hospital. He was the first African-American chief resident of OB/GYN at any major teaching hospital in the South.

In January of 2021 University Health opened one of the first and largest mass COVID-19 vaccination centers in Texas and delivered more than 500,000 shots through Spring of 2022.

transport media. University Hospital also became the largest enrollment site in the world for an important clinical trial for a medication that was ultimately approved to treat patients with severe COVID-19 complications. While there are numerous other examples of the University Health team's innovation and commitment to caring, perhaps its greatest pandemic-related contribution was the establishment of one of the largest COVID-19 vaccination centers in Texas. Centrally located in the Wonderland of the Americas shopping mall, the center delivered more than 500,000 doses of vaccine from January 4, 2021 through March 4, 2022.

A Place for Compassionate, Quality Care

University Health remains committed to the principles on which it was founded—to be compassionate professionals, fostering a culture of health excellence for the community, and treating all who enter its doors with kindness and respect. In doing so, it is nationally recognized for excellence as:

- South Texas' only three-time Magnet health care organization by the American Nurses Credentialing Center, considered the "Gold Standard" in patient care. As a Magnet hospital, University Health attracts the best and brightest health care talent from around the nation, providing patients the peace of mind they are being cared for by a nursing team with a proven track record of success.
- The first and only health organization in Texas to be certified as a Level 10 Most Wired health system by the College of Healthcare Information Management Executives (CHIME). Level 10 is the highest certification possible, and University Health has earned it for both its hospital and outpatient care centers. From electronic health records to online patient portals, University Health is at the forefront of improving outcomes for patients with digital tools.

A Focus on the Future

Looking to the future, the Women's & Children's Hospital will open in the summer of 2023. The new hospital will provide much-needed facilities to meet the needs of our growing community and region.

The Sky Tower at University Hospital opened in 2014, offering advanced care and the latest technologies in a beautiful, warm, and welcoming environment that promotes healing through its SaludArte: Art of Healing program.

This exciting addition to the University Hospital campus in the South Texas Medical Center includes:

- A 12-story, 300-bed hospital for women, babies, and children
- Dedicated Children's ER
- Dedicated unit for all OB/GYN emergencies
- Beautiful and state-of-the art Labor and Delivery Center
- Child Life Center
- Healing Arts throughout
- 900-space parking garage
- Conference Center

This will be a place where women, children and their families are surrounded with all of the experts and technologies to provide the highest level of compassionate care. It will be the only hospital in South Texas exclusively focused on the unique needs of women, babies and children.

Also on the horizon is the University Health Institute for Population Health and Health Equity. The Institute will organize and develop priorities around the population health needs of the growing Bexar County community. It will align public health services with medical care to better promote comprehensive population health objectives that support health equity, acute care, preventive care, and public health emergency response.

From its humble roots, University Health today is the premier and most respected health organization in San Antonio and South Texas—a hub of innovation and discovery, committed to delivering patient-centered, culturally competent, high-quality and compassionate care, based on a strong foundation of outcomes-based research and innovative teaching.

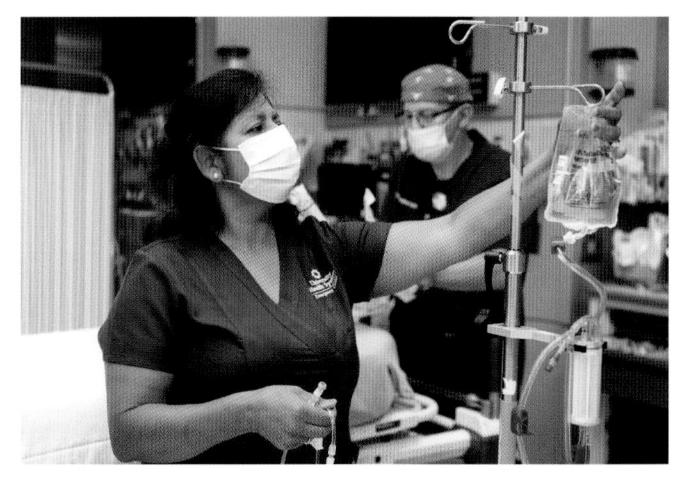

University Health is the first and only health system in South Texas to be designated as a Magnet by the American Nurses Credentialing Center (ANCC) for a third time and is now among an elite group of health care institutions that have earned this designation for more than 10 straight years.

The Clinical Pavilion at University Health's Robert B. Green Campus downtown opened in 2013. Now a hub of outpatient care including primary, specialty, and urgent care services, as well as pharmacy, lab and outpatient surgery, this campus was the birthplace of the University Health Mission.

Proud Past, Bright Future

When 25 young Army officers gathered at the Gunter Hotel in 1922 to establish USAA, none could have envisioned how iconic their little startup enterprise would become in San Antonio and around the globe.

Certainly, few at that meeting – or anywhere else – could have imagined what the future held for the new insurer's hometown, either. Although it was already 200 years old in 1922, San Antonio was still a frontier town tied to agriculture.

With a population of 165,000, it ranked 41st in the nation in size, well behind such cities as Toledo, Ohio, Richmond, Va. and Omaha, Neb.

My, how the two have grown together! Today, San Antonio—population 1.5 million—is firmly established among America's largest and most dynamic cities, with an increasingly diversified economy powered by tourism, health care, energy, aerospace, advanced manufacturing and cybersecurity. USAA, meanwhile, grew into one of the nation's largest and most admired financial-services institutions – and one of San Antonio's leading civic catalysts.

Powering the growth of both the city and USAA: a deep and unwavering commitment to the military community, here in Military City USA® and beyond.

That military community represents USAA's membership and its singular market focus. USAA now has more than 13 million members. Created to provide auto insurance to Army officers, USAA today offers a wide array of insurance and banking products to currently serving officers as well as enlisted in every branch of the armed forces, along with any veteran who left the armed forces in good standing, and their families.

Nearly 39,000 USAA employees serve those members, with about 19,000 in San Antonio —making USAA the region's second-largest civilian employer. With $37.5 billion in revenues in 2021, USAA ranks 96th on the Fortune 500, and is often described as one of the globe's most admired businesses.

"We have regional offices across the United States and Europe and members all over the world," said USAA President and Chief Executive Officer Wayne Peacock. "But San Antonio has always been our home. Our roots are here. Our heart is here. And I don't see that ever changing."

USAA was born amid one of history's most profoundly disruptive eras – the dawn of the automotive age. The exponential proliferation of cars and trucks sparked a cultural and economic revolution that reshaped America. Federal, state and local governments launched massive road-building campaigns. A new economy of gas stations, motor inns and roadside restaurants lined those roads. Established industries – steel mills, oil refineries and concrete plants – flexed to new markets and created countless new jobs. And some entrepreneurs moved to meet another market need: auto insurance.

▲ CEO Robert McDermott; John Akers, IBM Chief Executive Officer; Joan Holguin, policy service representative, 1988

◀ Grayson Street Building Policy and Ratings Departments, 1936

The Army officers who gathered at the Gunter found insurance hard to come by, however. Most insurance providers were local or regional, while the soldiers' lives kept them on the move worldwide. Insurance underwriting is a conservative practice; military men stare down danger. Some insurers wouldn't cover them at all. Others price-gouged, claiming that the military profession marked officers as inherently high risk.

What the officers couldn't obtain, they decided to create. They saw in each other what underwriters overlooked: honor and trustworthiness. So, led by a determined and persistent pilot named Maj. William Garrison, they gathered in downtown San Antonio on June 20, 1922, and pledged to pool resources and insure one another against risk.

Today's USAA remains deeply rooted in the foundation laid that day. The corporate structure remains one of member backing member, so profits remain secondary to service and satisfaction. Core values – service, loyalty, honesty and integrity – still underpin USAA's corporate culture. And the sense of trust and commitment shared among USAA's employees and members translates into rates of retention and willingness to recommend that are unrivaled in the field of financial services.

A similar loyalty binds USAA and the region, home to more than 71,000 active-duty service personnel and 210,000 veterans and host to 39,000 military-training graduates each year. USAA and its employees and retirees have been a powerful philanthropic force in the communities where its employees live, work and play – especially San Antonio. In 2021, the USAA family's total charitable support reached $52.7 million and 213,000 hours of volunteer time.

USAA leverages its philanthropic dollars strategically, teaming with civic and government leaders to tackle some of the region's most pressing problems. One high-profile example: USAA played a pivotal role in San Antonio's successful campaign to effectively end veteran homelessness, working with the city and several nonprofits and corporations. USAA's philanthropic support allowed nonprofits to provide housing placement, case management and other vital services. Other USAA-led initiatives over the years have included support for STEM education at area high schools; workforce training through area universities and community colleges; the establishment of a data-sciences program at the University of Texas at San Antonio; and initiatives

Photos on previous page:

In 1922, 25 Army officers gathered at the Gunter Hotel to establish USAA.

Portrait of USAA Founder, William Garrison

1926 Auburn, 8-in-line 4-door sedan with USAA logo ornament on grille. Donated by USAA member Harry N. Krenkel

aimed at closing wealth and achievement gaps that disproportionately affect underrepresented groups.

More broadly, USAA and its leaders have a long track record of engagement in San Antonio's economic development. The tone setter was retired Air Force Brig. Gen. Robert F. McDermott, USAA chairman and CEO from 1969 through 1993. While in that role, McDermott served as chairman of the Greater San Antonio Chamber of Commerce; co-created and chaired the San Antonio Economic Development Foundation; co-founded United San Antonio to promote social cohesiveness during the 1970s and 1980s; and co-founded the Texas Research and Technology Foundation, parent of the Texas Research Park. In the early 1990s, when the San Antonio Spurs were on the verge of being sold and moved, McDermott organized a group of local investors to buy the team and keep it in San Antonio. (The Spurs, of course, went on to win five NBA championships and build a die-hard fan base.)

USAA also has been instrumental in reshaping San Antonio's physical look and feel. Its real-estate arm, where Peacock began his career, pulled off a visionary transformation that turned an exhausted limestone quarry and its environs northwest of the city into the Shops at La Cantera, Six Flags Fiesta Texas and La Cantera Resort & Spa.

Less than six miles to the southeast, USAA's hilltop headquarters on Fredericksburg Road overlooks Interstate 10 – also known as McDermott Freeway. The 286-acre campus features 4.2 million square feet of office space – along with athletic fields, tennis and basketball courts, picnic pavilions, three gyms, reflective ponds and miles of running paths. Those amenities and a benchmark-beating total-rewards package are outward signs of USAA's belief that happy, healthy and highly engaged employees are the lifeblood of a culture of service that elevates USAA to the top of its industry

◀ In 2012, former CEO Joe Robles cuts a ceremonial 90th birthday cake with employees Marilyn Dworaczyk and Dustin Ottea, the longest tenured employee and the newest.

in third-party evaluations of customer satisfaction and loyalty.

Yet Peacock and other USAA leaders recognize that the association's century-long history of success does not guarantee an equally successful second century. As was true in 1922, powerful technological and social forces are disrupting today's economy and competitive landscape. Tech-empowered, price-conscious consumers expect ever-faster solutions, friction-free experiences and convenient self-service options.

To continue anticipating and meeting member expectations, USAA is investing heavily in modernizing talent, training and technology for the future. The company is also simplifying its operations and structure to concentrate on excelling in its core businesses of insurance and banking. Major elements of that simplification included divesting its mutual-funds business, its investment-management company and its controlling stake in USAA Real Estate Co. USAA returned a large share of the proceeds to members. The rest is being used to fund modernization initiatives and fortify USAA's reserves.

"I think our founders would be amazed at how their startup looks at age 100," Peacock said. "The times have changed dramatically, and change will only accelerate in USAA's second century. But what has remained constant, and will in the future, is our commitments to the military community and to our mission of facilitating the financial security of our members and their families.

"USAA has always differentiated itself by putting our military membership first, by being a company military families can trust, and by providing them with exceptional service," the CEO added. "We have a proud past. We will have a bright future. And we have a mission-driven commitment and a sense of purpose that make us want to come to work every day."

◀◀ Photos on previous page:

USAA employees gather to assemble 1,000 Comfort Crew for Military Kids care kits for children whose parents recently deployed.

San Antonio employees volunteering at the San Antonio Food Bank. Over 12,000 pounds of food and supplies were sorted and packaged in this effort

USAA Home Office campus on the Northwest Side along Interstate 10, or McDermott Freeway, named after the company's longest-tenured CEO.

◀ USAA President and CEO Wayne Peacock is leading USAA into its second century. Pictured at USAA's Home Office in San Antonio.

Familia and Community

The San Antonio Hispanic Chamber of Commerce (SAHCC) has been recognized for the vital work it has done on behalf of the area's Hispanic businesses. In addition to having been selected as one of the best-run Chambers in America, the SAHCC has been designated as a 5-Star Accredited Chamber from the U.S. Chamber of Commerce. It is the first Hispanic Chamber in the United States to be accredited by the U.S. Chamber of Commerce.

The SAHCC is the first organization of its type in the United States, having been originally chartered as the Mexican Chamber of Commerce in 1929. Today, there are about 35 Hispanic chambers of commerce in Texas and about 600 across the nation.

Born With a Mission of Service

Don Enrique Santibanez, Consul General of Mexico in San Antonio, became the first president of the Chamber at its founding. Given the deep historical and commercial ties between the U.S. and Mexico, the Chamber's primary emphasis in its early years was to promote trade, policy, and cultural harmony.

While the Chamber's leaders forged ahead to define modern Hispanic business, the social climate of the time posed many barriers. Minorities faced discrimination in business, employment, education, infrastructure, and access to capital and markets. These social issues necessitated that the Chamber go beyond the traditional scope for chambers of commerce and into one focusing on business advocacy and promotion of doing business within the Hispanic market.

Mission Accomplished

The SAHCC is now the largest Hispanic Chamber in America. Since its inception, the Chamber has been a strong advocate for Hispanic business, Hispanics in business, and the Hispanic market.

The Chamber lists more than 900 members, 80 percent of whom are local small businesses and non-profit agencies. Member benefits include participation in at least three networking opportunities hosted by the Chamber each month, along with quarterly Meet & Greet events, workshops, committee meetings, legislative update seminars, and roundtable discussions with elected officials.

The Chamber's small business members are particularly interested in finance, legal and HR, promotion and branding, and technology trends. Over the past year, SAHCC has provided countless member and community engagement events as supportive resources for members.

The international commerce and trade needs of the Chamber and its members are represented through Foreign Trade Missions. Chamber staff also works with foreign government entities, trade associations, other Chambers of Commerce, and civic/business groups to simulate foreign representation on behalf of the Chamber and its affiliates. The Chamber is currently planning a Trade Mission to Panama and Colombia for Fall 2022.

"As the oldest and largest Hispanic Chamber in the country, the San Antonio Hispanic Chamber of Commerce has a deep history of community enrichment, leadership development, and business support for Hispanics in business and those working within the Hispanic market," stated Marina Gonzales, J.D., the organization's President and CEO. "Our Chamber plays a vital role in ensuring that our small, minority-owned businesses can continue to prosper in San Antonio."

HOLT CAT San Antonio

Superior products. Legendary customer service. Unmatched capabilities.

FIVE GENERATIONS OF THE HOLT FAMILY HAVE PURSUED AND EXPANDED THE DREAM OF BENJAMIN HOLT WHO, IN 1866, ALONG WITH HIS BROTHERS CHARLES, AMES, AND WILLIAM, PRODUCED THE FIRST HORSE-DRAWN, LINK-BELT COMBINED HARVESTER. A SERIES OF ADDITIONAL INVENTIONS LED TO HOLT'S INTRODUCTION OF THE FIRST SUCCESSFUL track-type tractor in 1904, the Caterpillar®, which used self-laying tracks instead of wheels. Several mergers and acquisitions over the years led to the establishment of the Caterpillar Dealer Network.

Additional growth and expansion to meet the needs of companies in the construction, renewable energy, and manufacturing industries led the Holt family to establish deep roots in Texas. San Antonio's thriving cultural and family-friendly environment aligned perfectly with the mission and vision for their organization. The city's resource-based economy and centralized location provided ample opportunities for growth. San Antonio remains the headquarters for HOLT CAT.

HOLT CAT and the HOLT lines of business operate under a Values-Based Leadership philosophy. This philosophy is governed by the company's Mission, Vision, and Core Business Values. The Mission captures what HOLT does as a company; the Vision provides an ongoing purpose for completing the mission; and most importantly, HOLT's Core Values describe how the associates treat one another and their customers. These three elements provide each of HOLT's approximately 3,200 employees with guidelines for making daily decisions in their jobs.

HOLT CAT puts its people first and leads by a set of core values that connects customers, employees, and stakeholders.

Serving the Lone Star State and Beyond

HOLT CAT is the authorized Caterpillar® heavy equipment and engine dealer for 118 counties in South, Central, North, and East Texas. The company sells, services, and rents Cat® equipment, engines, generators, and trucks for construction, mining, industrial, petroleum, and agricultural applications. HOLT CAT has become synonymous with quality, integrity, and commitment to customer service. In addition to being the largest Caterpillar® dealer in the United States, HOLT sells used Caterpillar® equipment worldwide.

The company strives to not only provide superior and diverse service and products, but strategic opportunities that lead to growth, initiate change, and bring added value to customers and the community.

Adherence to those values has led to numerous awards, including:

- 2019 SABJ Best Places to Work
- Caterpillar® Global Dealer of Excellence Award in 2018.
- 2002 Dealer of the Year

Those values extend to HOLT CAT's commitment to the local community. In addition to matching monetary donations to the United Way from employees, HOLT is active in programs including Feeding Texas, various toy and book drives, back-to-school school supply drives, blood drives through the South Texas Blood and Tissue Center, and more.

Bill Greehey

A Man on a Mission, and Making a Profound Difference in the Mission City

"When I heard about this book, chronicling the growth and success of San Antonio's recent history, I immediately thought of the immeasurable ways in which Bill Greehey has helped transform our community. It's hard to imagine San Antonio without Bill Greehey's impact — without the thousands of good-paying jobs he created at Valero and NuStar and the hundreds of millions of dollars of support for virtually every nonprofit from both of these entities and The Greehey Family Foundation. Bill's fingerprints can be found on just about everything good in our city. So I know I speak for many when I say we are forever grateful for his unwavering support of our community."

Brad Barron, president and CEO of NuStar Energy L.P.

BILL GREEHEY. A MAN WHO CARES MORE THAN OTHERS MAY THINK IS WISE. A MAN WHO RISKS MORE THAN OTHERS THINK IS SAFE. A MAN WHO ACHIEVES MORE THAN OTHERS THINK IS POSSIBLE. A MAN OF VISION WHO EPITOMIZES THE AMERICAN DREAM. KNOWN FOR HIS FIERCE FAITH AND DEDICATION TO HIS EMPLOYEES AND THE COMMUNITY,

Greehey is a dealer in hope who has the confidence to stand alone, the courage to make tough decisions and the compassion to care about the needs of others. Through his vision and leadership by example, he has improved the lives of countless individuals. But Greehey did not set out to be a leader. Rather, he became one, by the quality of his actions and the integrity of his intent.

From Humble Roots

Greehey grew up in a small home in Fort Dodge, Iowa, with a roof over it, but not much more. His father worked for minimum wage in the local gypsum mill and from the time he was 12 years old, Greehey worked to help support his family, shucking corn at local farms and working at the gypsum mill by age 15.

But Greehey aspired for a life beyond Fort Dodge. And he knew that a college education was the key even though no one from his family or neighborhood had ever attended college.

Greehey joined the Air Force so he could attend college on the G.I. Bill, and was stationed at Lackland AFB. He soon married and had two small children, so in addition to his assigned military duties, he worked nights and weekends as a waiter and bartender at the base. Upon his discharge, he enrolled at St. Mary's University in San Antonio while working nights and weekends parking cars at the Nix Hospital in downtown San Antonio to provide for his young family.

Greehey still managed to earn his degree in just two-and-a-half years, making the Dean's List and receiving several other academic honors along the way, and graduated from St. Mary's in 1960. Armed with his degree and a fierce determination to succeed, Greehey was now prepared for his future.

Evolution to a Titan of the Energy Industry

Greehey's first jobs out of college were in accounting and auditing with Price Waterhouse and Exxon, and within a few years he was recruited to work in the finance division of Coastal Corp—a relatively young company with lots of growth potential. At the young age of 32, he was promoted to corporate controller, and just three years later he was senior vice president of finance.

Then, in 1974, a court-appointed board for LoVaca Gathering Company, a Coastal subsidiary that had contracted to sell more gas than it was able to deliver, asked Greehey to serve as the company's president and CEO. Most people in the oil and gas industry viewed his odds for succeeding at "zero." Greehey, however, viewed the challenge as yet another opportunity.

Over the next six years, Greehey worked tirelessly to negotiate a $1.6 billion spin-off

settlement of LoVaca, and before the settlement was even completed, moved the company from Houston to San Antonio. The settlement resulted in the creation of Valero Energy Corporation on January 1, 1980, with Greehey as its chairman and CEO, and it was the largest spin-off in U.S. history at the time.

Greehey grew Valero from a small, regional pipeline company into the largest refining company in North America that rose as high as Number 15 on the FORTUNE 500 ranking before he retired as CEO of Valero in 2006 and as chairman in 2007. The Harvard Business Review later named Greehey one of the best-performing CEOs in the world based on his tenure as CEO of Valero, ranking Number 12 among U.S. CEOs, and Number 31 among all CEOs in the world. And in the energy industry, he ranked Number two among U.S. CEOs and Number five worldwide.

Through the course of Valero's growth, he also directed the growth and success of Valero L.P., a limited partnership which was comprised of the company's petroleum pipeline and storage assets and operations. With both Valero Energy and Valero L.P. continuing to grow and prosper, the strategic decision was made for Valero L.P. to spin off from Valero Energy. This resulted in the creation of NuStar Energy L.P., one of the leading pipeline and terminal operators in the nation, where Greehey continues to serve as the company's chairman.

Greehey credits the success of Valero and NuStar to the culture he established at both companies. His mantra has always been, "If you take care of the employees, they'll take care of the company, the communities and the shareholders." Greehey's personal commitment to providing the best career opportunities and compensation for his employees at Valero and NuStar earned the companies consistent rankings among the nation's top employers, including Valero reaching Number three on Fortune Magazine's "100 Best Companies to Work For" list before he retired from the company, and NuStar has since earned the ranking 12 times.

Greehey has also made community service a guiding principle at the companies he has led. Under his leadership, Valero and NuStar have been recognized as the nation's top donors to United Way based on employee per capita giving, and for supporting countless charitable and civic causes in San Antonio and other communities where they have operations.

Bill Greehey

A Titan of Charitable and Civic Endeavors

Greehey's contributions to the San Antonio community run far beyond creating two major companies that have created thousands of good-paying jobs that provided tens-of-thousands of volunteer hours to support the community each year.

He chaired the Citizens for the Dome campaign that resulted in voters approving construction of the Alamodome and was influential in the creation of the Alamo Bowl. He played a key role in the purchase of the San Antonio Spurs by local businesses to keep the team in San Antonio. And he led the charge to raise funds for the city's renowned new Central Library. In the early 2000s, the PGA Tour's Texas Open golf tournament, which has been hosted in San Antonio since 1922, was going to leave San Antonio due to its poor attendance and poor fundraising efforts. Greehey pledged Valero's title sponsorship, and quickly helped take it to the top of the Tour in charitable contributions. Greehey has also been a major supporter of the United Way and the Boy Scouts of America and has served in local and national leadership capacities for both organizations. And he is past chairman of the San Antonio Economic Development Foundation.

In 2004, Greehey established The Greehey Family Foundation and he has funded it with over $200 million, and between the foundation and his personal giving he has given hundreds-of-millions of dollars to hundreds of charitable causes, most of which are in the San Antonio area. This includes more than $32 million to the University of Texas Health Science Center to fund research and treatment for children's cancer and to discover a cure for Alzheimer's. He has also given more than $31 million to create The Greehey School of Business at St. Mary's University. And, he has invested $8 million to establish scholarships for first generation college students at six universities in the San Antonio area.

However, his greatest legacy will likely be the creation of Haven for Hope, known as the national model in the fight against homelessness, which provides every resource needed to help the homeless transform their lives. Greehey raised over $101 million to build Haven, which opened in 2010. He has given $44 million of his own money to support Haven and its partner agencies, and with the help of NuStar employees and business partners, he has raised over $50 million to fund Haven's operations over the past 14 years. Greehey has served as Haven's chairman of the board since the organization's inception, and he remains very active in its operational, planning, and fundraising efforts. At Haven, all are treated with dignity, respect, and unconditional love. More than 15,500 individuals have transitioned from homelessness to living in permanent or supportive housing, and gone on to live happy, independent lives.

Greehey has received numerous local and national awards for his professional and civic achievements and contributions. In 2000, he was presented the "Golden Plate Award" from the American Academy of Achievement and was inducted into the Museum of the American Dream. That same year he was one of 10 individuals inducted into the Horatio Alger Association, which recognizes individuals who come from humble beginnings to achieve tremendous success. In 2002, he was inducted into the Texas Business Hall

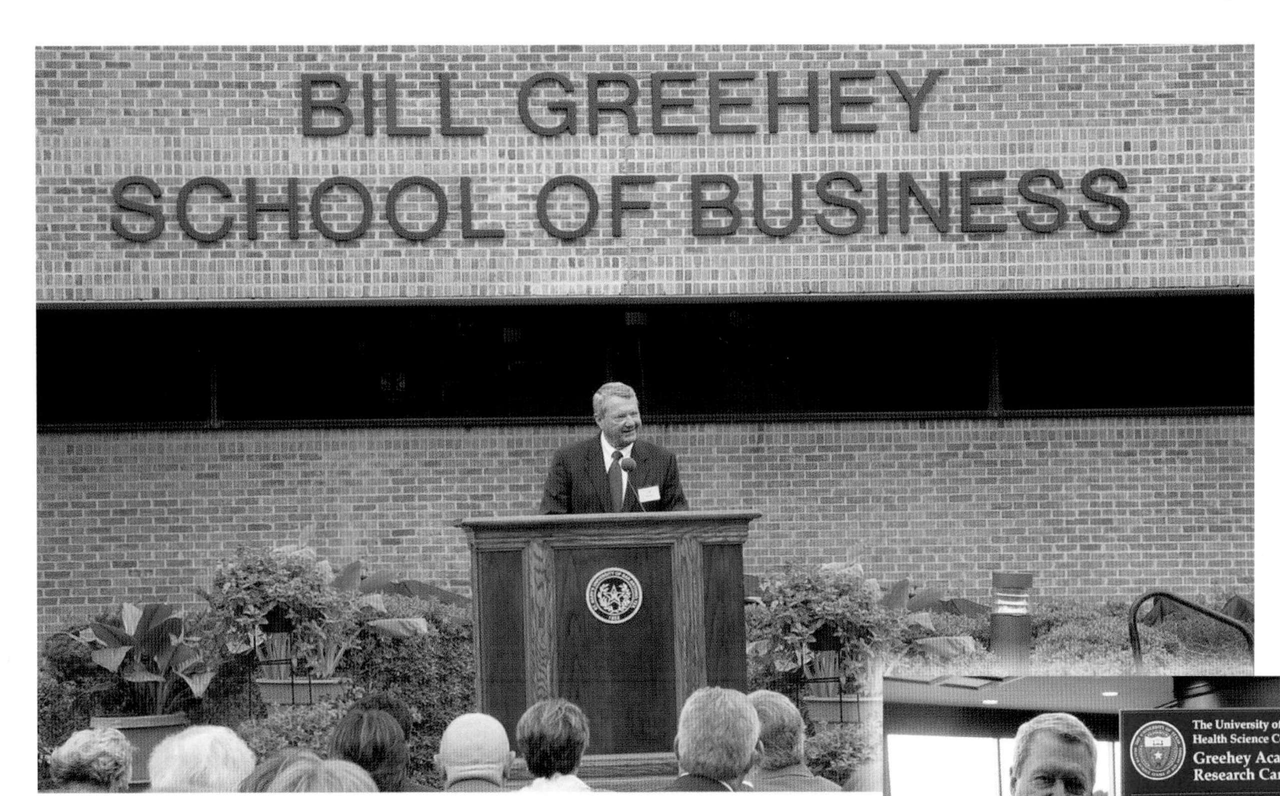

of Fame. And he has received numerous honors based on his contributions to education, including an honorary doctorate of social work from Our Lady of the Lake University and an honorary doctorate of philosophy from St. Mary's University.

The Definition of Success

The professional, personal and civic successes that Greehey has achieved in his life are unparalleled, but he has a very unique perspective on success.

"The most important thing I learned from the Marianists at St. Mary's is that you are never truly a success until you share that success with others."

Greehey has certainly lived up to that statement and the San Antonio community is a better place thanks to his vision, leadership and generosity.

Broadway Bank

Serving the Financial Needs of South Central Texas

The entire management team and the almost 650 dedicated professionals at Broadway Bank begin each working day with a question - "How do we make it easier for customers to bank with us?" Since the bank first opened its doors more than eight decades ago, those Broadway Bankers have remained focused on answering that question. Their expertise and their commitment to providing unsurpassed customer service have resulted in Broadway Bank being recognized for providing the best new products, new services, and new experiences to its customers whether they choose to access those products and services online or at their local Broadway Financial Center.

Broadway Bankers take great pride in matching and exceeding the broad range of financial services offered by the big national firms. However, there is one major difference. As a locally-based institution, Broadway Bank team members live and work in the communities and neighborhoods they serve. They know the financial needs of their friends and neighbors and stand ready to assist in meeting those needs. And they can offer the latest digital banking services available from the industry giants. Utilizing the latest financial technology, Broadway Bank has worked hard to become a future-ready bank, committing money and resources for innovation and technology.

Broadway Bank's legion of satisfied customers has come to rely on a modern banking experience that is locally sourced and personally delivered. And they have come to appreciate the best-in-class customer service that Broadway Bank offers. Each Broadway Banker welcomes the opportunity to serve each customer with financial advice, wealth management, personal and business banking, and more.

A Proud Past

While Broadway Bank today is the largest independently owned bank headquartered in San Antonio, its birth was in a small storefront in the city's Alamo Heights neighborhood in 1941. Charles E. Cheever, Sr. was an Army captain stationed at Fort Sam Houston in 1937 when he came up with the idea of creating a bank that would serve the civilian and military personnel in the Alamo Heights area. Cheever and his wife, Elizabeth, envisioned a financial institution that would serve the hundreds of military families who were migrating to San Antonio because of the war effort, and the businesses which would serve those new residents.

Their dream was realized with the opening of Broadway National Bank in 1941. The Bank's modest beginnings were made even more difficult with America's entry that year into World War II. Cheever was called to duty in Europe, where he achieved the rank of colonel and spent the war years working as a Judge Advocate for General George S. Patton. Elizabeth Cheever was left "to hold things together" at home and the bank, serving on the board of directors until her husband returned.

During the post-War era, Broadway Bank set numerous "firsts." In 1959, it was the first San Antonio bank to establish a mortgage lending division and it was the first to extend its banking hours to help working families. The bank again entered uncharted waters in 1983 by being the first in the city to offer on-site brokerage services. Broadway's successful Wealth Management Division was established the following year. In 1996, Broadway Bank acquired financial centers in Fredericksburg, Kerrville, Boerne, Castroville, Hondo, and Seguin, Texas.

Charles E. "Charlie" Cheever, Jr. followed in the banking footsteps of his mother and father. Born on an army base in Manila, Philippines in 1928 where his parents were stationed, Charlie was a 1949 graduate of the U.S. Military Academy at West Point and a 1957 graduate of The University of Texas School of Law. Intending to practice law in his wife Sally's hometown of El Paso, Charlie opted for another career path when the largest law firm there offered him only half of what Sally was making as a schoolteacher. His parents offered an alternative. "If you're going to starve that way," they told him, "we can starve you." With four children under the age of three, Charlie accepted their offer and started at Broadway Bank as a vice president.

He never looked back. When Charlie joined Broadway Bank, the institution had one location and total deposits were just more than $11 million. With Charlie's vision, a great leadership team, and cutting-edge innovation, Broadway Bank's assets have grown to $5 billion with over 30 branch locations today across San Antonio, Austin, the Hill Country and Dallas.

His success was noted locally and industry-wide. Charlie was elected President of Broadway Bank in 1961 and Chairman & CEO in 1982. He served as the Chairman of the Texas Bankers Association, Director of the San Antonio Branch of the Federal Reserve, and Regional Director of the American Bankers Association.

In 2004, Charlie was honored to be inducted into the San Antonio Business Hall of Fame and, twelve years later, into the Texas Bankers Hall of Fame and the Texas Business Hall of Fame.

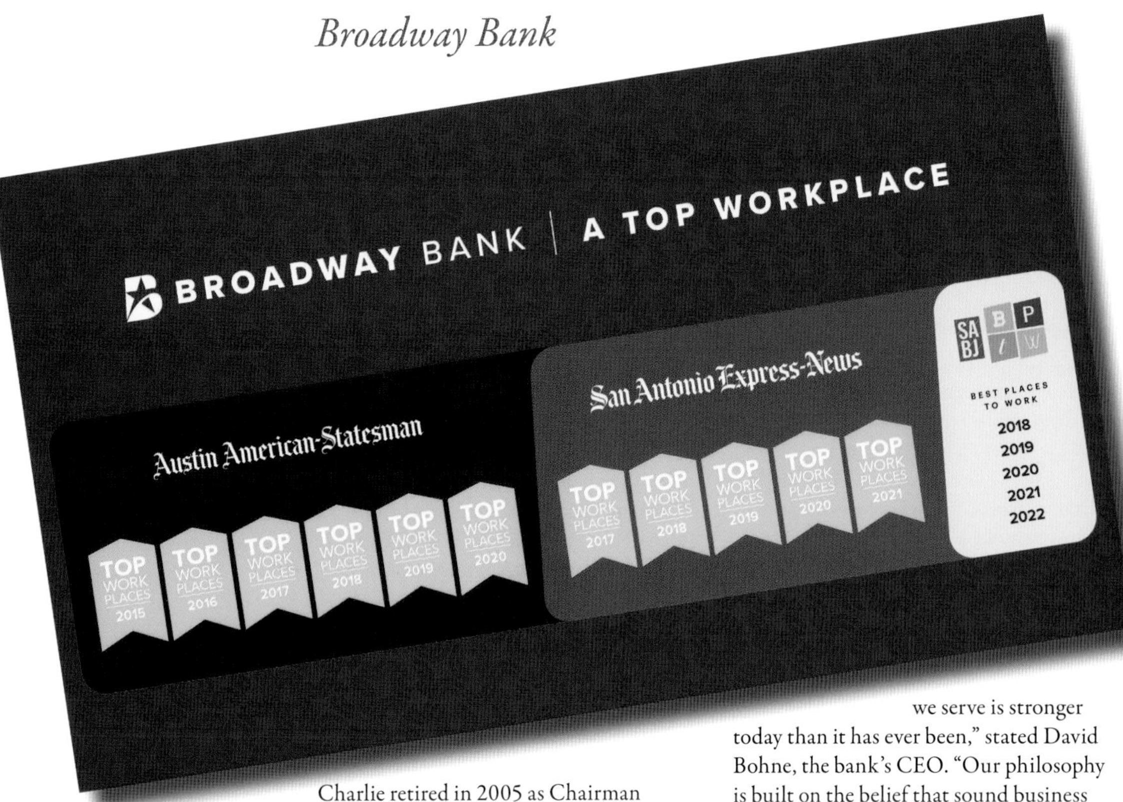

Charlie retired in 2005 as Chairman Emeritus of Broadway Bank. He passed away in 2021 and is remembered as a successful banker, civic leader, philanthropist, and devoted family man.

A Bright Future

"As an integral part of South Central Texas for more than 80 years, Broadway Bank's commitment to the communities we serve is stronger today than it has ever been," stated David Bohne, the bank's CEO. "Our philosophy is built on the belief that sound business decisions will always be in the best interest of our customers, our employees, and ultimately our communities. It is through this philosophy that we have withstood the test of time, evolving into one of the largest privately-owned banks in the state with more than $5 billion in assets.

"Part of what makes us special is our ability to transform to meet our customers' evolving needs and the shifting digital landscape while remaining true to our values and our roots. As we look toward the future, we are constantly innovating with the products and services we offer, be it online or in person at any of our financial centers. In addition to enhancing our online and mobile banking platforms, we are developing financial centers with modern and open layouts designed to enhance the customer experience and provide access to our financial experts."

The core values on which Broadway Bank was founded—trust, excellence, teamwork, community, friendliness, and creativity—continue to identify the bank today. These values personify the bank's mission, vision, and business strategy and are embodied by every Broadway Banker. Those values underscore the bank's commitment to delivering excellence by creating a positive customer experience and productive work environment. They identify the way each banking professional treats their customers—helping them with their financial needs and building long-term relationships. Those relationships form the cornerstone of what Broadway Bank stands for as an institution.

The management team at Broadway understands that nurturing those relation-

ships involves giving back to the community. They have formed partnerships with friends and neighbors that truly look out for each other.

Despite the numerous challenges brought on by the pandemic, Broadway Bank again led the way in service to the San Antonio area. In 2021, Broadway Bank employees donated 6,272 hours to various nonprofit organizations in San Antonio, Austin, and the surrounding communities. Care Corps employee volunteers supported 44 charitable projects in addition to projects they supported individually. In 2021, Broadway Bank's corporate contributions were more than $858,000.

Employees donated upwards of $361,000 to the United Way Capital Campaign in 2021. Along with the Bank's contribution of $135,000 to the campaign, almost a half-million dollars in total were raised to benefit local programs.

Realizing the importance of education as a path to success, Broadway Bank was pleased to award $15,000 in scholarships to high school graduates as part of the San Antonio Education Partnership program.

During his time as Chairman Emeritus of Broadway Bank, Charles E. Cheever, Jr. remarked on the vision his parents had when they founded the bank and how it has evolved into the successful and respected financial institution it is today—a team of committed professionals providing universal expertise in helping customers make more informed and effective decisions for themselves and their businesses.

"We at Broadway Bank will look to the future," he stated, "remembering our past, and doing what is best for our customers, employees, and stakeholders."

Broadway Bank
Member FDIC
Equal Housing Lender

Familia, Comida y Cultura: Making the American Dream Come True

There were no newspaper headlines and probably little attention paid to the restaurant that Pedro and Cruz Cortez opened in an abandoned market area in San Antonio in 1941. Only a few years removed from the Great Depression, Europe had been at war for two years and people in the United States were focusing on when, and if, America would enter the conflict.

Pedro and Cruz, however, were following their dream of creating a three-table café the city's Latino community could point to with pride. Imbued with a fierce work ethic, the couple decided to go against conventional wisdom and invested $150 in their dream. They purchased the Jamaica No. 5 Café, a small three-table café in San Antonio's Market Square. From day one, the café's doors would remain open 24 hours a day, seven days a week to cater to the various needs of the community, including the farmers who rose before the sun, the workers who labored late into the evening, and the night owls who celebrated into the night.

The couple overcame difficult times during the post-World War II recession years and persevered. By 1947 the business had become established, and the couple even replaced the cigar boxes they used for cash drawers with an actual cash register. Adding air conditioning to the café was a true rarity in that time.

A Treasure of Sights, Sounds and Smells

Looking to grow their business, Pedro and Cruz purchased in 1951 what had been the Toyo Café in Market Square. Inspired by the beauty and vibrancy of his home Guadalajara, Mexico, Pedro named the couples' second restaurant Mi Tierra, reflecting his love for his native country and the strong cultural similarities that San Antonio's Mercado shared with the historic San Pedro Tlaquepaque whose name was derived from the ancient language of the Aztecs meaning the "best of everything.".

Mi Tierra Café now serves as a beacon in San Antonio's Historic Market Square. The neon sign continues to light the way as it welcomes hungry guests to enjoy its famous food, fabulous margaritas, and unparalleled décor, including a world-class expansive al fresco mural, celebrating Latino and community leaders.

After bringing their children Manuel, Jorge, Rosalinda and Ruben into the business, in 1981 the family opened La Margarita Restaurant & Oyster Bar, also located in Market Square. Additional expansions saw the family adding the Mariachi Bar to Mi Tierra and renovating and rebranding another restaurant to meet San Antonio's growing culinary demands, the newly renamed Restaurante Pico de Gallo located one block west in downtown San Antonio across from UTSA's original downtown campus. Like the popularity of the family's other restaurants, Pico de Gallo quickly became another success story for La Familia Cortez Restaurants. The most recent addition to the Cortez family of restaurants is Mi Familia, located on the northside of San Antonio in the RIM.

More than two million guests visit La Familia Cortez Restaurants each year, not simply for their mouth-watering food. More than restaurants, they are a feast for the senses that celebrates Latino culture and fantastic cuisine at every turn, creating instant memories for everyone who walks through the door. A living, breathing tradition unlike any other in San Antonio, Mi Tierra Café delivers nostalgia with family photos and memories decorating every wall. Paired with the strolling trio musicians and the authentic flavors that only come from scratch-made recipes passed down through generations, La Familia Cortez's authentic culture and sincere hospitality never fail to make every guest feel like familia.

Four generations of La Familia Cortez continue the dream of the founders. And the original three-table café now encompasses almost an entire city block and seats more than 650 guests.

An Enduring Legacy

The legacy of Pedro and Cruz Cortez continues to live on through their children, grandchildren, great-grandchildren and more than 500 loyal team members united to provide the highest quality food, authentic culture, and sincere hospitality while robustly supporting the San Antonio community. Today, La Familia Cortez Restaurants celebrates more than 80 years of proud service to San Antonio and, based on Restaurant Business Magazine's latest "Top 100 Independent Restaurants," Mi Tierra ranks in the Top 25 largest independently-owned restaurants in the nation.

"As a proud immigrant from Mexico, my grandfather proudly said, 'I'm an American by choice, not by chance,'" shared Pete Cortez, the eldest member of the third generation. "My grandparents believed in preserving San Antonio's Mexican culture through our passion for hospitality and cuisine. Our second generation's commitment to their vision played an important role in the revitalization of the Historic Market Square and the surrounding Zona Cultural. Once considered a blighted area, our family worked with the City of San Antonio and community stakeholders to help revitalize the area. Now, it is one of the most popular tourist destinations in San Antonio – and we are still deeply committed to helping enhance downtown culture to this day."

The family's support of numerous local charities and cultural events along with the many awards they have received are a testament to their success. "Above all, our mission is to glorify God by honoring the vision of our founders," Pete added. "Together we work as familia with our dedicated team members to create a special connection with our guests and with the community."

photo by AL Rendon

Alamo Colleges District

Making Higher Education Accessible and Affordable For All

Like its namesake, Alamo Colleges District has its own inspirational impact on society. From its origin as a community college district in 1945 through decades of change and expansion, the Alamo Colleges have fought to make higher education accessible and affordable for all.

Today, five colleges fulfill this promise with a vast array of courses and two-year degrees — St. Philip's College (established 1898), San Antonio College (established 1925), Palo Alto College (established 1985), Northwest Vista College (established 1995), and Northeast Lakeview College (established 2007).

Serving an eight-county area, the Alamo Colleges is the largest provider of higher education in South Texas with more than 90,000 students taking credit, workforce, and continuing education courses annually.

A Journey of Excellence

The Alamo Colleges District is on a journey of excellence, receiving major recognition annually from national, state, and local organizations. As a testament to its dedication to student success and performance excellence, the Alamo Colleges District was a 2018 recipient of the Malcolm Baldrige National Quality Award, marking a significant milestone in the district's ongoing journey to achieve the highest level of student success and performance excellence. The Alamo Colleges District is one of only five organizations to receive the award and is the first community college system to achieve this level of recognition in the history of the program.

Palo Alto College was named a Rising Star of the 2019 Aspen Prize for Community College Excellence. In 2020, Alamo Colleges was named part of the Achieving the Dream Network to earn Leader College of Distinction status for student outcomes and narrowing equity gaps. The following year, San Antonio College was named the top community college in the nation by The Aspen Institute's College Excellence Program.

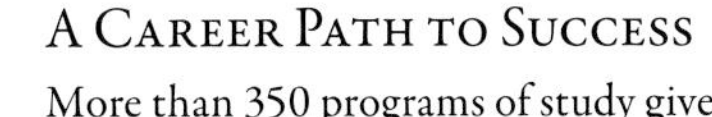

A Career Path to Success

More than 350 programs of study give students diverse options for the future they want. Alamo Colleges partner with a consortium of universities and work hard to streamline the transfer process so students don't lose credit or time. Alamo Colleges also have more than 12,500 high school students in its high school programs, including early college high school and CAST career academics that give them a head start on college.

The AlamoPROMISE program provides tuition-free college to thousands of eligible seniors. It also ensures that tuition and mandatory fees at the Alamo Colleges are covered for students who graduate from participating high schools. As last-dollar funding, AlamoPROMISE covers the gap between financial aid and the cost of tuition for up to three years.

"At the Alamo Colleges, we encourage continuous improvement and innovation for our award-winning district and

economic and social mobility for our students," said Alamo Colleges District Chancellor Dr. Mike Flores. "We look forward to the future as we strive to empower our diverse communities for success."

A recent $450 million capital improvement project has allowed Alamo Colleges to create some of the best facilities for teaching and learning in the country and well poised to service students for years to come.

Building A Better Tomorrow Today

INNOVATION IN SCIENCE AND TECHNOLOGY HAS BEEN A HALLMARK OF SOUTHWEST RESEARCH INSTITUTE (SwRI) SINCE TOM SLICK'S VISION FOR CREATING A "SCIENCE CITY" IN SAN ANTONIO RESULTED IN HIM FOUNDING THE COMPANY IN 1947. IN ITS 75-YEAR EXISTENCE, SwRI HAS GROWN TO RANK AMONG THE LARGEST INDEPENDENT, NONPROFIT research and development laboratories in the U.S. SwRI's mission is to advance science and applied technology for the benefit of government, industry, and all of humankind. The company's staff of approximately 3,000 scientists, engineers, analysts, and support staff members specialize in the creation and transfer of technology in engineering and the physical sciences. Over 4,000 projects were active at the Institute at the close of fiscal year 2021.

Adventurer, philanthropist, and oilman Thomas Baker Slick Jr. founded SwRI on a South Texas ranch, where he challenged a team of scientists and engineers to seek advancements through science and applied technology.

As a recognized leader among independent, nonprofit research and development organizations, SwRI professionals continue to accomplish outstanding fundamental and applied science and engineering and perform research for clients from diverse segments of government and industry. They have garnered worldwide attention by leading NASA missions such as the New Horizons mission to Pluto, Juno mission to Jupiter, Magnetospheric Multiscale (MMS) mission, and others currently underway. And they take great pride in leading the way in fuel and energy efficiency, geosciences, turbomachinery, automated driving systems, and energy storage. Throughout its history, the Institute's success has been based on a multidisciplinary, collaborative approach to successfully solve their clients' most challenging problems.

The Vision

Thomas Baker Slick Jr. founded SwRI on a ranch just west of San Antonio in 1947 after returning from service in World War II. Many residents were no doubt puzzled as to Slick's decision to launch his enterprise in their city. A number of nonprofit research institutes already existed at that time, but they were located in cities with either a major university or a large industry to support their research. San Antonio in 1947 was not an industrial center. It had no state university or even a college with a graduate engineering program. San Antonio was more of an agricultural center and was more than 100 miles from the nearest seaport.

While San Antonio certainly did not have a reputation as a "science city," it did have Tom Slick Jr.

The oldest son of legendary Oklahoma oilman Tom Slick Sr., who was known as the "King of the Wildcatters," Tom Slick Jr. was only 31 years old at the time he launched SwRI, but was already into his third scientific enterprise. Shortly after graduating from Yale University, where he earned Phi Beta Kappa honors as a pre-med student, Slick began acquiring South Texas ranch lands for what he called the Essar Ranch, phonetic for the initials of "Scientific Research." It became his first science laboratory, helping to develop the Brangus cattle breed, combining the Brahman breed's heat resistance with Angus beef quality. It also tested exotic and improved grasses, crops, and farm equipment to advance South Texas farms and ranches.

A man of many interests, Slick had also founded the Foundation for Applied Research, which survives today as the prestigious Texas Biomedical Research Institute and would later launch the Mind Science Foundation that focused on investigating the science of consciousness. The ranch eventually provided room for the spacious campuses of his biomedical and physical-science research centers.

Although SwRI concentrated at first on serving the booming Texas oil and gas industries and postwar military research, over the succeeding seven decades, it has diversified to include nine technical divisions with research extending from "Deep Sea to Deep Space®, and everywhere in-between."

Staff members progressed from a laboratory setup to a small indoor pilot unit to this outdoor pilot plant in an effort to help a client develop innovative uses for natural gas.

Slick's vision for SwRI was to concentrate on applied research in the physical sciences and to earn its way through contracts with government and industry clients. After recruiting talent from across the nation, he challenged his team of scientists and engineers to seek revolutionary advancements through advanced science and applied technology.

"That spirit lives on today," said Adam L. Hamilton, P.E., the President and CEO of SwRI. "Our staff is just as committed today as our founder, Thomas Baker Slick Jr., was in 1947 when he proposed that the betterment of mankind depends on the use of advanced science and technology. His dream of building an internationally respected institution working in research and development has, I believe, been more than realized."

Chemists perform analyses of petroleum products for the automotive industry. The automotive sector is one of SwRI's largest program support areas.

◀ SwRI staff members test a submarine glass dome at high pressure to ensure it will not leak during real-world deep sea use.

Services for a Diverse Clientele

SwRI is proud to provide a broad range of services to a very diverse range of clients:

Government. In the government sector, SwRI is well versed in government contracting, working with a wide range of government agencies, including the U.S. Department of Defense (DoD). The company's work includes operating a U.S. Army laboratory since 1957, providing state-of-the-art research, development, and engineering services for the Army's fuel and lubricant needs.

SwRI is one of the nation's leading organizations for providing medical and pharmaceutical research for the DoD. SwRI also evaluates weapons and armors including both large and small ballistics and explosives. That also involves performing work in cyber security, radio frequency systems, and signal analysis equipment to advance industry network and homeland security. SwRI professionals provide world-class aerospace and aircraft solutions, and develop highly advanced, custom defense systems, myriad antennae, and sophisticated armors. Working with the aerospace and defense sectors, the Institute provides world-class facilities to perform hypersonic research, modeling, and flight test solutions.

Private Sector. Clients in the private sector have long turned to SwRI for solutions relating to the automotive, healthcare, robotics, chemical, energy, energy storage, and other fields. In the automotive field, SwRI has assisted in difficult technical issues to improve automotive performance, solving fuel and lubricant issues through evaluations and analytical services.

The Institute's biomedical researchers support the healthcare industry from biomaterials and pharmaceutical development to food safety and microencapsulation. They provide product design and development, modeling and analysis, testing and evaluation, manufacturing assistance, and failure analysis.

Since chemicals and materials are part of our everyday lives, SwRI's team of scientists, analysts, and engineers works diligently to find solutions to difficult technical challenges that help improve safety, health, and product performance. The company employs advanced analysis technologies to develop and improve materials that enhance the performance of client products.

SwRI is collaborating with Phoenix International Holdings and other partners to create a rescue system for the Royal Australian Navy similar to this U.S. submarine rescue vehicle, the Pressurized Rescue Module Falcon.

photo courtesy of Phoenix International Holdings

photo courtesy of NASA/JPL/SwRI

SwRI leads NASA's Juno mission to Jupiter, which entered orbit around Jupiter in 2016. The knowledge gained is building on humankind's knowledge of the planet and gas giants in general.

A two-stage light-gas gun helps researchers achieve launch velocities up to 7 kilometers per second. Scientists use these speeds to advance knowledge on impact and penetration events related to armors used on land, sea, air, and space.

In the twenty-first century, energy fuels the global economy from the power plants driving heavy industry to the refining of conventional resources that drive transportation for land, sea, air, and even space. From oil and gas to nuclear and renewable resources, SwRI is a leading provider of technical solutions that improve the efficiency, performance, and safety of energy across fuel cycles and supply chains. And as interests shift to electrified powertrains, SwRI is helping lead the way.

SwRI's research efforts explore mysteries from deep sea to deep space. Here at home, SwRI scientists explore the geological secrets of our own planet and apply expertise in deep-water systems to adapt components for harsh ocean environments. The Institute designed and built a new, titanium crew chamber for the U.S. Navy's deep-diving Alvin research submersible, and, more recently, is developing a remotely operated submarine rescue system for the Royal Australian Navy.

One of the most visible projects is the SwRI-led New Horizons spacecraft mission, which produced historic close-up photos of Pluto and its satellite Charon in 2015. In early 2019, New Horizons celebrated another first: visiting the Kuiper Belt Object now officially named Arrokoth, four billion miles away, the farthest, most primordial object ever explored.

These and other projects help make SwRI's motto, "Deep Sea to Deep Space®," not hyperbole but everyday reality. They have also led to numerous industry awards, including 50 R&D 100 Awards, sometimes called the "Oscars of Innovation," sponsored by *R&D Magazine* to recognize the year's 100 most significant technical innovations. The Institute holds more than 1,400 patents and last year submitted 48 invention disclosures, filed 46 patent applications, and received 25 patent awards.

photo by NASA/SwRI

SwRI engineers designed and built a constellation of eight microsatellites for NASA's Cyclone Global Navigation Satellite System (CYGNSS) mission. The satellites launched in 2016 and continue their mission to peer through the clouds to observe hurricane formation and activity.

Partnering with San Antonio

SwRI is among the top five largest private employers in San Antonio contributing more than $1 billion to the local economy. Part of SwRI's 1,500-acre campus hosts a 50-acre demonstration solar farm for San Antonio's local power utility, CPS Energy, with 17,000 solar panels producing five MW of power. The facility includes four battery storage containers that are capable of powering about 400 homes.

In other community activities, SwRI volunteers participate in events like the local United Way campaign, "Meals on Wheels," and work at the San Antonio Food Bank. Over 1,000 staff members donated blood in 2021. In addition, SwRI professional staff serve as mentors to students in local Science, Technology, Engineering and Mathematics (STEM) programs and as adjunct and adjoint professors at local colleges and universities.

"The impact of SwRI's work is felt far beyond San Antonio," related Adam L. Hamilton. "The growing science, engineering, and technology sectors in this city are important for the Institute's continued success. Together, San Antonio and Southwest Research Institute are creating a more balanced workforce by adding high-paying STEM opportunities that complement other strong employment sectors in our city."

photo courtesy of NASA/JHUAPL/SwRI

The groundbreaking New Horizons mission to the Pluto system is helping to write the textbooks on Pluto, its moons, and the Kuiper Belt world Arrokoth, the farthest bodies ever explored by humankind. SwRI leads the NASA mission.

Setting the Hospitality Industry Standard

HEMISFAIR '68, THE OFFICIAL WORLD'S FAIR HELD IN SAN ANTONIO, WAS TIMED TO COINCIDE WITH THE 250TH ANNIVERSARY OF THE FOUNDING OF THE CITY. MORE THAN 30 NATIONS AND 15 CORPORATIONS HOSTED PAVILIONS AT THE FAIR. THE EVENT AND THE CATERING SERVICES REQUIRED FOR THOSE PAVILIONS PROVED TO BE THE CATALYST that would help catapult a small local business into a one-stop hospitality service for events across the nation.

Rosemary and Hank Kowalski opened Uncle Ben's Bar B-Q in 1946 on San Antonio's West Side. As events were growing in popularity in the post-World War II era, so too was catering. The business morphed into Rosemary's Catering, which blossomed after successfully handling the catering needs of the majority of the 112 pavilions at HemisFair '68. Shortly afterward, the company became the caterers of San Antonio's Convention Center, where it has managed the facility's food operations for the past 50 years.

Today, Rosemary's Catering is just one of the many hospitality divisions that make up The RK Group, which also includes::

- Illusions Tents, Rentals & Event Design
- National Structures & Event Services
- The Sandwich Factory
- RKIII Culinary Group
- RK Signature Services
- The RKD Studio & Print Lab
- Flair Floral
- RK Strategic Management Solutions
- RK Emergency Management Support
- Mobile Kitchens & Event Support
- Circa Destination Management
- RK Cares
- The Red Berry Estate

GROWING WITH GOOD TASTE

While Rosemary and Hank Kowalski may have been novices in the food business in 1946 when they pooled Hank's muster money from his military service to purchase Uncle Ben's Bar B-Q, they were keenly aware of the importance of fresh ingredients, innovative menus, personalized service, and attention to detail in every meal they served. Strict adherence to their unwavering dedication to excellence led to success.

Rosemary's Catering grew to become the preferred caterer for the most prestigious social and business events around San Antonio. In 1989, Rosemary officially turned the leadership over to her son Greg, and the firm was rebranded under a new name—The RK Group. With Greg at the helm, the leadership team of The RK Group began to diversify even more with the founding of Illusions Rentals & Design, Flair Floral, Circa Destination Management, The RKD Studio & Print Lab, National Structures, The Sandwich Factory, RK Emergency Management Support, and other specialized hospitality services that could offer a national reach.

That tradition of personalized service that would meet and exceed the expectations of each individual client endures to this day as the third generation of the family continues to build on the legacy of the founders.

CONTINUED GROWTH AND EXPANSION

The RK Group operates today as a one-stop hospitality company that continues to expand its integrated specialized service offerings to clients across the United States, from tenting to culinary and everything in between. With the constant growth, it soon became clear that the business needed to be under a single roof. In May 2020, The RK Group and its 15 divisions moved into a new home.

The campus today overlooks a beautiful lake and the San Antonio skyline. The picturesque and custom-built space includes a 168,000-square foot facility with an industrial-scale kitchen, event décor warehouse space, floral, woodshop, print

lab, and much more to provide one-stop service for event planners. There is also an adjacent 50,000-square foot facility that operates a fresh grab-and-go meal production for clients including universities, hospitals, and airports across the nation.

What satisfied clients have found that truly sets The RK Group apart from the competition is its attention to detail, quality, and top-notch service provided daily. Each service is individually tailored to each event, client, and occasion.

Another distinctive quality is The RK Group team itself. Each of the more than 1,000 team members is passionate and dedicated to exceeding client expectations through high-end service, innovative design, and a presentation that "wows."

These team members, inspired by leadership, have become instruments of change and innovation, not only in the hospitality industry, but also for the economic impact on the city. The RK Group has indeed been a catalyst for growth and job creation in the area.

The admirable reputation that San Antonio has received for its superb hospitality service can largely be attributed to The RK Group. For more than a half-century, it has provided food service to thousands of convention visitors at the Henry B. González Convention Center and has helped set the standard for top-notch client service. This partnership has also helped bring substantial revenue to the city through the convention center sales.

The exclusive venue services of The RK Group have also had a major impact on the hospitality industry, not just in San Antonio, but across the nation. The company's extensive portfolio of satisfied clients includes being the exclusive provider at the following: the Kentucky Derby Museum in Louisville; the food provider for the Etter-Harbin Alumni Center at UT Austin; and the tent provider for Barrett-Jackson Scottsdale, among others.

Each division of the company is trend-setting and each team member serves as a thought leader in the industry. Year after year, the company and team continue to elevate the art of hospitality.

In 2019, The RK Group purchased from the City of San Antonio The Red Berry Estate, a 14,000-square-foot mansion set on 80 magnificent acres on San Antonio's east side. Transforming the residential home built in 1951 required massive upgrades to the mechanical, electrical, and plumbing systems. Completed in 2020, the team's design and renovation efforts led to the mansion's re-birth to honor its

glory. Featuring the most luxurious design and elegant touches, The Red Berry Estate is now recognized as one of the city's most popular event venues.

The company's broad range of services has been applauded across a variety of stages by numerous satisfied clients.

"This was hands down the best cuisine that we have ever had for our conferences!" stated Christine Montgomery, Global Meeting Manager, Association of Clinical Research Professionals after The RK Group handled their event.

Her comments were echoed by Marie McDaniel, Logistics Manager of Premiere Inc. "Everything that they did really just set the mark," she noted.

Among the most impressive of the many accolades that The RK Group has garnered over the years comes from Sheryl Sculley, San Antonio's City Manager from 2005 to 2019. "The RK Group is more than a catering company," she stated. "Their product and service are a total experience, from high-quality food to superior service and attention to detail concerning event themes and special events. No other company can come close to measuring up to the superior quality of The RK Group. And that statement comes from my experience managing three cities with convention centers and attending hundreds of conferences and meetings in convention centers and hotels across the country for many years. Their

attention to detail is exceptional in every respect."

Success on Numerous Stages

The RK Group's turnkey solutions have helped hospitality providers set and maintain attractive standards for their food and beverage programs, maximize profitable operations, and quickly respond to the changing needs of area markets while seamlessly delivering food and beverage banquet catering services.

In addition, leveraging the company's deep experience with off-premise catering, equipment rentals, destination management, and hospitality services, The RK Group's multi-disciplinary teams deliver dedicated management and enhanced logistics capability to assist federal, state, and municipal government agencies and their primary contractors. RK Strategic Management Support, an integrated member of The RK Group is designed to respond within 48 hours to provide emergency and contingency assistance with temporary food services, shelter operations, and facility support services.

For 75 years, The RK Group has grown its portfolio and continues to expand year after year. The Kowalski family is proud to continue its tradition of assisting a broad range of clients to help them create their own special memories.

Building Better Lives

ONE HAS ONLY TO LOOK AT THE SAN ANTONIO SKYLINE TO SEE THE IMPRINT THAT BARTLETT COCKE GENERAL CONTRACTORS HAS HAD ON THE CITY THE COMPANY HAS CALLED HOME FOR MORE THAN 60 YEARS. BARTLETT COCKE'S IMPRESSIVE SIGNATURE IS ON THE CHRISTUS SANTA ROSA SAN ANTONIO CHILDREN'S HOSPITAL.

The company was selected for the reconstruction of the main building at Our Lady of the Lake University after it had been destroyed by fire. Project managers again turned to Bartlett Cocke for the Central Academic Building and Frank Madla Multipurpose Building at Texas A&M University–San Antonio. Bartlett Cocke General Contractors has also been tasked to construct many of the landmark corporate facilities in San Antonio, including USAA, Toyota Motor Manufacturing, Wells Fargo, and Citi Corp. In addition, the company has had a significant presence in the construction of some of the most notable healthcare facilities in the city, including:

- The South Texas Blood and Tissue Center
- Greehey Children's Cancer Research Center
- The United Health System Downtown Robert B. Green Campus

Add to those successfully completed projects numerous buildings on the UTSA Campus and multiple PreK-12 schools throughout the city and greater San Antonio region and it becomes evident why the Bartlett Cocke name ranks among the most trusted general contractors in the region.

In fact, Bartlett Cocke General Contractors has grown to become one of the largest general contractors in San Antonio and among the largest commercial building contractors in Texas. Each year the Bartlett Cocke signature is placed on more than $750 million in construction projects.

LAYING THE CORNERSTONE

Bartlett Cocke General Contractors was founded in 1959 in San Antonio by Bartlett Cocke, Jr. A native of the city, he was the son of an architect, but soon realized that he was a builder at heart. He decided to venture out on his own and founded his construction company upon

his return from service in the United States Navy.

Cocke quickly found his niche. He specialized in building residential porches and grew the company over the next six decades. He expanded his range of services, resulting in Bartlett Cocke General Contractors evolving into one of the largest commercial building firms in Texas.

The cornerstone that Bartlett Cocke, Jr. laid in 1959 remains the heart of the business today. The fact that more than 80 percent of the company's business is derived from repeat clients is perhaps the finest testament to Bartlett Cocke's pursuit of excellence and attention to detail on each project the firm undertakes.

In addition, the company's success has been attributed to the lasting partnerships the firm's professionals have established with owners and their design teams, many of which span decades and even generations. Throughout Bartlett Cocke's growth and evolution as builders, the company has applied the input and advice from owners and designers as it strives to be responsive to each client's goals, building facilities that set a standard for quality regardless of project type.

A Successful Business Model

The primary service area of Bartlett Cocke General Contractors includes the IH-35 Corridor from Waco south to Laredo; the I-10 corridor from San Antonio to Houston; and the Highway 6 corridor from Houston to Waco. The company also works in Corpus Christie.

Bartlett Cocke serves its clients through four regional offices, including its San Antonio headquarters which employs more than 200 construction professionals and trade craft. The Austin office includes a 30,000-square foot, two-story building. Additional locations in Houston and in Baytown, which services the petrochemical industry, round out the firm's facilities.

"Our success as construction managers is attributable to our ability to team with owners, architects, engineers, and end users to align budgets, schedules, building systems, and performance from project kick-off to close-out," states Jerry Hoog, the firm's Chairman of the Board. "Our efforts include working together to optimize design documents for constructability from sitework to window details using collaborative digital design review processes. Estimates are prepared in a thorough and transparent way, and we apply a construction administration environment that is open and executed with an emphasis on stewardship of a project's financial resources."

(continued on next page)

From Initial Design to Project Completion

From initial planning sessions with each client through to project completion, the Bartlett Cocke fully integrated preconstruction and construction teams offer a single source of communication for the project owner, streamlining the entire process. This collaborative approach allows for flexibility in overlapping phases of the project for a reduced schedule and greater overall value for all stakeholders.

Bartlett Cocke accepts every project with the intention of exceeding client expectations for safety, quality, functionality, and aesthetics—ultimately delivering finished products that stand the test of time. The company's value begins long before breaking ground and endures long after project delivery.

The company's Integrated Project Delivery method requires a high level of collaboration between the architect, contractor, owner, and stakeholders. To ensure a smooth project, the Bartlett Cocke team has implemented processes and technologies that enable them to stay current and provide a transparent environment for all to push the project forward.

"What sets Bartlett Cocke General Contractors apart from our competitors is our core purpose of building better lives for our employees, clients, business partners, and the people who inhabit the spaces that we build," Hoog adds. "We are a values-based company with four core values that define who we are and what we do.

"First, we are family. We are stronger together. We respect and support one another, and we value the family unit. Before everything else, we seek to send everyone home safely to their families.

"Second, we take ownership. We take initiative to do the right thing and we stand behind our work.

"Third is to make it happen. We move forward with a sense of urgency, grit, creativity, and innovation while being fair and respectful along the way.

"Lastly is our belief that quality matters. We never lose sight of our goal of building projects that enhance our communities and provide lasting value."

Weaving all this together, Bartlett Cocke operates as an employee-owned company with more than 110 employee owners. It is normal for project teams to include two to three employee owners who have a personal and financial stake in the performance of their projects.

A Track Record of Success

Numerous satisfied clients have lauded Bartlett Cocke's work. Among the most telling testimonials is a note from Jon Hall, the Project Manager for the Texas

A&M University System. "I was relieved to learn that Bartlett Cocke is the General Contractor for our next large project on campus," Hall noted. "I look forward to this project with an optimism that comes from knowing we have a proven winner on board with us."

Hall's comments were echoed by Alamo Architects. "Bartlett Cocke has demonstrated leadership and the ability to manage and coordinate a large and complex project from pre-construction activities through post-occupancy warranty periods."

The company's success in construction of healthcare facilities was underscored by UT Health San Antonio. "Erecting a building, especially a medical or research facility is a very complex undertaking. Bartlett Cocke has proven themselves to be a strong team member who has managed projects with professionalism, trustworthiness, and dependability."

The management team is keenly aware that along with the company's success comes responsibility. "Bartlett Cocke General Contractors is very engaged in the communities we work in," Hoog adds. "Our employees participate in various and multiple charities, civic, and professional trade organizations including Texas public school district educational foundations throughout the state, serving on the boards of the Greater San Antonio Chamber, the North San Antonio Chamber, the New Braunfels Economic Development Foundation, greater:SATX Regional Economic Partnership, Opportunity Austin, the Round Rock Chamber of Commerce, Texas A&M San Antonio Development Foundation, and the American Heart Association. We also have a leadership presence within our industry in San Antonio having had four previous Presidents of the Associated General Contractors local San Antonio Chapter."

At 92 years young, Bartlett Cocke, Jr. is no longer actively involved in the daily business of the company he founded. He continues to drop by the office on a regular basis, however, and keeps in touch with many of the firm's employees.

He can be justifiably proud of the realization of his dream.

FUN

Helping San Antonio Regional Businesses Become Greater

SINCE 1975, GREATER:SATX, FORMERLY KNOWN AS THE SAN ANTONIO ECONOMIC DEVELOPMENT FOUNDATION, HAS WORKED TO GROW QUALITY JOBS IN SAN ANTONIO. THE ORGANIZATION WAS FOUNDED BY GENERAL ROBERT F. MCDERMOTT OF USAA AS A WAY FOR BUSINESSES TO PRIVATELY FUND THE RECRUITMENT OF COMPANIES TO SAN ANTONIO. TODAY, greater:SATX continues this legacy with an expanded scope of services to help local businesses thrive and ensure that the region has the workforce employers need today and for the future.

As a regional economic partnership, greater:SATX serves the eight-county San Antonio-New Braunfels Metropolitan Statistical Area. Partners include economic development entities throughout the region working together to make the San Antonio region the ideal destination to live, work, and do business.

A Region on the Move

San Antonio is a majority-minority community that represents the demographic future of the U.S. As one of the largest metropolitan areas in the nation with room for growth, San Antonio continues to attract new residents. On average, 130 people moved to the San Antonio region each day in 2021—70 percent of whom were under age 50.

Emerging from the COVID-19 pandemic, San Antonio ranked number four nationwide in jobs retained in the U.S. The city is also on track for expected job growth with more than 2,500 new jobs paying six figures expected in the region by 2025. What's more, those high-paying jobs go further as the region's cost of living sits below the national average.

Fueling its phenomenal growth is Greater San Antonio's position as a region of choice. Military, blue collar, white collar, hikers, bikers, students, foodies, animal lovers, techies—people from all walks—love living in the area. The broader eight-county region offers a high quality of life and options for every style, whether that be dense urban living or suburban neighborhoods, hill country open spaces or sky-high tower views.

The San Antonio region was among the first to fully integrate its workforce development initiatives within the economic development team. SA WORX is committed to bridging the gap between education and industry and meeting the demand of our employers in the short- and long-term. Workforce being the top priority for companies exploring relocation opportunities, San Antonio will continue attracting and retaining quality employers.

greater:SATX has helped hundreds of companies establish roots in the area, including:

- Toyota Motor Manufacturing Texas – truck manufacturing plant
- Navistar – commercial truck manufacturing
- Victory Capital corporate headquarters
- Boeing – maintenance, repair and overhaul including U.S. Navy Super Hornets
- DeLorean–electric vehicle headquarters

"greater:SATX is committed to growing strategically to the benefit of our residents here today and those we will attract in the future," stated Jenna Saucedo-Herrera, the organization's President and CEO. "We are well-positioned to become a mega-regional powerhouse in the coming decade. With our regional partners and businesses in support, San Antonio is achieving its even greater future."

VIA Metropolitan Transit

Keeping San Antonio Moving

PUBLIC TRANSPORTATION IN THE SAN ANTONIO REGION HAS COME A LONG WAY SINCE 1878 WHEN THE SAN ANTONIO STREET RAILWAY COMPANY STARTED THE FIRST HORSE-DRAWN STREETCAR SERVICE FROM SAN PEDRO SPRINGS TO ALAMO PLAZA. ELECTRIC STREETCARS WITH OVERHEAD POWER LINES WERE INTRODUCED IN THE 1890S, AND WERE THE primary mode of public transportation for nearly two decades. By the 1930s, automobiles had replaced the streetcars. Buses, which were city-owned since 1917, became increasingly popular at that time and were effective in moving people into and out of San Antonio military bases.

Today, VIA Metropolitan Transit provides mobility options that connect more than a dozen member cities in and around San Antonio and Bexar County. VIA service puts opportunity within reach, moving more people faster, supporting economic vitality, and enhancing quality of life throughout the region. From its founding in 1978, the successor to the city-run San Antonio Transit System, VIA has grown to be the largest bus-only transit system in the nation.

In 2020, VIA rolled in a new era of mobility for the communities it serves and entered a crossroads of change. With overwhelming voter approval to increase dedicated funding for transit service in the region, VIA moved ahead with projects designed to modernize public transit for nearly two million people living and working in its service area. The Keep SA Moving plan includes a network of rapid transit corridors, on-demand models, and other service innovations that will transform the bus company and San Antonio.

A Focus On Service

Realizing that an equitable and accessible transportation network is part of a city's economy, VIA Metropolitan Transit was created on November 8,1977 by voters in Bexar County. Its mission today remains the same as its founding more than a half-century ago - providing public transportation services that improve mobility for people and increase access to places of employment, business, education, services, and recreation.

VIA began operating in 1978 as a political subdivision of the State of Texas rather than a department of any city or county government. VIA is governed by an 11-member Board of Trustees that meets regularly and is dedicated to responding to the community's transportation needs. The Board takes great pride in working with individuals and groups to plan and implement the best transit service possible.

VIA currently serves an approximately 1,200 square mile area that includes 14 member cities and the unincorporated areas of Bexar County.

VIA operates seven days a week on 79 routes, with complementing VIAtrans paratransit service and VIA Link on-demand options. More than 500 buses operating on those 79 routes deliver approximately 36 million passenger trips through seven transit centers, eight park and ride facilities, and more than 6,800 bus stops.

VIA's leadership maintains a sharp focus on improving the customer experience with programs designed to decrease wait times, provide quicker transfers, and offer faster trips with a commitment to delivering service innovations. They are also constantly exploring efficiencies within the existing transit network and offering more convenient first/last mile connections. Examples include expanding its VIA Link on-demand service model and integrating in-app options to book complete trips with bus and bike options.

Service at VIA doesn't just mean miles traveled. The agency's VIA Cares volunteer program matches VIA employees with opportunities to serve non-profit and charitable organizations from throughout San Antonio, including support for the local food bank, Meals on Wheels, the Texas Diaper Bank, City Parks & Recreation, United Way, and others.

VIA In the Future

The phenomenal growth that San Antonio and Bexar County have experienced since the 1970s is expected to continue in the future. The city ranked highest nationally for growth in 2022. Over the next 20 years, Bexar County is expected to add an estimated 1.6 million new residents. Upwards of three million people are expected to call San Antonio home by the year 2040.

Vision 2040 is VIA's strategic plan developed to guide the agency through the next 20 years of rapid growth and change. The overall goal to improve public transit across the San Antonio region was crafted through two years of extensive public outreach in which upwards of 50,000 area residents offered insight and feedback. The key concepts from the Vision 2040 and VIA Reimagined plans became the cornerstones for Keep SA Moving, which also implements strategies to address the ever-changing community.

As the population ages, services such as VIAtrans and VIA Link will help maintain mobility for older adults and persons with a disability.

When COVID-19 became a global pandemic and struck the San Antonio area, VIA realized the need to revise its plans. Routes and schedules were quickly adjusted in response to changing demands and conditions. Recovery is possible only when we can connect with one another, and VIA's services proved vital to keep our community moving forward.

In 2020, voters approved funding for VIA's Keep SA Moving plan in support of projects designed for a modern mass transit system in San Antonio and Bexar County. The initiative is designed to provide innovative transit solutions like on-demand service zones, a rapid transit system designed to move quickly through key corridors, and a better bus system with reduced wait times, easier trips and expanded real-time information.

Connecting the community remains at the heart of VIA's mission and vision. Economic mobility comes from actual mobility. With a renewed focus on delivering a more modern transit system for a growing region, VIA is putting opportunity within reach to transform the way San Antonio moves and grows.

Helping Build America's Future

Stretching across the 1,900 acres that once spanned Kelly Air Force Base, where chapters in aviation history have been written since the dawn of flight, is one of America's leading innovation destinations. Located just minutes southwest of downtown, Port San Antonio is where people are connecting with transformative opportunities in their careers, educational paths, and entrepreneurial ventures. Here, groundbreaking technologies in aerospace, cybersecurity, robotics, defense, applied technologies, and global logistics are being developed by an array of local startups who work together with marquee names in industry, education, and research based at the vast tech innovation campus and throughout the region.

Driven by a framework known as *Tech Port*, the organization is leveraging the campus as a strategic place to develop connections and collaborations focused on innovation. That effort, conducted together with Port customers and an array of educational, public sector and other partners across the region, has resulted in the creation of over 6,000 new jobs on the campus since 2018, bringing it to a total of more than 16,000 on-site workers, employed by more than 80 tenant customers, by the summer of 2022.

During the same timeframe, ambitious development projects have been underway to accommodate the expansion of existing Port customers, welcome new customers, and prepare for big near- and long-term growth. In 2018 the organization completed Project Tech Building 1, which was shortly thereafter fully leased by leading cybersecurity operations that include Lockheed Martin, Northrop Grumman, CNF Technologies, CACI and Novetta Solutions. Here, these firms are in proximity to the Air Force's leading cybersecurity headquarters—the 16th Air Force—as well as to other regional company clients who require expertise in safeguarding national and commercial digital assets. In 2020, Project Tech Building 2, a facility more expansive in size than its predecessor, was completed as the latest modern office space on the property and was fully leased prior to construction being finalized.

Flexible office/commercial spaces completed in 2018 have become home for an array of new customers, including the Alamo Regional Cybersecurity Operations Center (ARSOC)—a collaboration between the City of San Antonio and CPS Energy to safeguard municipal, utility, and other community digital assets. It is the first operation of its kind in the nation, taking a wholistic and collaborative approach toward protecting various entities within a local community against the rising threat of cyberattacks. The same

Completed in 2017, Project Tech Building 1 provides modern and secure facilities for leading named in cybersecurity and government customers in immediate proximity to large Department of Defense operations on the Port campus and across the region.

photo by Port San Antonio

photo courtesy of Port San Antonio /City of San Antonio

complex is also home to locally based Plus One Robotics, which integrates artificial intelligence (AI) and sensor technology into industrial robots and has become one of the most successful tech startups in the history of San Antonio.

Transforming the Aviation Industry

Tech Port has ushered in a new era for recent newcomers to the campus such as Knight Aerospace and XYREC, whose integrated products are transforming the aviation industry. Netherlands-based XYREC established its North American headquarters at the Port in 2019, where it now operates the world's largest industrial robot. Outfitted with a laser, the new technology can remove paint from an airplane fuselage in a fraction of the time required by traditional methods that often make intensive use of water and harsh chemicals. The XYREC robot provides operators an important opportunity to return their aircraft to their service fleets in a faster timeframe. And the eco-friendly innovation, which utilizes a laser reducing the paint removed from a large aircraft into a powder approximately the size of a coffee can, will be a boon to the environment as it is adopted globally.

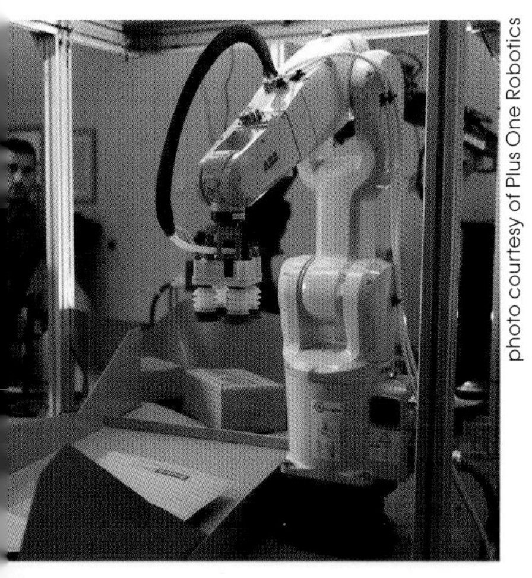

photo courtesy of Plus One Robotics

▲ Headquartered at the Port since 2017, Plus One Robotics is among the most successful technology startups in San Antonio history. The company specializes in integrating industrial robots with visual and AI technology to assume tasks in dynamic industrial environments, such as large e-commerce operations run by client FedEx. In the process, the company has created new career paths, including those of "crew chiefs" who can remotely oversee and manage robotic networks anywhere in the world.

Similarly, San Antonio-based Knight Aerospace relocated its headquarters to the Port in 2019, where it creates an array of modular systems that are rolled onto several different types of commercial and military cargo aircraft and can convert the hold into multiple uses, including traditional rows for passenger seating, kitchen galleys and self-contained VIP suites for heads of state and other clients. With the global onset of the COVID-19 pandemic, Knight pioneered the development of state-of-the-art aeromedical modules that serve as "flying emergency rooms" in safely transporting seriously injured or ill patients.

In addition, Boeing and StandardAero, which have been operating at the site since the Port began redevelopment activities more than 20 years ago, have recently expanded their operations significantly. StandardAero specializes in the maintenance and modernization of engines that power numerous commercial and defense aircraft, including those flown by the U.S. military as well as allied nations.

▲ In 2021, the Alamo Regional Security Operations Center (ARSOC) began activities in a custom-built facility within one of the Port's commercial/industrial complexes. In 2022, the Cybersecurity Manufacturing Innovation Institute (CyManII) announced they will open a training facility within the same building.

Boeing, which operates the company's largest sustainment site at the Port's industrial airport at Kelly Field, similarly provides multiple services to support important U.S. military, allied, and commercial fleets. Much of the company's work at the Port focuses on supporting the C-17 platform, which is the backbone of global defense logistics operations. And the U.S. Navy has entrusted modernization of a large part of its F/A-18 Super Hornet fighter fleet to Boeing's San Antonio site. Likewise, an array of commercial 787 aircraft, the world's most modern

photo courtesy of XYREX, SwRI

▲ The world's largest industrial robot — which was developed by XYREC and its developmental partner Southwest Research Institute — offers leading edge robotic technology for painting and de-painting large assets, including aircraft and sea vessels.

◀ StandardAero's campus at the Port includes a highly specialized array of facilities to test commercial and military aircraft engines.

photo courtesy of wikimedia commons

▲ Among the projects undertaken at Boeing's Port San Antonio site are upgrades and modifications to 787 passenger and cargo aircraft.

commercial airliner, are undergoing important modifications at the Port.

Education

Education has been a foundational pillar of the *Tech Port* strategy. As this framework was initially being adopted, the Port welcomed the San Antonio Museum of Science and Technology (SAMSAT), itself a startup operation at the time, onto the campus in 2016. In addition to housing a world-class collection of transformative innovations that in some cases date more than 100 years, including examples of light bulb prototypes pioneered by Thomas Edison and the world's first camera cell phone and personal computer, the museum is sharply focused on inspiring and guiding young people on educational paths and future careers tied to the innovations that are thriving on the campus and across the community.

Multiple new hands-on exhibits and educational programs delivered by the museum connected with more than 80,000 area students within the first five years since launching at the Port. From a state-of-the-art cybersecurity simulator that engages students with real-world scenarios to project-based educational curricula in space technology, conducted in partnership with Port-based WEX Foundation, students are invited to participate in addressing many of the same challenges as the growing industries that surround them while developing new solutions.

To scale the proven strategic framework launched by the Port, in 2022 the organization completed its most ambitious development project to date: Tech Port Center + Arena. The 130,000-square foot facility is like none other in the country, with integrated state-of-the-art spaces that establish and reinforce the key connections to educational, career, and business opportunities.

The cornerstone of the facility is a 3,000-plus seat arena. The space, the most modern events space in the nation, can be

photo courtesy of Port San Antonio / SAMSAT

▼ The first Knight Aerospace medical module as it is loaded onto a Royal Canadian Air Force aircraft at Kelly Field in early 2021—ready to undertake life-saving missions in Canada and around the world.

▶▼ Interior of Knight Aerospace's medical module.

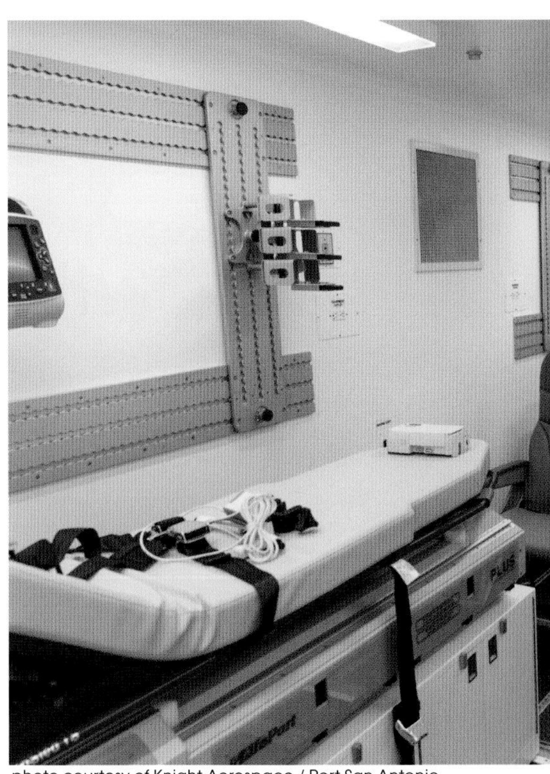
photo courtesy of Knight Aerospace / Port San Antonio

configured to meet many different needs. As an entertainment venue, it can host everything from concerts to esports competitions (and it is the first large competitive video gaming facility in the nation designed and built from the ground-up to host the fast-growing sport). The same arena can serve technology demonstrations, such as robotics and drone competitions, and product launches (which can be broadcast worldwide via integrated A/V technology). Additionally, thanks to retractable seating capabilities, the arena can also serve as a convention center.

Next door to the laboratory space is the new home for SAMSAT, where additional space allows the organization to expand its roster of exhibits and will significantly increase the numbers of students it connects with every year. The same space also serves as an industry showroom, where entities at the Port and beyond can demonstrate their innovations to the public and, in the process, also connect with future buyers.

Additionally, Tech Port Center + Arena is a gathering place that simultaneously connects people who work at the Port and visitors from afar. Amenities include a food hall that features several local dining options and a state-of-the-art LAN gaming center, a place where individuals, school-sponsored teams, and other enthusiasts can gather in their shared passion for video gaming while they sharpen their skills.

Collectively, Port San Antonio, its growing number of advanced technology customers and partners and the *Tech Port* vision that provides the strategic underpinnings that connect people with opportunities have created one of the most vibrant innovation destinations in the world—a place where people from across the region are building their futures and taking part in an exciting world of opportunities.

▲ The first esports event at Tech Port Center + Arena—Battle for Texas—took place in 2022. The event marked the launch of the 2022 Overwatch Season and saw the Houston Outlaws face off against the Dallas Fuel.

◀◀ In early 2020, SAMSAT launched a realistic cybersecurity simulator exhibit—helping young students to see first-hand the roles they can play within the industry and sharpening necessary skills, including analytical thinking, communications and teamwork.

▼ Tech Port Center + Arena

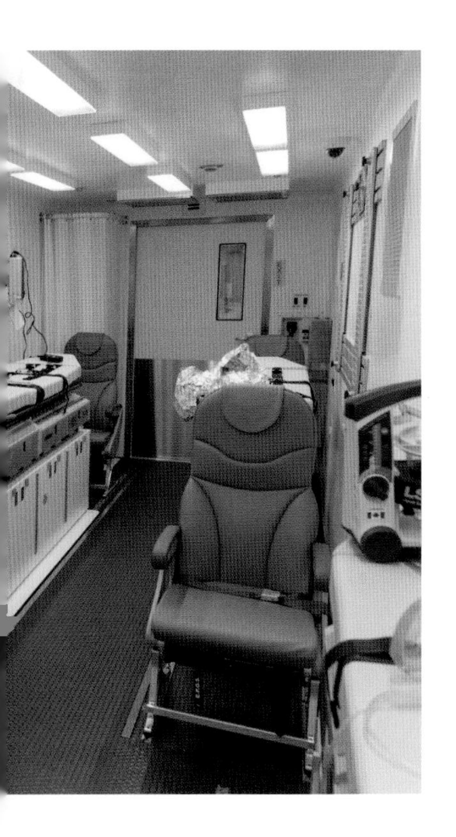

San Antonio Water System

Delivering Responsible Water Services for Life

A SAFE SUPPLY OF HIGH-QUALITY WATER IS AMONG THE RESOURCES MANY PEOPLE NEVER THINK ABOUT, BUT IT RANKS AS ONE OF THE MOST IMPORTANT IN DAILY LIFE. AND THE PROVISION OF THAT RESOURCE AND ENSURING THAT IT REMAINS SECURE AND AVAILABLE FOR FUTURE GENERATIONS IS A DETERMINING FACTOR FOR THE GROWTH AND development of a metropolitan area. Accepting that responsibility and the unwavering commitment to provide the highest quality water to its residential and commercial customers is the San Antonio Water System.

San Antonio Water System (SAWS) is a public utility owned by the City of San Antonio. It was created in May 1992 through the consolidation of three predecessor agencies: the City Water Board (the previous city-owned water supply utility); the City Wastewater Department (a department of the city government responsible for sewage collection and treatment); and the Alamo Water Conservation and Reuse District (an independent city agency created to develop a system for reuse of the city's treated wastewater). SAWS also owns and operates a separate utility – the former City Water Board's chilled water plant, which is a centralized cooling system for the buildings in and around HemisFair Park.

An important component of SAWS' planning role is the responsibility to protect the purity of the city's water supply coming from the Edwards Aquifer, including enforcing certain city ordinances related to subdivision development. The Edwards is recognized as one of the most abundant artesian aquifers in the world and was the site of Native-American encampments in the San Antonio area centuries ago and the reason that the Spanish established the settlement in 1718.

A Commitment to Service

San Antonio Water System is one of the largest water/wastewater providers not only in Texas but in the U.S., serving two million people in Bexar County as well as parts of Medina and Atascosa counties. The population includes more than 516,000 water customers and 462,000 wastewater customers.

The service area for water supply includes most of Bexar County, several suburban municipalities, and adjacent parts of the county. In addition to serving its own retail customers, SAWS also provides wholesale water supplies to several smaller utility systems within this area.

SAWS headquarters is located north of downtown San Antonio in two office buildings that once were home to Valero HQ. SAWS additionally oversees four operations centers, three water recycling plants, two payments centers, two district cooling operations, and an inland desalination plant and aquifer and storage facility at SAWS' H2Oaks Center.

A Tradition of Excellence

SAWS' track record and the work of its 1,700 dedicated professionals has been recognized across the industry:

- San Antonio is the only U.S. city to reuse all three wastewater treatment process byproducts: recycled water, organic biosolids, and methane gas. SAWS humbly refers to that distinction as the environmental "trifecta."
- SAWS has the nation's largest direct recycled water system. More than 130 miles of pipeline deliver highly treated recycled water to industrial and commercial users, golf courses, municipal parks, universities, military, etc.
- SAWS brokered the first public-private water project called the Vista Ridge Pipeline. The deal protects ratepayers by locking in today's water prices and secures the city's water needs for the next 50 years.

- SAWS has the largest inland desalination plant in the U.S.

In addition, SAWS is an inducted member of the international organization, Leading Utilities of the World. The utility has been named a Top Workplace in San Antonio by *The San Antonio Express-News* eight times since 2011. SAWS has also been recognized nationally with the 2016 National Environmental Achievement Award for its Impact high school education program. The utility also garnered the 2020 Government Social Media Golden Post Award for Best Facebook Presence. SAWS is also nationally and internationally known for its novel and effective water conservation programs which are often duplicated elsewhere.

A Focus on Community

In addition to its commitment to providing the highest quality water service to its customers, SAWS maintains a sharp focus on being a good corporate citizen in the communities it serves. SAWS has an annual corporate charity campaign that raises upwards of $100,000 to benefit local United Way agencies. The company also operates SAWS Cares, a robust volunteer program where employees participate in beautification projects, school supply and food drives, mentoring, and volunteering to the San Antonio Food Bank. SAWS also established Project Agua, a bill payment assistance program for customers needing help with their water bill. Throughout the year, SAWS raises funds through Fiesta medal sales, employee charitable giving, and fundraisers.

SAWS values close interaction with its customers. The utility's Community Experience Committee maintains an important dialogue with its neighbors by educating and seeking feedback from a diverse group of community-oriented individuals on a range of topics to improve the overall customer experience.

San Antonio Water System's Board of Trustees has adopted mission, vision, and values statements that serve as a foundation to move the utility forward through 2050 and reinforce San Antonio's much-deserved reputation as Waterful. SAWS is committed to its leadership role in delivering responsible, sustainable, and affordable water services for life.

Transforming Lives One Student at A Time

As a proud contemporary university reflective of the diverse and heritage-rich community it serves, Texas A&M University-San Antonio (A&M-SA) transforms lives and the local community by delivering a quality higher education experience that is accessible and inclusive, and by empowering students for academic success, rewarding careers, and engaged global citizenship.

Founded in 2009 as the first upper-division institution of higher education in South San Antonio, A&M-SA today is a comprehensive four-year university offering affordable, high-quality education. A&M-San Antonio has become a beacon of the South Side of San Antonio, delivering for the first time in the city's history, high-caliber, affordable bachelor's and post-graduate degrees in a historically underserved community. Since becoming a standalone university, from Fall 2009 to Fall 2021, enrollment grew 196 percent. A&M-SA is the fastest-growing university in the A&M System.

The San Antonio area is the nation's eighth fastest-growing metropolitan area with about 65 percent of the city's population identifying as Hispanic. A&M-SA is only one of three public universities in San Antonio and the only A&M institution of higher learning in a metropolitan area. Designated a Hispanic-Serving Institution, A&M-SA is the first comprehensive public university on San Antonio's historic South Side, providing critical access to education and opportunities to people in that area.

Nearly 80 percent of the student body is from Bexar County. In addition, A&M-SA is a "Military Embracing™" campus community with one in six students being military connected.

The University currently serves nearly 7,000 students and has graduated more than 14,000 alumni. The student body is 64 percent female and 77 percent Hispanic, and approximately 72 percent of students are the first in their family to attend college. A full 98 percent of students receive some sort of financial aid while upwards of 70 percent qualify for non-paying tuition.

Through the University's 29 undergraduate degrees and 14 graduate degrees, students can pursue a wide variety of in-demand fields, such as education, business, information technology and cyber security, criminology, and biology. A&M-SA prepares and empowers students with knowledge and marketable skills that prepare them for responsible global citizenship and lifelong learning.

The Seed Is Planted

A&M-SA has traveled an interesting road to reach its present position within the A&M System. Before his untimely death in 2006, Texas Senator Frank Madla had been a tireless advocate for the establishment of an institution of higher learning on the South Side of San Antonio. Beginning in 1997, he requested proposals from the Texas Tech University System, the University of Texas System, and the Texas A&M University System. The Texas A&M University System responded with a proposal, and Madla collaborated with Senator Joe Farias for 12 years to bring Texas A&M-San Antonio to the forefront.

In 2005, Madla wrote the bill later passed by the Texas Legislature authorizing the creation of A&M-SA. Further, during the special legislative session of 2006 he convinced his fellow legislators to pass $40 million in tuition revenue bonds to make Texas A&M-San Antonio a reality.

Greg Garcia, while working as Assistant Vice Chancellor for Governmental Affairs with the Texas A&M University System, was another unrelenting champion of higher education representing several Texas A&M University institutions. Garcia worked tirelessly to garner support

from elected public servants, community leaders, chambers of commerce, and academic leadership to bring the Texas A&M University-San Antonio dream to life. Dr. Maria Hernandez Ferrier was named the inaugural president of Texas A&M-San Antonio in 2010. Dr. Cynthia Teniente-Matson currently serves as the University's president.

The University in the 21st Century

"Texas A&M University-San Antonio was born of a mission to serve all students — particularly those from South San Antonio's underserved population — with access to a high-quality, affordable education," stated John Sharp, Chancellor, Texas A&M University System. "Because of this mission, and our dedication to it, Texas A&M University-San Antonio has not only become the fastest growing university in the Texas A&M University System, but the entire State of Texas."

A&M-SA is home to a community of distinguished faculty members with regional, national, and global connections. Today, 223 full-time and 147 part-time faculty prepare students for the paths they will travel. These faculty members instill in their students the fact that they are not just students, but important members of the A&M-San Antonio Jaguar family. They quickly become part of a dynamic, innovative, and community-connected University that is eager to help each student become tomorrow's entrepreneur, researcher, and leader. A&M-SA has structured its resources to become recognized as a national model of student success. With faculty and staff that are student-focused, coaches that provide individualized support, and affordable degree programs designed for timely graduation, today's students soon become proud alumni of A&M-SA.

A&M-SA students in the University's undergraduate and graduate degree programs participate in internship opportunities with local partners for experiential learning, research, community learning, and valuable practical skills. These experiences help students develop their skills, knowledge, and values. These special courses expand the student experience beyond the traditional academic setting.

The Mays Center for Experiential Learning and Community Engagement supports a variety of experiential learning courses that have intentional projects, partnerships, or service components that can also connect students to local businesses and non-profits. Through experiential and service-learning, students can see the practical application of their academic knowledge through real-world problems and contexts. The A&M-SA community also is provided opportunities to volunteer and discover civic events with more than 70 community partnerships. Among them are:

- Alzheimer's Association
- Any Baby Can
- Boys & Girls Clubs of San Antonio
- Goodwill
- Down Syndrome Association of South Texas
- Girl Scouts of South Texas
- Haven for Hope
- SAMMinisitries
- San Antonio Food Bank
- United Way of San Antonio and Bexar County.

A Relentless Pursuit of Excellence

In its mission to provide the finest learning opportunities with hands-on experience in the real world, A&M-SA has garnered numerous awards. In 2021, the University received the Seal of Excelencia, the nation's premier authority on efforts to accelerate Latino student success in higher education. In 2020, A&M-SA was honored with the national Well Work Place Silver Award for its Jaguar Strong-Get Fit Wellness program. In addition, the Society for Human Resource Management (SHRM) awarded a 2018-2019 Superior Merit Award designation to the A&M-SA SHRM student chapter for providing superior growth and development opportunities to its student chapter members.

As a result of San Antonio's recognition as "Military City USA" the University takes great pride in having been recognized for its establishment of a Military Cultural Competence Training program. This professional development program for faculty and staff introduces the need for increased cultural awareness and understanding of the transition military members face when returning to civilian life. In 2020, A&M-SA jumped from number 77 to number 35 on the "Best for Vets: Colleges 2020" ranking in the *Military Times* out of 134 four-year institutions.

"A&M-SA embodies the rich culture and heritage of the surrounding San Antonio communities," noted Dr. Cynthia Tenient-Matson, President of Texas A&M University-San Antonio. "At A&M-San Antonio, we are audacious in our thinking, and we are here to serve students throughout Texas and the nation in their pursuit of discovery and lifelong learning.

"University campuses are a place where the important work of advancing equity and inclusion is done in earnest. At A&M-San Antonio, we strive to embody the core values of diversity and inclusion that America's public universities foster and revere. And, as a public Hispanic-Serving Institution, we have a special purpose to ensure students from historically underrepresented communities are growing Con Fuerza—with strength—and with the equitable support they need to face the challenges and opportunities before them."

Big Sun Solar

Energy for a Renewable Future

A chance meeting through mutual friends in 2015 brought together two founders who would have an indelible impact on San Antonio and the future of solar energy. Robert Miggins and Jason Pittman were both contemplating career changes. While one was leaving a long technology career, the other was looking to bring the benefits of sustainability directly to households. Both were focusing on clean energy and looking for a meaningful way to build a more renewable future for the next generation of Texans.

The result of that meeting was the founding of Big Sun Solar to drive the mass adoption of solar energy by making it affordable, accessible, and understandable to all. Their mission was to build a team that shared that same passion for building a renewable future and to fulfill that passion in San Antonio.

Staying consistent to the "City on a Mission" atmosphere in San Antonio, the founders realized they were in the perfect location to launch their new initiative. With plentiful sunshine and a city with an appetite for renewable energy, San Antonio allowed them to build a high-growth solar energy business, create meaningful jobs, bring the benefits of renewable energy to the community, and be leaders in environmental stewardship.

Achieving the Dream

Communities across the country are demanding more renewable energy options from their utilities. Historically, the benefits of solar energy had been out of reach to most San Antonio households and businesses due to cost and the lack of access to suitable rooftops. Big Sun Solar eliminated the barriers to solar adoption by leveraging innovation while giving back to the San Antonio community that Miggins and Pittman both call home. The company focused on creating a partnership with utilities to develop and implement innovative solar programs that make financial sense for the community and the utility.

Big Sun Solar found a willing partner in CPS Energy to create and launch the Big Sun Community Solar program that allowed residential and business customers to purchase solar panels. Instead of installing the panels on the rooftop, Big Sun Solar installed them on solar carport structures throughout the city.

Historically, community solar was typically deployed in rural areas as "solar farms." Big Sun Solar found a way to utilize large, open parking lots to provide shade for cars and, at the same time, support solar panels to be used in a community solar program. San Antonio's openness to innovative and new ideas

made it the perfect launching pad for Big Sun Solar.

In addition to community solar programs and with a goal of deploying as many solar panels as possible, Big Sun Solar partners with large commercial and industrial customers. Commercial customers include rooftop projects such as storage facilities and multifamily developments plus solar carport structure for car dealerships and medical offices across central Texas.

Over the past decade, many electric utilities have embraced solar programs. Big Sun Solar partners with utilities to develop and integrate renewables into customers programs in a reliable and cost-effective manner. The final group of projects are merchant solar facilities. Big Sun designs, builds and owns solar farms to sell electricity in the real time market to ERCOT.

"Big Sun Solar has successfully leveraged innovation to bring more solar energy to the San Antonio community," stated San Antonio Councilman Mario Bravo. "With solar energy being a relatively young technology, Big Sun Solar has set the standard for community involvement and customer education."

A Mission-Driven Organization

The leadership team at Big Sun Solar believes that prosperity is not solely delivered through financial performance, but also by making a positive contribution to society. In its first year of operation, Big Sun Solar saved community solar customers over $1 million on their energy bills. The company is also doing its part to not only help the environment, but also the business community by helping customers see a significant return on their solar investment and creating jobs in the new clean energy economy.

In addition, Big Sun Solar has taken the "One Percent Pledge" where one percent of the company's gross profit is given back to the community as donations ranging from in-kind services to educational partnerships.

The company's local imprint has been evident since 2017 when Big Sun Solar donated services and equipment to the Will Smith Zoo School resulting in the facility achieving LEED Platinum certification. With the belief that solar energy should be available to everyone regardless of socioeconomic status, Big Sun Solar launched in 2019 the "Solar Assistance Program" for families that fall under the 80% Area Median Income threshold.

And during the difficult economic times brought about by the COVID-19 pandemic, Big Sun Solar assisted a local eatery by purchasing enough gift cards to cover staff salaries during their temporary closing. Big Sun Solar is committed to continuing their mission of bringing more renewable energy to the city of San Antonio.

Index

D

E

F

G

H

I

U

V

W

X

Y

Z